CANCELLED 0 4 JUL 2022

First published in Great Britain in 2013 by

The Policy Press
University of Bristol
Fourth Floor
Beacon House
Queen's Road
Bristol BS8 1QU
UK
Tel +44 (0)117 331 4054
Fax +44 (0)117 331 4093
e-mail tpp-info@bristol.ac.uk
www.policypress.co.uk

North American office:
The Policy Press
c/o The University of Chicago Press
1427 East 60th Street
Chicago, IL 60637, USA
t: +1 773 702 7700
f: +1 773-702-9756
e:sales@press.uchicago.edu
www.press.uchicago.edu

British Library Cataloguing in Publication Data
A catalogue record for this book is available from the British Library.

Library of Congress Cataloging-in-Publication Data
A catalog record for this book has been requested.

ISBN 978 1 84742 799 1 paperback
ISBN 978 1 84742 800 4 hardcover

Cover design by Qube Design Associates, Bristol
Front cover: image kindly supplied by www.alamy.com
Printed and bound in Great Britain by Hobbs, Southampton
The Policy Press uses environmentally responsible print partners.

FSC
www.fsc.org
MIX
Paper from
responsible sources
FSC® C020438

Contents

Ann Marie Gray:
To my granddaughter Chloe

Derek Birrell:
To my granddaughter Lucy

List of boxes, tables and figures

Boxes

Tables

Figures

List of abbreviations

ADASS	Association of Directors of Adult Social Services [England]
ADSS Cymru	Association for Directors of Social Services Cymru [Wales]
ADSW	Association of Directors of Social Work [Scotland]
CHP	community health partnership
COSLA	Convention of Scottish Local Authorities
CQC	Care Quality Commission
DASS	director of adult social services
EEA	European Economic Area
GP	general practitioner
GSCC	General Social Care Council
HCPC	Health and Care Professions Council
ISA	Independent Safeguarding Authority
JIT	Joint Improvement Team
LGA	Local Government Association
LINk	Local Involvement Network
NHS	National Health Service
NICE	National Institute for Health and Clinical Excellence
NMDS-CS	National Minimum Data Set for Social Care
PALS	Patient Advice and Liaison Services
PCT	primary care trust
POPPs	Partnerships for Older People Projects
RQIA	Regulation and Quality Improvement Authority
SCIE	Social Care Institute for Excellence
UK	United Kingdom
UKHCA	UK Home Care Association
ULO	user-led organisation
WLGA	Welsh Local Government Association

Acknowledgements

We would like to thank Liz McNeill for her invaluable administrative assistance. Grateful thanks to Emily Watt, Jo Morton and the production team at The Policy Press for their support and efficient management of the process.

ONE

Introduction

Overview

Adult social care has emerged as a distinct area of provision following the separation from children's services after 2006. This decision was driven by concerns relating to children's social care and services, not to adult services. In the first instance this meant organisational separation from the area of child protection and children and family services in local authorities in England. Social care in general had had a distinct existence from the National Health Service (NHS) in the United Kingdom (UK) from 1948. The separation from children's services was to lead quickly to a clear focus on the notion of 'adult social care' as a distinct entity and the use of the term became established in most governmental, professional and academic writing. The term 'adult social care' has largely replaced the former general terms of 'personal social services' and 'community care' with new attempts to define the term. The distinctiveness of adult social care services has not, however, meant a reduction in the importance given to the relationship of adult social care to health or other cognate services. Adult social care services are expected to work closely in partnerships with the NHS, other public services and the independent sectors. As adult social care has become established as an area of provision, a number of factors have pushed adult care into a major issue on the government agenda and in public debate. These include demographic change, growing needs, pressure on public expenditure, welfare retrenchment, promoting independence and the balance with health. The debate on problems, principles and policy options has led to the adoption of major strategies in terms of modernisation, vision statements and more recently a transformation of care. Underpinning principles under debate relate to the balance of responsibilities between the individual and the state, the role of contracting out and funding arrangements and changes, reliance on unpaid care and law reform. The potential for further transformation lies in developing the emerging key values of personalisation, integration and user participation. Further key delivery issues relate to safeguarding, outcomes, diversity, the role of carers and the nature of the workforce.

Definitions of adult social care

The emergence of the distinct area of adult social care led government bodies to define the area for official purposes. The Department of Health adopted originally a broad enabling definition in the key paper *Our health, our care, our say* (DH, 2006a). This defined adult social care as 'the wide range of services designed to support people to maintain their independence, enable them to play a fuller part in society, protect them in vulnerable situations and manage complex relationships' (2006, para 2.5). Attempts at definitions have tended towards purpose-based statements rather than a listing of provision. Thus, the current definition used by the Department of Health refers to promoting people's wellbeing and independence and giving them control over their lives (DH, 2012a, p 8). The Law Commission, in a major study of the legal status of social care, decided that it was not possible to provide a single definition. It examined a service-orientated definition that adult social care means the care and support provided by local authority social services pursuant to their responsibilities towards adults who need extra support (Law Commission, 2011, para 1.5). Also examined was an approach based on tightly defined processes, which served to determine the scope of adult social care, for example, community care assessments and care planning. In the end the Law Commission preferred to define the purpose of adult social care as 'promoting or contributing to the well-being of the individual' (Law Commission, 2011, para 2.1), although it also noted the developing range of non-traditional services such as art therapy, personal assistance and life coaching. Other contributions to definitions have stressed the importance of social care. In 1998, the landmark White Paper *Modernising social services* (DH, 1998a) noted that social services are an important fabric of a caring society, while over a decade on, the new Coalition government's White Paper *A vision for adult social care* (DH, 2010a) noted that social care is an essential human need. The latter White Paper also quoted the Seebohm Report (Great Britain Ministry of Housing and Local Government, 1968) in saying that social care should enable the greatest possible number of individuals to act reciprocally, giving and receiving services for the wellbeing of the whole community. A rather different approach has focused on unique features of adult social care as a service. This again has continued from community care where some definitions stressed the residual nature of the services (Baldock, 1994) for those in greatest need, as the majority of vulnerable people had no contact with statutory services. The *Caring for our future* White Paper (DH, 2012a) makes the point that care and support enable people to do the everyday things that most of us take for granted: dressing, cooking, seeing friends, caring for others and being part of the community. Newman et al (2008) identify three features of adult social care that distinguish it from other public services: the blurring of public and private boundaries; the extensive use of market mechanisms and diffuse nature of providers; and the role of users in the co-production of social care.

Definitions used by the Scottish and Welsh governments also are purpose based but are written rather generally. The aim of adult care and support in Scotland is described as to improve the quality of life for adults in receipt of social care and there is a reference to a shift in the balance of care so that more people can live in their communities (Scottish Government, 2012a, p18; Self-directed Support [Scotland] Bill 2012). The Government of Wales Act 2006 identified social care services provided in connection with the wellbeing of any person as residential or non-residential services; information, advice, counselling or advocacy services; and financial or other assistance. The Welsh government has seen adult social care as designed to protect a range of people whose lives would be poorer for the absence of the services, listing responsibilities for planning, assessing, commissioning and delivering adult social services. The consultation on the Welsh Social Care Bill examined a definition in terms of the need to maintain wellbeing, covering if an individual is unable to achieve a reasonable standard of wellbeing, or their wellbeing would be impaired without the provision of social care or they need protection (Welsh Government, 2012a).

Groups covered by adult social care

There is more agreement and clarity on the nature of the groups of people who are included in the term 'adult social care'. Although the groups covered can range widely, the core groups are normally listed as follows:

- older people – some 76% of older people will need care and support at some point in later life; furthermore, 51% of people receiving state-funded social services are over the age of 65 and 75% of adults in residential care are over the age of 65;
- people with physical disabilities, sometimes also specifically including sensory disabilities;
- people with learning disabilities, sometimes using the alternative term 'intellectual disabilities';
- people with mental illness.

A number of other groups, smaller in number, can be categorised as vulnerable groups who may be eligible for care and support, but who may or may not be included in listings. These groups include:

- people misusing drugs and alcohol;
- people with HIV/AIDS;
- asylum seekers and refugees;
- homeless people;
- ex-offenders;
- minority ethnic groups, for example, Travellers;
- people who are terminally ill.

Some groups may be identified separately on occasions rather than included in the above categories, for example, adults with autism. Some groups are only occasionally identified as a distinct group, for example, the victims of domestic violence. It has also been pointed out that some people may fall into several of these categories and experience multiple disadvantages (Larkin, 2009). Studies in adult social care and lists of groups catered for in provision also often include unpaid carers as a separate category.

Nature of adult social care services

The traditional forms of social care services have not changed significantly from the time of the expansion of care in the community, but there have been some significant shifts in emphasis and the introduction of new services and the nature and scope of services can range widely. A current production of a categorisation of adult social care can be suggested along the lines presented in Box 1.

Box 1: Adult social care services

- Residential care, including the specialist category of nursing homes.
- Domiciliary or home care covering assistance and facilities in the home, including home helps and meals on wheels.
- Other care in the community, usually provided on a day basis, including drop-in centres, day centres and clubs.
- Supported housing care covering different formats of housing for special needs, including provision of caretakers and support facilities and workers – sometimes now referred to as supported living.
- Reablement developed as a strategy for helping people regain independence, usually after leaving hospital, by learning or relearning skills necessary for daily living; based on short-term interventions.
- Intermediate care, usually accommodation in an institution to bridge hospital to home.
- Direct payments, individual budgets and other forms of self-directed support.
- Social work services, support and advice, the traditional roles of assessment, care planning, counselling advice and advocacy.
- Safeguarding services, protection and safety, as a relatively new dimension. This gives protection against the risk of abuse, harm or neglect, covering both institutional and community safety.
- Support for carers, including services, financial support, advice and respite care.

This list is not exhaustive and varies in provision as well as innovation and experimentation, which are characteristics of adult social care.

Growth in demand for adult social care

The scale of social care provision has grown substantially in recent years, with almost two million adults in England using social care services (House of Commons Health Committee, 2010). In 2008/09, it was estimated that 1.78 million people received care and support, with 1.54 million people receiving non-residential care, 319,000 people receiving residential care and 86,000 receiving direct payments (Law Commission, 2011, para 15). In a six-year period in England, expenditure increased by 16%, from £14.5 million in 2003/04 to £16.8 million in 2009/10 (Audit Commission, 2011, para 7). There has been a continuing rise in demand for new services. In 2011 in England, the number of new contacts to councils responsible for social services rose by 4% to 2.12 million. Of these, just over half resulted in a further assessment or commissioning of a service (CQC, 2012). *Caring for our future* (DH, 2012a) suggested that in England, 1.1 million people are receiving care at home, with around 380,000 people in residential care and around five million people caring for a family member or friend. Some 1.8 million people are employed in the care and support workforce. Spending on all adult social service groups has increased, with the greatest increase in spend on people with learning disabilities, followed by older people. See Figure 1 for expenditure by user group for 2011/12.

Figure 1: Expenditure by user group on adult social care (England) (2011/12)

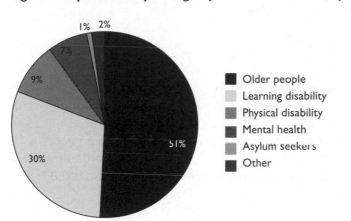

The key expectation is that in future more adults will need care and support. This mainly reflects demographic change, with older people living longer. The absolute numbers of older people are increasing and their proportion of the population is also rising. (See projected populations by age group in Table 1.) The numbers of older people aged over 85 in England will almost double between 2010 and 2026, from 1.2 million to two million (House of Commons Health Committee, 2010, para 1.7).

There is more uncertainty about the precise increase in disability-free life expectancy, that is, without limiting illness or disability, and this of course will also be a determinant of future levels of need for care and support. There is evidence of increasing numbers of older people with dementia and more adults with autism. A further uncertainty exists about the number and role of carers as family break-up, population movement and other social trends may affect provision by carers, for example, already less care than previously is provided by neighbours and friends.

Despite some degree of uncertainty, it has been argued that on all reasonable assumptions the adult social care system will face considerable increased pressures in the decades to come (House of Commons Health Committee, 2010, para 71). It has been suggested that eight out of 10 people aged 65 will need some care and support in their later years and there will be large increases in the numbers of older people, people with dementia and the number of young disabled adults (DH, 2012a, p 16).

Table 1: Projected population by age group (UK) (thousands)

Age	2015	2020	2025	2030
0–14	11,497	12,231	12,455	12,279
15–29	12,619	12,168	12,192	12,809
30–44	12,545	13,185	14,037	14,108
45–59	13,018	13,161	12,514	13,338
60–74	9,709	10,353	10,925	11,807
75+	5,388	6,093	7,279	8,051

Source: ONS 2010 based population projections

In Scotland, it has been suggested that 25% of Scotland's population will be aged over 65 by 2033 and the numbers aged over 75 will grow by 10,000 a year (Scottish Government, 2012a, p 13). In Wales, a growing but ageing population and a rise in the numbers of people with limiting life-long conditions and people with dementia are projected (Welsh Government, 2010, p 15). In Northern Ireland, the number of people aged over 75 will increase by 40% by 2020 (DHSSPS, 2011a, p 21).

Devolution and social care

This book examines policy and provision of adult social care throughout the UK. The establishment of devolved governments in Scotland, Wales and Northern Ireland in 1999 has become an increasingly significant factor in the study of adult social care, as adult social care is a devolved matter in these countries. It is the Scottish Government and Parliament, the Welsh Government and Assembly and the Northern Ireland Executive and Assembly that determine legislative provision, administrative and delivery structures and policies and strategies (Birrell, 2009). Divergence in social care policy and provision between the four countries of the UK did exist before 1999 as forms of administrative devolution through the Scottish Office in Edinburgh (Mooney et al, 2006) and the Welsh Office in Cardiff (Drakeford, 2005) did produce differences, particularly in structures but also in some policy areas, while Northern Ireland had long experience of the use of devolved powers in health and social care. Devolution in 1999 brought more potential for policy divergence throughout the UK, in relation to both health and adult social care and also children's services and housing services. As devolution has developed, divergence in policy, provision, strategies and delivery structures has grown. Of particular importance has been Scotland's adoption of free personal care for older people and generally a strong commitment in Scotland to social change and social justice (Dumbleton and McPhail, 2012). Writing of Wales, Scourfield et al (2008) have referred to a distinctiveness from England in terms of language and national identities and increasingly independent social policies. Northern Ireland has long had a distinctive structure of integrated health and social services organised outside local government. A separate administrative structure for adult social care is more pronounced in England than in Scotland, Wales and Northern Ireland. In studying social care in the UK, it is very important to be continually aware of these territorial differences and that the policies of the Department of Health in London only cover England. In recent years, all four administrations have embarked on major reviews impacting on the role of social work and social care, the restructuring of the delivery of social care in relation to health and the development of new strategies for social care. As devolution has impacted on all aspects of adult social care, the subject is considered at appropriate points throughout the book rather than in a separate chapter. In the book there is a focus on major strategies, policies and provision discussed or introduced for England. Highlighted is whether these feed through in policy copying or transfer to Scotland, Wales and Northern Ireland or whether divergent policies have emerged.

Sources

As the book has a focus on the development of policy and provision of adult social care, a major source of material has been government papers, strategies, legislation and guidelines. Those produced by government departments in Whitehall, mainly the Department of Health, apply now to England only. Thus, papers produced by the devolved departments and directorates are also important. The work of parliamentary committees in the House of Commons is useful for contemporary analysis, especially arising from inquiries and scrutiny by the Health Committee and also by the Public Accounts Committee. Some similar work is produced by the relevant committees of the Scottish Parliament and the Welsh and Northern Ireland Assemblies. The four parliamentary bodies also have research and briefing facilities, which have produced reports and papers on aspects of social care. A number of reports especially commissioned by government have also been significant documents in the development of policy, in such areas as the costs of residential care, reviewing the law on adult social care in England and Wales and reviewing free nursing and social care in Scotland. Reports from public regulatory bodies are also of significance and this category of reports includes those by the Audit Commission and the Care Quality Commission (CQC) in England and the equivalent bodies for Scotland, Wales and Northern Ireland. On occasions, reports from the statutory equality and human rights bodies may have significance for aspects of adult social care. Use is also made of the traditional academic sources in terms of books, research reports, occasional papers, journal articles and conference proceedings. A number of non-governmental bodies have contributed to the body of evaluative, analytical and practice-based studies. The output of the Social Care Institute for Excellence (SCIE) has been substantial, especially for England. A number of research institutes and think tanks have also made contributions in the field of adult social care, particularly the Joseph Rowntree Foundation, the Nuffield Trust and The King's Fund. Representative and professional bodies produce much contemporary analysis, particularly the Association of Directors of Adult Social Services (ADASS), the British Association of Social Workers and the NHS Confederation as well as, on occasions, the local government representative bodies in England, Scotland and Wales. A number of journals/magazines representing practitioners also produce much detailed contemporary commentaries. A large number of voluntary organisations operate or have interests in adult social care and provide another source of reports, evaluations, policy analysis and comment. The main provider bodies, whether local councils, trusts or boards, independent sector organisations or partnerships, also publish extensive documentation and have websites. With adult social care moving into the political spotlight, at times commentary in the social and public media can be focused and critical.

The structure of the book

The book is organised by major themes in policy and practice rather than by user group, provider or country of the UK. The introduction explains the rationale for the book in terms of the emergence of adult social care as a distinct policy area, and by the major focus of government on the direction of agendas for adult social care. The introduction briefly examines the nature and scope of adult social care, including definitions and the range of groups falling within social care services. There is a summary of the reasons for the growth and development of adult social care and the importance of the introduction of devolution is explained. An account is given of the main sources used and the organisation of the book.

Chapter Two provides a summary of the major developments since the 1960s in the area of the personal social services and community care. This identifies the main trends in policy and practice, which form the background to the emergence of adult social care.

Chapter Three sets out the main issues that currently concern the delivery of adult social care. The chapter begins by noting the main shortcomings that have been identified in a range of assessments and analyses and proceeds through what have emerged as major issues in policy and practice. These include integration, personalisation, user participation, the costs of long-term care, providers, safeguarding and quality, the workforce, reduced resources, and transformation and change agendas.

Chapter Four examines the multi-level institutions of governance that are involved in the formulation of policy and the delivery of services. These include government departments and directorates and executive agencies in the UK government and the devolved administrations. The continuing important role of local authorities, increasingly as commissioners of care, is explained. It is noted that a wide range of public bodies or quangos have a role in the provision of adult social care, from some direct provision to regulatory and advisory functions.

Attention is also paid to the expanding role of partnerships, both across health and social care and where led by local authorities. The considerable impact of restructuring in different ways throughout the UK is also considered.

Chapter Five looks at the origins of the personalisation agenda in adult social care and considers it from the perspective of national and local policy and in relation to all areas of social care. It examines implementation issues, including funding mechanisms, commissioning and personal budgets, support mechanisms and the paid and unpaid caring workforce. The chapter also considers differences as a result of devolution.

Chapter Six discusses the impact on adult social care in the last 10 years of much closer collaboration between health and social care. The various ways in which this has been facilitated through legislation, structures and frameworks are set out. Joint working and partnership working in England and Wales is described as is the experiment with the particular model of care trusts. The somewhat different model in Scotland of health and social care partnerships is also discussed and particular attention is paid to the very different model in Northern Ireland of structurally integrated trusts and boards. There is an assessment of the evidence for the impact of the promotion of integrated working in various modes and a consideration of what can facilitate further integration. The challenges for integration within the reformed health structures in England are also discussed.

Chapter Seven focuses on unpaid carers. The vast majority of people who ever require care are looked after by family or friends and the chapter begins by looking at the scale of unpaid caring and the issues impacting on carers. It examines the challenges to assumptions about unpaid carers and the development of the policy response, including the role of carers' organisations in advocating for support. A major preoccupation of research and policy discussions is the reconciliation of paid work in the labour market and unpaid caring work and there is a discussion of the extent to which carers have real choices about work and care. The chapter also reflects on the sustainability of unpaid care in the face of increasing demand and the social and economic factors that may reduce the number of unpaid carers.

Chapter Eight looks at the paid social care workforce, which is predicted to expand massively in coming years. It begins by considering the changes to the regulation of professional social work training and goes on to discuss the diversity of the social care workforce. Despite the centrality of the workforce to the success of contemporary social care policies, it is a workforce with significant problems in terms of recruitment, retention and the lack of value attached to it and the implications of this situation are considered. The chapter looks at workforce training and professional development issues and the workforce challenges presented by the personalisation agenda.

Chapter Nine focuses on participation and the making and delivery of social care policy through user involvement. The chapter considers the rationale for user and public participation and the values underpinning these concepts. Participatory initiatives are described, covering national and local initiatives and links to specific user groups. The nature and extent of user participation in different areas of social care are described and new developments in the identification of experts by experience, the role of user organisations, participation by carers and the growth of advocacy are examined. Differences in approaches in the devolved administrations are examined and the changes in structures to be introduced in England are noted.

Chapter Ten examines the extent to which the delivery of social care is subject to inspection and regulation. It explores the remit of inspection bodies and the powers they exercise. The structures are strongly affected by devolution, with each of the four countries of the UK having separate inspection systems and bodies and the differences between these are assessed. Both residential and home care have been the subject of scandal and inquiries, which have given rise to criticism of regulatory bodies but have also raised questions about more fundamental attitudes towards users. The chapter looks at the policy response to these criticisms and the argument that there should be an increasing emphasis on human rights in adult social care. With regard to safeguarding, issues of protection and risk are discussed, including the difficulty of balancing choice and control with risk and protection.

Chapter Eleven then concludes the book, identifying a number of transformational changes in adult social care and the underlying influences.

Terminology

Throughout the book, the term 'UK' refers to England, Scotland, Wales and Northern Ireland and the term 'Great Britain' refers to England, Scotland and Wales. The term 'UK government' is used to refer to the London government; its responsibility for adult social care normally extends only to England.

TWO

History of adult social care

Overview

The adoption of the term 'adult social care' was a response to decisions about children's services and related organisational changes and was not associated with any major new policies or strategies or particular new services. This meant that the developments and changes in adult social care built upon and emerged from existing patterns and trends. This chapter outlines the main historic trends that had influenced the shape and content of the services that were seen as composing adult social care at the time it became established as a more distinct area of provision.

Developments in welfare services in the post-1948 period, following the establishment of the NHS, marked the first grouping of what came to be identified by the 1960s as the personal social services. The process was led by the Children Act 1948, which gave local authorities responsibility for the establishment of children's departments. The National Assistance Act 1948 emphasised the reform of public assistance institutions and their replacement with local authority residential homes but other welfare support such as domiciliary care was slow to develop and at the discretion of local authorities (Means and Smith, 1998). The growth of disparate social services was originally mainly related to older people and mental health. There was a contrast between the muddled package of general community health and welfare measures in local councils and the new children's departments with a clear remit (Hill, 2000). A major development with a process of closing mental hospitals came with the Mental Health Act 1959 but the consequent closures were not always matched with care and support in the community (Johnson, 1999). Also, residential institutions for older people, including local authority homes, had attracted criticism for their admissions practices and often poor conditions, particularly in the significant *Last refuge* study by Townsend (1962).

Statutory unified social services approach

A government review of local authority social services between 1965 and 1968 was to mark the beginning of what has been described as a dramatic turnabout in the previously relatively low profile of local authority personal social services (Adams, 1996) in their fragmented state. The Seebohm Report (Great Britain Ministry of Housing and Local Government, 1968) recommended the creation of unified all-purpose local authority social services departments, based on existing children and welfare departments. The Seebohm proposals were enacted almost in their entirety and comprehensive social services departments came into existence following the Local Authority Social Services Act 1970, covering mainly children, families, older people and mental health and providing community-based and family-orientated services. The 1970 Act required local authorities to appoint a director of social services and set up social services committees. A Chronically Sick and Disabled Persons Act 1970 also placed a responsibility on local authorities to assist disabled people. A further consequence of the Seebohm Report was the adoption of a generic social worker approach rather than specialist approaches. With the implementation of the Seebohm recommendations in the 1970s, it has been argued that the personal social services came out of the shadows they had occupied and their activities could not be ignored in policy debates (Hill, 2000, p 32). With more resources, a higher-profile and more locally organised personal social services could move from an adjunct of health care to providing what was described as a more comprehensive, less stigmatising and more accessible service for the whole community (Adams, 1996, p 40).

Action had already been taken in Scotland to move to comprehensive local authority departments for social services, mainly through the Social Work (Scotland) Act 1968 which followed the *Social Work and the Community* report (Scottish Office, 1966). Strong campaigning by social work interests and a key issue of promoting a social work approach to offending by children were factors in Scotland. Local authorities in Scotland, undergoing reorganisation at the time as in England, established distinct unified social work departments. They differed in title from the Seebohm social services departments.

It was local government reorganisation that also led to reforms to the structure of personal social services in Northern Ireland. Unified welfare departments had actually existed since the 1950s, with children, families, older people and mental health being the responsibility of the county councils and county boroughs, but the outbreak of civil disturbances in 1968/69 led to major structural changes. As part of a programme of administrative reform, major functions were removed from local government, requiring a decision about the future location of welfare services. The outcome was legislation in 1972 to establish unified health and social service bodies for the planning and delivery of health and social care. Government narratives at the time made little reference to any principles of social care delivery (Heenan and Birrell, 2010). Consequently, since 1972, Northern Ireland has developed an integrated system of health and social services, with social services outside local government control. Historically, the nature of actual service provision remained generally in parity with Great Britain.

The restructured social service departments across the UK were seen as putting a heavy emphasis on new residential care, with a growing dependent population and a growth of an independent residential and nursing home sector (Means et al, 2002, p 53). Economic crises, reduced public expenditure and pressure on local government meant the slow development of care and support services. Financial pressures also played a major role in attention turning to the promotion of home-based care and the extension of family and community support (Johnson et al, 2010, p 27) as well as to the potential of greater involvement by the voluntary sector. Henwood (1992) identified three factors influencing the emerging of a new model of community care:

- demographic trends;
- criticisms of the reality of community care;
- the new managerialism and value-for-money agenda.

Consequently, a policy priority developed around avoiding institutional care and developing new, efficient means of attaining social care and welfare objectives.

Community care and mixed economies of care

Care in the community was mainly identifiable as a policy as opposed to care in institutions. 'Community care' had first begun to be discussed and developed in relation to people with mental illness and the running down of mental hospitals. The term had a much wider meaning than just a shift from care in institutions, covering domiciliary care, day care, counselling, supported housing and adaptations to assist independent living. Gladstone (1995) argued that the term 'community care' was ambiguous and often complicated the analysis of social care settings but did note the key distinction between institution and home. However, it has been suggested that the meaning of community care became refined over time and came to mean non-residential care, as opposed to just non-hospital care (Evandrou et al, 1991, p 244).

The 1980s saw a greater impetus towards community care with the closure of many residential institutions and the encouragement of community care for groups thought to need residential care (Young, 2000, p 221). Between 1979/80 and 1987/88, the number of places in residential homes rose by 47% and the number of beds in private nursing homes doubled. In the same period, staff of local authority home help services increased by 27%. The amount of home care and available resources was limited and a report on services for older people noted that care in the community really meant care by the community, by family, friends and neighbours (DHSS, 1981). A more influential and critical report was published in 1986 by the Audit Commission: *Making a reality of community care* (Audit Commission, 1986). This strongly criticised the very slow movement of people with mental health problems, people with learning disabilities and older people in hospital to community-based provision (Means et al, 2002). The report identified problems with the mismatch of resources, the lack of bridging funds, organisational fragmentation, inadequate staffing and the perverse effects of social security with no provision for social security to support care in the community. The financial arrangements allowing social security payments to meet care costs provided a perverse incentive for local authorities to use residential care (Johnson et al, 2010, p 27). The UK government responded to such criticisms by establishing a strategic review of community care, focusing on the ways in which public funds supported community care policy and advising on options to improve the use of these funds. The Griffiths Report (Griffiths, 1988) concluded that community care policy was in need of reform and radical steps were necessary. This view was based on a number of key findings:

- that central government had failed to develop any link between the objectives of community care policy and the resources made available;
- that responsibilities between different bodies at local level were not clear, including between health and local authorities;
- that subsidising residential and nursing home places through the social security system was wasteful;
- that choice and efficiency could be developed through a mixed economy approach.

The Griffiths Report made a number of recommendations and the key recommendations are listed in Box 2.

Box 2: Griffiths Report – key recommendations

- Social service authorities should be the lead agency for all the main community care groups and be given the role of planning and coordinating social care.
- There should be a mixed economy of care provision involving public, voluntary and private sectors.
- Provision would be determined by packages of care arrangements and annual community care plans.
- The funding system should change with social services meeting care costs subject to a means test and with local authorities receiving earmarked monies.

Source: Means et al (2002, p 4)

The UK government made no formal response to the Griffiths Report but acted a year later – a delay caused by government doubts about an increased role for local authorities (Sharkey, 2000). A government White Paper *Caring for people* (DH, 1989) set out six key objectives for what it called community care:

- to promote domiciliary, day and respite services to enable people to live in their own homes;
- to ensure support for carers has high priority;
- to have proper assessment of need and packages of care;
- to promote a flourishing independent sector;
- to clarify the responsibilities of agencies;
- to introduce a new funding structure for social care.

The six objectives had different purposes or rationales and Lymbery (2010) notes that two related to care principles, two were primarily administrative and two expressed an ideological preference.

The government proposed a number of policy changes, which in practice broadly followed the recommendations of the Griffiths Report. The proposals can be grouped into four elements:

- Local authorities would become responsible for assessing individual need, designing care arrangements and producing plans for the development of community care services.
- Local authorities would be expected to make maximum use of the independent sector and promote a mixed economy of care.
- Local authorities would take responsibility for the financial support of people in homes over and above social security entitlements. There would be a new grant to develop social care for people with mentally illness.
- Local authorities would be expected to establish inspection and registration units.

Caring for people was somewhat unusual at the time in that it took into account differences between the four countries of the UK. Separate chapters relating to Scotland and Wales were included and there was a separate policy paper for Northern Ireland. *Caring for people* described the aim of community care in Scotland as enabling those who need care to live as independently as possible in their own homes and to reduce the reliance on residential care. It was noted that the development of community care was well established. Between 1979/80 and 1988/89, expenditure on community services rose by 43% and between 1979 and 1987 the number of people with learning disabilities in institutions fell by 21%, the number of long-stay hospital patients with mental illness fell by 13% while the number of clients of home-help services rose by 35% (DH, 1989, p 79). Three main priority aims for community care were identified:

- to clarify the responsibilities of agencies;
- to develop services that allow for a range of options for those in need of care;
- to ensure that residential care is used appropriately.

It was also particularly noted that there had been joint working between Scottish local authorities and health bodies in shifting the emphasis from institutional care to domiciliary and other community-based services. It was recognised that, unlike in England, local authorities in Scotland were likely to remain major providers of care facilities for the time being. The UK government still wished local councils to make greater use of the voluntary and private sectors and expected them to also move to an enabling role rather than that of a direct provider. Proposals for care assessments, packages of care, community care plans and registration inspection of residential homes were similar to England. There was also a call for closer collaboration between general practitioners (GPs), health boards and local social work departments. Overall, there was an emphasis on the development of domiciliary and day care services as an alternative to residential care, which could be provided by local councils or the private or voluntary sectors.

Caring for people also separately recognised the remarkable development and growth of social services in Wales, particularly for the most vulnerable. While it was argued that most of the proposals for England applied equally to Wales, it was accepted that Wales had distinctive needs and circumstances. Particular attention was paid to services in Wales for people with mental illness or learning disabilities, which were seen as imbalanced and poorly distributed across Wales (DH, 1989, p 93). Joint plans were to be prepared by health and social services authorities within the framework of an all-Wales strategy. Also proposed for Wales was the preparation of what was called a 'social care plan' as a fairly comprehensive approach, to include contributions from social services authorities, health bodies, GP services, housing bodies and voluntary sectors and to take account of the views of users of services. However, it was proposed that social services authorities should have the responsibility and the budget for social care. A new system of quality assurance would include a Social Services Inspectorate Wales.

A separate paper was produced for Northern Ireland by the UK government – *People first: Community care in Northern Ireland in the 1990s* (DHSS, 1990) – based on the Griffiths Report. The number of people in independent residential care receiving social security support in Northern Ireland rose from under 300 in 1979 to some 3,500 in 1989 and over the same period the number of places in statutory care homes rose by 24%. The arrangements for public funding were seen as having a built-in bias towards residential and nursing home care rather than services for people at home. The principles underpinning the government's approach to community care were given as follows:

• Services should respond flexibly to the needs of individuals.
• Services should offer a range of options.
• Services should intervene no more than necessary.
• Services should concentrate on those with the greatest needs.

Despite this more residential emphasis in principle, the main changes to the way in which community care was to be delivered were similar to those set out in *Caring for people* and included:

• health and social services boards;
• making use of the independent sector;
• assessing individual needs;
• tailoring care packages to meet needs;
• introducing a new funding structure;
• establishing registration and inspection units;

- monitoring and evaluating more clearly community care services (DHSS, 1990, p 6).

The implementation was to differ in certain respects from Great Britain, with no prescribed purchaser–provider divide and less independent sector involvement in domiciliary, day and respite care.

Returning to *Caring for people*, most of the proposals in the White Paper were included in the NHS and Community Care Act 1990, although the measures were not fully implemented until 1993. Responsibility for assessing community needs, community care plans and individual care management passed to local authorities. With the Act it was suggested that personal social services experienced the most far-reaching changes since the Local Authority Social Services Act 1970 (Johnson, 1999, p 82). McDonald (2006, p 20) notes that the 1990 Act produced no new entitlements to services that were not provided under existing legislation and retained the confusing distinction between powers and duties. Underpinning the proposals were the principles of reducing the role of the state and introducing a quasi-market. The major change under the Act was the purchaser–provider split. Local authorities ceased to be the main providers of community care and changed their role to assessing social care needs and commissioning or purchasing community services from a variety of sources. Much more use was to be made of the voluntary and private sectors and consequently the 1990 Act led to a more mixed economy of care. One of the most significant government interventions was its insistence that 85% of the transitional money be spent on independent providers of social care (Sharkey, 2000, p 4). Thus, Hill (2000, p 36) describes the 1990 Act as incorporating a move towards the partial privatisation of all existing local authority services in the area of community care. The community care reforms introduced by the Act were seen by many as undermining a rights-based and free system of care, being replaced by means testing and charging (Means et al, 2002, p 27). People in residential care were no longer funded from social security benefits. The transfer of a budget to be administered by local authorities put an end to continuing growth in the numbers entering residential care (Lewis and Glennerster, 1996). Competition among independent agencies was expected to reduce the cost of services and offer a wider choice to users (Langan, 1998, p 165).

The 1990 Act did introduce some other measures. The role of the Social Services Inspectorate was strengthened and new complaints procedures were introduced. Also, the Act required local authorities to consult with service users and carers in assessing needs and developing plans and priorities. Although the Act strengthened the voices of users in its provisions, it has been suggested that it did little to reconcile policy statements on user involvement with the reality that most users experienced (Adams, 1996, p 125).

Local authorities had to introduce a complex package of reforms at a time of financial, organisational and political uncertainty (Means et al, 2008, p 60). They adopted the changes at different speeds. There was also a view in some authorities that care management became a process of rationing resources (Ellison and Pierson, 1998, p 169). An Audit Commission report in 1992 – *Community care: Managing the cascade of change* – highlighted the scale of organisational change and the need to develop new assessment and management systems, with research identifying a spread of approaches (Lewis and Glennerster, 1996). The impact on provision seemed greater for services for older people than for services in the areas of mental health and learning disability. The development of the mixed economy also varied between local authorities. There were some clear trends, as the independent sector became more important as a provider in care services for adults rather than for children and families but also as the independent sector developed a stronger role in residential provision than in domiciliary care. The voluntary sector also responded in diverse ways as pressure was put on smaller groups and the traditional role of specialist provision changed to mainstream provision and bidding for contracts became a major activity. In the period 1992–96, the voluntary sector contribution in domiciliary care was small, remaining mainly stranded in day care (Kendall, 2000).

By far the majority of social care was still provided by the informal sector and social services departments agreed to support carers in their community care plans. Legislation in 1995 gave carers the right to separate assessments and to further packages of support. However, in the mid-1990s, financial pressures and expenditure cuts were putting strains on the planned developments in community care and local authorities began to respond in a number of ways: tightening eligibility, cutting services, reviewing charges and limiting funding on care packages (Sharkey, 2000, p 13). It has been argued that the implementation of community care became more resources-led rather than needs-led or user-led (Adams, 1996, p 124). From the 1980s, the emphasis on community care had promoted not only the voluntary sector but also the role of unpaid carers. The 1990 Act specified that the needs of carers had to be taken into account. It has been argued that there had been a shifting of carers from the wings to centre stage in a short period of time (Offer, 1999, p 38). The 1990 Act applied to Scotland and Wales as well as England. Research in Scotland showed obstacles to development, including the fact that participation by GPs was not widespread (Titterton, 1994). It has been suggested that social work departments in local authorities in Scotland were much slower in developing a mixed economy of care (Sharkey, 2000, p 9) and support for statutory provision was high, with widespread opposition to markets and competition. Social work departments in Scotland were able to carry out community care assessments, develop services to allow people to remain in their own homes and become enablers rather than providers of services (Cavaye, 2006, p 253).

Moving to the end of the 1990s, the new direction to community care and the mixed economy of social care had become well established, but the system was largely a quasi-market with the characteristics of purchaser–provider distinction, state bodies as purchasers, state funding and services largely free to the user but with some means-tested charges. Although the Conservative governments of the 1980s and 1990s might have been thought of as not well disposed to local authority social services departments and social workers both expanded under Conservative governments (Langan, 1998, p 161). It has been noted that the focus of *Caring for people* was on avoiding admission to residential care but not the other emerging dimension of replacing acute medical beds with community care (Wistow, 1994).

Modernisation of social care

Despite the changes, it was apparent by 1997 when a Labour government came to power that the objectives set out in *Caring for people* had at best only been partly met (Means et al, 2000, p 82). It was also suggested that there had been too much emphasis on structures and procedures rather than on outcomes (Lewis and Glennerster, 1996). The new government identified a major need to reform and modernise social care and produced a major policy document: *Modernising social services* (DH, 1998a). This stated the government's intention to undertake reforms that would lead to improvements in services and rejected the previous government's commitment to privatisation of care provision but also rejected a return to near-monopoly local authority provision. This was defining a New Labour Third Way for social care, moving the focus away from those providing care to outcomes for individuals and carers (DH, 1998a, p 8). It has been noted that *Modernising social services* is one of the few documents that actually defined the Third Way in relation to specific policies (Netton, 2005, p 89). As to why modernisation was needed, the White Paper listed failings in social care. These are listed in Box 3.

Box 3: Failings in adult social care

Protection
People with learning disabilities or older people were neglected or mistreated.

Coordination
There was poor joined-up working in relation to people leaving hospital.

Flexibility
There was inflexibility in providing what suits the service rather than what suits the person needing care.

Clarity of role
There was no definition of what users can expect and also a lack of clarity in objectives and standards.

Consistency
Social services differed between localities, with inconsistencies in eligibility and standards.

Efficiency

There was scope for authorities to get more for what they spend.

Source: DH (1998a)

Box 4 sets out the key principles and recommendations for social care provision that were set out in the White Paper.

Box 4: Key principles and recommendations in social care provision
- Care should be provided in ways that support people's independence and use their capacities and potential.
- The system should be more centred on the service user, with people having more say.
- Everyone should be safeguarded against abuse, neglect and poor treatment.
- Services should be provided in a more consistent way in every part of the country.
- There should be improved partnership working through integrated working with health and with the independent sector.
- There should be improvements in the workforce, with staff sufficiently trained.

Source: DH (1998a)

In an interesting approach, given what was to happen organisationally in the future, *Modernising social services* went on to identify separate national objectives for adult services from children's services as part of a wider exercise in setting national service frameworks. The objectives for adult social services were presented as:

- promoting the independence of adults;
- enabling people to live safe lives in their own homes;
- helping people to remain in employment;
- avoiding unnecessary admission to hospital;
- assisting informal carers;
- planning and commissioning services;
- assessing needs and care practices.

With partnership and community both important concerns for New Labour, social care policy reflected both local authorities working together and a proactive approach to establishing a framework for care in the community (Malin et al, 2002). The scope of New Labour's approach was wide and complex and had the potential for a further cascade of change. The main strategies can be divided usefully into three.

The first trend can be seen in policies that very much reflected major principles and values of Third Way initiatives. With partnership a major feature of New Labour policy, *Modernising social services* devoted a full chapter to partnership and particularly the health and social care interface. This was seen as being crucial in the future for reducing the need for long-stay beds and for the primacy of care in the community as well as having benefits through addressing overlaps in care. After 1997, successive Labour governments were to produce what has been called a stream of policy guidance, legislation, strategies and resources (Clarke and Glendinning, 2002), all to encourage joint working. The empowerment of stakeholders was a further emphasis of New Labour, linked closely to ideas of participation and partnership. New Labour also promoted ideas about reinventing government through collective action within the community (Malin et al, 2002) and an increasing role for service users and carers became a further important feature of social care policies (Beresford, 2002). Evidence-based policy making was to be articulated as a key factor in the wider New Labour approach to public service delivery and modernisation and this view also had an impact on social care provision. This led to a number of initiatives, such as the establishment of the Social Care Institute for Excellence and personal social service research units in several universities.

A second trend in the implementation of *Modernising social services* can be interpreted as a continuation of policies operated by the previous Conservative administration. This was most apparent in the continuation of the mixed economy and the growth of contracting out of services to the independent sector. The shift was clear in home care provision where, by 2002, 64% of home care provision in England was supplied by the independent sector. Action to improve performance and efficiency and drive up performance through assessment and inspections was also largely a continuation in policy. New Labour did replace compulsory competitive tendering with a Best Value regime but the aim was to drive up service quality.

A third trend can be seen in policies that demonstrated mainly a view that adult social services were at the heart of the welfare state and the quality of provision should be strengthened. This was reflected not only in extra resources and a modernisation fund but also in delivering more support for carers and assessing the needs of carers, in policies to improve the workforce including new regulatory bodies and in national service frameworks to promote the standards of care and new modes of care.

Anti-oppressive practice and rights agenda

Issues of discrimination and inequality in the provision and outcomes of community care and social care more generally emerged as an important issue in the 1980s and 1990s. Questions relating to racial discrimination, prejudice, treatment of minority ethnic groups and what was defined as anti–oppressive practice were identified and analysed by an increasing number of researchers, academics, practitioners, managers and politicians. Such issues had received little attention in the *Caring for People* (DH, 1989) paper beyond a brief reference to minority ethnic groups, or in the major government strategies. Williams (1996) comments that connecting racism to the history of community care is no easy task and records of experiences are relatively recent. Analysis in terms of race identified a number of aspects of the treatment of black and minority ethnic people which can be listed as:

- the disadvantages that minority ethnic groups experience in accessing or knowing about services;
- direct discrimination in the delivery of services, meaning some groups experience unequal treatment;
- the impact of wider discrimination and abuse that service users may experience in the wider community or even in care settings;
- patterns of discrimination in employment in the social care and social work sectors – in 1997, it was reported that only 4% of senior staff were from minority ethnic groups and in 1999 there was only one black social services director in England (Balloch and McLean, 2000, p 94);
- the potential for racist attitudes emerging as a factor in relations between a care worker and user;
- the need for social care to recognise and be sensitive to the circumstances and culture of minority ethnic communities;
- a number of studies indicating that black people's experience of mental health services differed from that of the white population (Watters, 1996).

The term 'oppression' arose in relation to defining disadvantage, inequality and disadvantage in these terms (Ahmad and Atkins, 1996). The debate on anti-oppressive practice opened up more wide-ranging issues and analysis. Anti-oppressive practice could be related to deeper structural inequality in society and all social care interpreted as having a role in maintaining patterns of inequality and oppression (Dominelli, 2002). Racial discrimination was only one form of anti-discriminatory practice: people and users could also suffer disadvantage on grounds of disability, mental health, gender, age or religion or forms of double oppression. Social care in Northern Ireland had to contend with similar issues but based on religious discrimination and sectarian prejudices (Heenan and Birrell, 2011, p 23).

These agendas were related to a number of outcomes that had a developing impact on adult social care. Two developments had particular significance. First, the government introduced anti-discrimination legislation, mainly through the Race Relations Act 2002, which imposed a duty on public authorities in Great Britain not to discriminate on grounds of race, colour, ethnic or national origin and covered both direct and indirect discrimination. Public authorities also had a duty to promote racial equality. Secondly, there was training in anti-discriminatory, anti-oppressive and anti-racist practice. This was based on what was called a 'collectivist' professional approach with at the time the social work profession taking responsibility to eliminate oppression from its own practice, through education and training requirements. Training requirements in anti-sectarian practice were also introduced in Northern Ireland.

Box 5: Adult social care policy timeline, 1968–97

Year	Policy/legislation	Main provisions/developments
1968	Seebohm Report	Outcome of government review of local authority social services. Recommended all-purpose local authority social services departments
1970	Local Authority Social Services Act	Required local authorities to appoint a director of social services and set up social services committees
1970	Chronically Sick and Disabled Persons Act	First legislation to place a responsibility on local authorities to, after assessment, assist anyone covered by the legislation with practical assistance such as adaptations to homes
1986	Audit Commission Report *Making a reality of community care*	Influential report critical of slow progress in moving people from institutions to community-based provisions
1988	Griffiths Report *Community care: agenda for action*	Report of review established by government in the wake of criticisms about community care. It provided recommendations on future of community care policy
1989	Publication of White Paper *Caring for People* (A paper setting out similar provisions was published for NI in 1990: *People First*)	Set out key objectives for community care policy including assessment of need and packages of care and promotion of mixed economy of care
1990	NHS and Community Care Act	Implemented most of the proposals contained in the 1989 White Paper and signified the move towards a mixed economy of care. Introduced a statutory framework for community care
1995	Carers (Recognition and Services) Act	Gave carers the right to a separate assessment of need

Conclusions

Accounts of the development of social care tend to make a differentiation in terms of either key distinctive themes or government ideology. For example, in relation to the former approach, Adams (1996, p 19) identified three main themes as treatment, consumerism and empowerment. Treatment means diagnosing and prescribing services to tackle people's problems. Consumerism is the managed markets of personal social services. And empowerment involves the importance of user involvement with an emphasis on control, participation and choice. Other overviews reduced the major themes to two: the shift to community care and the introduction of quasi-markets (Sharkey, 2000; Means et al, 2002). The latter approach is to define distinctive themes more clearly in terms of political ideology. Such accounts usually make a distinction between New Right approaches, mostly related to the Thatcher government, and New Labour, exemplified in the policies adopted by respective governments. On occasions a wider perspective of rising neoliberalism is invoked or Old Labour policies or Fabianism may be separately identified. An interesting typology has also been developed by Greer (2004) in analysing mainly health developments but including some reference to social services. His distinctions also accord with a key divergence between each of the four countries of the UK. He sees trends in England dominated by increasing reliance on markets; in Scotland, the strength of professional bodies has been key; in Wales, localism and local government dominance has been key; and in Northern Ireland, Greer identifies a prevailing permissive managerialism with little policy innovation and a desire to keep services running.

It is clear that the period from the 1960s to the end of the 20th century saw shifts and developing trends in the provision of social care. A number of these dominated during this period (see Box 6).

Box 6: Developing trends in the provision of social care
- The change from institutional to community care.
- The development of the mixed economy and the increasing role of the independent sector.
- The acceptance of charging for social care.
- The importance of carers and support for carers.

A number of other important themes emerged during this period but these can be seen as continuing to develop and becoming more important in the period after 2000. These can be listed as:

- the growing significance of health and social care collaboration;
- the growth of personalisation of care;
- the further development of quasi-markets and the independent sector;
- the importance of equality and rights agendas;
- the promotion of user involvement and public participation;
- the development of standards inspection protection and safeguarding.

Wider socioeconomic factors also had an influence at times, in particular pressures on public expenditure and the state of local government finances in Great Britain.

Sources

The shift from institutional to community care is well covered by Means and Smith (1998), and Means et al (2008) deal with the development of community care under New Labour. For discussion of the emergence of the mixed economy of care, see Malin et al (2002) and Hill (2000) for analysis of policy making in relation to social services.

Questions

- What factors have led to adult social care becoming a distinct area of provision?

- How significant has the idea of a mixed economy of care been in government approaches to adult social care?

- Were there notable differences between policies on adult social care between Labour and Conservative administrations?

- Were there major differences in adult social care policies between the four countries of the UK?

THREE

Contemporary issues in adult social care

Overview

The emergence of adult social care as a more distinct area of provision since 2005 has facilitated the easier identification of major issues and debates that have been of central concern to governments, users, carers, providers, managers, practitioners, academics and other commentators. Since 2005 a significant number of government reports and papers specifically on adult social care have been published as part of what all recent governments have seen as a need for a new vision, reform and transformation. Parliamentary reports, academic work and other research and policy reports have also addressed the direction that adult social care should take. This chapter traces the major policy developments and debates in government reports and White and Green Papers, lists the main shortcomings and problems that have been identified and reviews the key points of analysis, and summarises the issues for debate about future direction and delivery.

Transformation, vision and change agendas

The period marking the development of adult social care as a distinct entity has seen a series of major governmental inquiries and policy recommendations, which have been aimed at setting new directions and new principles for delivering adult social care. These strategic documents (listed below) have covered Labour and Conservative/Liberal Democrat administrations in the UK, demonstrating some continuity in thinking between them and also policy development by the devolved administrations. It can also be noted that this process has not yet ended and some more significant UK government papers are likely.

The period 2005–12 was noteworthy for what was encompassed by a transforming adult social care agenda in England. The Green Paper *Independence, well-being and choice* (DH, 2005) has been seen as a watershed in the UK government approach to adult social care (Roulstone and Morgan, 2009) and as pivotal to a new vision for adult social care (Lymbery, 2010). It set out a largely developing emphasis on increasing users' independence, giving greater individual choice and control, and pushed forward the personalisation agenda, including direct payments and pilots for individual budgets. The 2005 Green Paper was seen as introducing three shifts in the modernisation of adult social care:

- putting service users more in control;
- an emphasis on prevention and wellbeing
- a greater emphasis on users, carers and the workforce (Newman et al, 2008, p 539).

The adoption of a transforming adult social care approach was to be more closely associated with the government White Paper *Our health, our care, our say: A new direction for community services* (DH, 2006a). This White Paper claimed a new and ambitious vision for the future of community services. Underpinning this vision was a view that community services needed to take centre stage in the health and social care system, rather than acute services, and that there should be a fundamental shift to provide care closer to home, with a seamless health and social care system to support this. The White Paper also advocated the development of a personalised approach to the delivery of adult social care. The new direction that was set out proposed making adult social care higher quality, more responsive to people's views, more cost effective with better prevention, more choice and voice, support tailored to individual needs and more flexible support. A concordat – *Putting people first* (DH, 2007) – was an agreement between central and local government in England to implement this agenda over the following 10 years. The transformation of adult social care would be based on partnership working between central and local government, social care professionals, providers and the regulator. *Putting people first* was underpinned by four key themes and a number of goals, as presented in Box 7.

Box 7: Key themes and goals in the development of adult social care
- Access to universal services and information, advice and advocacy.
- Prevention and early intervention to help people stay healthy or recover from illness.
- Choice and control so that people can design support themselves and have a choice about how they receive support and who manages it.
- Promotion of social capital by making sure that everyone has the opportunity to be part of a community.

Putting people first set out a vision and commitment to the transformation of adult social care, with the values and elements of a personalised adult social care system. Four main goals were specified in the concordat:

- better prevention and early intervention for improved health, independence and wellbeing;
- more choice and a stronger voice for individuals and communities;
- tackling inequalities and improving access to services;
- more support for people with long-term needs.

The transforming adult social care programme led to an extensive structure of coordination groups, partnerships and networks (Improvement and Development Agency, 2009) to oversee its implementation. There was a strong emphasis on better delivery through inter-departmental and inter-agency cooperation and an increasing importance given to delivering personalised care.

The emergence of distinct adult social care departments in local councils coincided with three major transformation strategies:

- the transfer of resources from secondary health care to community health and social care;
- increased collaboration and joint working between health and social care;
- implementation of the personalisation agenda through a person-centred approach, greater choice, direct payments and individual budgets.

Following on from *Putting people first*, the UK government, then led by Gordon Brown, launched a wider initiative of a national engagement process to ask people who use care and support, their carers, people working in care and support and the public for their views on the future care system. The outcome was the Green Paper *Shaping the future of care together* (DH, 2009a). Pressures for change were identified from changes in life expectancy and changing demographics and also rising expectations, which meant that people expected more choice and control over services. The Green Paper identified challenges around people who do not get help towards paying for care, that care was often only provided when people had developed high levels of need, and people with the same needs received different levels of care depending on where they lived. Other problems identified with the care system were the different parts not working together, the system being confusing and the system not being tailored to people's needs. The Green Paper set an aspiration for the future of a vision of a national care system for England that was fair, simple and affordable for everyone, underpinned by national rights and entitlements but personalised to individual needs. Some more fundamental thinking was reflected in ideas that money could be better invested in prevention, rehabilitation and keeping people active and healthy, and that people who need services are often the experts in their own care and the system for the future must respect this. *Shaping the future of care together* acknowledged problems with the current system in terms of uncertainty about costs, variations in the standards and quantity of care and funding pressures.

A further White Paper – *Building the national care service* (DH, 2010b) – set out six founding principles and six pillars of the national care service, as presented in Box 8.

Box 8: Founding principles and pillars of the national care service

Founding principles
- Be universal – supporting all adults with an eligible care need within a framework of national entitlements.
- Be free when people need it – based on need, rather than the ability to pay.
- Work in partnership – with all the different organisations and people who support individuals with care and support needs day-to-day.
- Ensure choice and control – valuing all, treating everyone with dignity, respecting an individual's human rights, personal to every individual's needs, and putting people in charge of their own lives.
- Support family, carers and community life – recognising the vital contribution that families, carers and communities make in enabling people to realise their potential.
- Be accessible – easy to understand, helping people make the right choices.

Source: DH (2010b, p 13)

Pillars
- Prevention and wellbeing services to keep you independent.
- Nationally consistent eligibility criteria for social care enshrined in law.
- A joined-up assessment.
- Information and advice about care and support.
- Personalised care and support, through a personal budget.
- Fair funding, with a collective, shared responsibility for paying for care and support.

Source: DH (2010b, p 14)

This vision for the future suggested a need for three main changes:

- more joined-up working, particularly between the national care service and the NHS, free at the point of need;
- a wider range of services in care and support and more choice;
- better quality and innovation.

With a change of government the idea of a national care service in England was dropped but the idea of a new vision for adult social care was to continue. In 2010, the new Coalition government produced a document *A vision for adult social care: Capable communities and active citizens* (DH, 2010a), which claimed to set a new agenda for the reform of adult social care in England. The Coalition's vision for adult social care focused on three commitments:

- to break down barriers between health and social care funding to incentivise preventative action;
- to extend the roll-out of personal budgets to give people and their carers more control and purchasing power;
- to use direct payments to carers and better community-based provision to improve access to respite care.

The emphasis on personalisation, direct payments and carers was seen as in tune with three values of freedom, fairness and responsibility, which underpinned the Coalition government's vision for social care.

The policy content of the vision was to build on seven principles:

- *prevention*, empowering people and helping people to retain and regain independence, with carers at the first line of prevention;
- *personalisation*, with individuals not institutions taking control of their care with direct payments provided for all eligible people;
- *partnership*, between individuals, communities, the voluntary and private sectors, the NHS and councils to deliver care and support;
- *plurality*, with diverse service provision and a market of service providers;
- *protection*, with sensible safeguards against the risk of abuse or neglect;
- *productivity*, with local accountability driving improvements and innovation to deliver higher productivity and high-quality care and support services;
- *people*, with a workforce to provide care and support with skill, compassion and imagination.

In the discussion of this new vision, clear differences with the thinking of the previous administration were drawn. The new vision was described as not simply looking to the state for answers but devolving power from central government to communities and individuals and shifting power to people so that they have the freedom to choose services from a vibrant plural market. The vision document specifically identified with a 'Big Society' approach to social care, using the creativity and enthusiasm of local communities (DH, 2010a, p 10).

Two major reports were published in 2011 following inquiries that had been launched previously. The Dilnot Commission was an independent inquiry reviewing the funding system for care and support (Dilnot Commission, 2011). The current system of funding social care was seen by many as being unfit for purpose, with growing levels of unmet need. It was perceived as unfair because of the variation of eligibility thresholds across local authorities and because of the means-testing system, which meant that people over a certain income had to pay in part or in full for their care. For some people this amounted to thousands of pounds and involved them having to sell their home. The Dilnot Commission found the current funding system in urgent need of reform, identifying the key issue of people being left exposed to potential catastrophic care costs. The commission made recommendations, some of which are presented in Box 9.

Box 9: Dilnot Commission recommendations

- An individual's lifetime contribution should be capped at £35,000.
- The means-tested threshold for liability for full costs should be increased to £100,000.
- There should be national eligibility criteria and portable assessments.
- The integration between social care services and other services should be increased and more emphasis should be placed on the preventative aspect of social care.

Source: Dilnot Commission (2011)

The Coalition government gave a cautious response to the estimated costs to government and proposed further consultation, which would lead to a new White Paper.

The second major report in 2011 came from the Law Commission and an investigation into adult social care law. It was found that existing legislative provisions were outdated, disparate, complex and fragmented (Law Commission, 2011). The law reform was based on the approach presented in Box 10.

Box 10: The Law Commission report on social care approach to social care law

- A three-tier structure of statute, regulations and guidance with a single statute for adult social care for England.
- A requirement for ministers to revise a code of practice for guidance to social services authorities in England.
- That separate legislation for Wales was now necessary.
- The adoption of an overarching principle that adult social care must promote and contribute to the wellbeing of individuals and that individuals should be involved in planning care.
- *Source:* Law Commission (2011)

A series of recommendations was made, covering:

- information provided by local authorities;
- community care assessments;
- eligibility frameworks for users and carers;
- charges for services;
- adult protection;
- portability between local authorities;
- an enhanced duty imposed on each social service authority to cooperate with other organisations.

Source: Law Commission (2011).

In 2011, the government launched the strategy: *Caring for our future: Shared ambitions for care and support* (DH, 2011a). This was seen as an opportunity to bring together the recommendations from *A vision for adult social care* (DH, 2010a), the Dilnot Commission (2011) on funding and the Law Commission (2011) in order to get reform right (DH, 2011a). This was to take the form of an engagement with service users, carers, local councils, care providers and the voluntary sector about the priorities for improving care and support and helping people to live independent, active and healthy lives. The government noted that making changes to care and support was not simple.

Six key areas covered were:

- *quality* – how can we improve the quality of care with the right workforce?
- *personalisation* – how can we give people more choice and control over the care and support they use?
- *shaping local care services* – how can we ensure there is a range of local organisations responding to people's needs and choices?
- *prevention* – how could we support more effective and early prevention?
- *integration* – how could we build better connections locally?
- *role of financial services* – role of financial services in supporting care users and carers.

The *Caring for our future* engagement and evidence led to a White Paper entitled *Caring for our future: Reforming care and support* (DH, 2012a). Alongside the policies in the White Paper was a draft Care and Support Bill, to enact many of the proposals and also consolidate an adult social care statute, closely informed by the recommendations of the Law Commission (DH, 2012b). The government identified two core principles at the heart of the White Paper: first, we should do everything we can – as individuals, as communities and as a government – to prevent, postpone and minimise people's need for formal care; and second, people should be in control of their own care and support. The White Paper again used the language of transformation in setting out a new vision for a reformed care and support system. The main problems identified in the current system are presented in Box 11.

Box 11: *Caring for our future* **and main problems in the current system**
- Too often the system only reacts to crisis.
- Not enough use is made of the skills and talents in communities.
- Access to care varies across the country.
- Carers have no clear entitlement to support.
- The quality of care is variable and inconsistent.
- There is often no joined-up health, care and support.
- There is increasing pressure of a growing and ageing population.

Source: DH (2012a)

Principles that were listed as underpinning the White Paper contained a mixture of well-rehearsed phrases alongside some more innovative expressions of principle and were limited to six, as presented in Box 12.

Box 12: Principles underpinning the *Caring for our future* **White Paper**
- The health, wellbeing, independence and rights of individuals are at the heart of care and support, with timely and effective interventions.
- People are treated with dignity and respect and are safe from abuse.
- Personalisation is achieved through giving a person real choice and control over the care and support they need.
- The skills, resources and networks in every community are harnessed to support people to live well.
- Carers are recognised for their contribution to society as vital partners in care.
- A caring, skilled and valued workforce delivers quality care and support.

Source: DH (2012a)

The last two principles are very familiar to social care papers and it is not surprising that personalisation, independent living and safeguarding should appear as core principles of government strategy. There are more innovative references to prevention and the values of the Big Society.

A seven-point list of objectives of the reformed system, which accompanied the White Paper, used rather more traditional language and categories of policies, noting that the new system will:

- focus on people's wellbeing and support them to stay independent for as long as possible;
- introduce greater national consistency in access to care and support;
- provide better information to help people make choices about their care;
- give people more control over their care;
- improve support for carers;
- improve the quality of care and support;
- improve integration of different services.

Key policy initiatives set out in *Caring for our future* describe policy initiatives in 12 areas:

- strengthening support within communities;
- housing and new housing options;
- better information and advice;
- assessment, national minimum eligibility threshold, and portability;
- carers' support;

- defining high-quality care;
- improving quality;
- keeping people safe;
- a better local care market;
- a skilled workforce;
- personalised care and support;
- integration and joined-up care.

These policy areas can be seen as reflecting a greater or new priority to certain areas by the Coalition government in terms of the involvement of:

- communities and networks;
- better information;
- national eligibility;
- a diverse range of providers;
- the importance of quality standards;
- housing support.

Particular innovations included ensuring the portability of assessments, piloting the use of direct payments in residential care and improving mechanisms for the early identification of care. As part of the wider consultation process on the strategy, a study of the views of users was carried out (Beresford and Andrews, 2012). Some concerns accorded with government aspirations relating to the quality of the workforce, support for users and lack of integration but much concern was expressed at privatisation and the impact of public spending cuts on personalisation and user involvement.

The draft Care and Support Bill (DH, 2012b) placed a number of clear duties on local authorities in England, setting out entitlements, processes, frameworks and administrative mechanisms. The major provisions included creating a single, clear duty on local authorities to carry out assessments and determine whether a person has eligible needs, and using a national threshold for eligibility, that is, establishing an entitlement to care to meet need. There is a new duty on local authorities to provide a care and support plan and this planning process will take place between the person, any carer and the local authority. The draft Bill also creates a legal entitlement to a personal budget. Previously only direct payments have had a place in law. The draft Bill also sets out carers' legal rights to assessments and support for them in their caring role. After deciding whether a carer has eligible needs, the local authority and the carer need to think about what type of support the carer might benefit from.

The draft Bill includes the key provisions as outlined in Box 13.

Box 13: Key provisions of the draft Care and Support Bill 2012

- New statutory principles, which embed the promotion of individual wellbeing as the driving force underpinning the provision of care and support.
- Population-level duties on local authorities to provide information and advice, and prevention services, and shape the market for care and support services.
- Clear legal entitlements to care and support, including giving carers a right to support for the first time to put them on the same footing as the people for whom they care.
- Set out in law that everyone, including carers, should have a personal budget as part of their care and support plan, and give people the right to ask for this to be made as a direct payment.
- New duties to ensure that no one's care and support are interrupted when they move home from one local authority area to another.
- A new statutory framework for adult safeguarding, setting out the responsibilities of local authorities and their partners, and creating safeguarding adults boards in every area.

Source: Long and Powell (2012)

It had been anticipated that the White Paper and the draft Bill might have contained a response to the recommendations of the Dilnot Commission on funding reform for long-term care. Instead, the government published a progress report on social care funding reform (DH, 2012c). This report stated that the government agrees that the principles of the Dilnot Commission's model – financial protection through capped costs and an extended means test – would be the right basis for any new funding model. However, the government expressed the view that the right place to consider the introduction of a new system was at the next Spending Review. In the meantime the progress report committed to introducing a universal deferred payments scheme to ensure that no one would be forced to sell their home to pay for care in their lifetime.

The White Paper reforms as listed were broadly welcomed, including the new statutory duties and entitlements in the draft Bill. Measures relating to national eligibility criteria, personalisation, support for carers, assessment, involvement, quality and safeguarding can be seen as building on work already done. Some specific criticisms were directed at the absence of commitments to advocacy and in relation to information and advice. However, critical comment was dominated by one issue in the responses of local government, and voluntary and non-governmental bodies, that the White Paper did not address the reality of the growing crisis in adult social care and the subsequent financial pressures.

Reform strategies and policies have also been produced by the devolved administrations in the period since 2007. In Wales, strongly focused documents on adult social care have been published. The Welsh Assembly Government (2007) published *Fulfilled lives, supportive communities: A strategy for social services in Wales over the next decade.* There was a distinctive support in the rationale for a Welsh approach based on welfare, social justice, social inclusion, a rights-based approach and being citizen centred. The key themes identified were:

- users and carers at the centre;
- a simpler system to improve access;
- a higher profile for social services;
- promoting social inclusion and independence;
- continuity of care and supporting people through vulnerability;
- local authorities remaining both commissioners and providers;
- a better-qualified workforce.

This report was followed by an independent commission (Independent Commission on Social Services in Wales, 2010), which engaged people across Wales in looking at what they wanted from social services and the challenges presented. The main proposals involved a more efficient means of collaboration, intelligent commissioning and an emphasis on preventative services built around the service user, their families and their carers. The new Welsh Government set out a way forward, stating that high-quality, responsive, citizen-centred social services are essential to a successful Wales. A strategy of retrenchment was rejected in favour of renewal, based on delivery and innovation. The strategy – *Sustainable social services for Wales: A framework for action* (Welsh Government, 2011) – set out the priorities for action, a vision based on building on strengths and a number of key principles. These included:

- a strong voice and real control;
- supporting each other;
- safety and protection;
- respect;
- recovery and restoration;
- adjusting to new circumstances;
- stability;
- simplicity;
- professionalism.

The Welsh Government has proceeded to a new Social Services Bill, which has been seen as an attempt to set up a national social care service in Wales, with all-Wales eligibility thresholds, a national contract for care homes, and more regionalised commissioning arrangements and delivery instead of 22 councils doing everything separately. The Welsh Government has, however, rejected the vision of personalisation adopted in England as too closely associated with a market-led model of consumer choice, although there is a commitment to increase the use of direct payments.

As well as providing the legislative basis to take forward sustainable social services for Wales, the Bill is aimed at enacting a legal framework for social services (Welsh Government, 2012a). This follows the recommendations of the Law Commission for separate Welsh legislation. The overall Welsh review differs from England in continuing with children's social care as part of social care and the new Bill includes aspects of children's services, for example, adoption. The Bill is based on a central principle that social services are provided in Wales through a general duty to maintain and enhance the wellbeing of people in need. The Bill gives a statutory right of assessment of need for people of all ages and provides a new legal framework for the management of care and support plans. Similar to England, there will be a national eligibility framework and provision for the portability of assessments. Other key aspects of the Bill are an extension of the duty on local authority social services and the NHS to collaborate in the delivery of integrated services with power to strengthen partnership working. The Bill gives people the right to access information, advice and assistance in finding out about services. The legislation also seeks to provide people with a stronger voice and real control. It will extend the range of services for which people have the right to a direct payment where that is their wish. Also included in the provisions is the power to establish a national outcomes framework and to set standards for social services. In a separate exercise, the Welsh National Assembly is undertaking an inquiry into residential care for older people, covering the capacity and quality of the sector, alternative community-based services and alternative funding models.

In Scotland, the Scottish Government has tended to focus on particular categories of care and strategies and legislation on mental illness and learning disability appeared shortly after the introduction of devolution. There has also been major innovative legislation on adult protection and support – in 2007. Social services have been mainly addressed in the document *Changing lives: Report of the 21st century social work review* (Scottish Executive, 2006). *Changing lives* largely dealt with social work and included children's services but did engage with wider issues of increasing demand for social services, better use of skills, integration and work with other services, and delivery principles of choice and control. In a number of cognate strategies related to social care, the Scottish Government has pursued issues of personalisation and co-production, integration and partnership working, the social care workforce, early intervention and a mixed economy of care (Berry, 2008).

Reshaping care for older people was a programme for engagement with people for an approach based on shifting the balance of care from hospital services into local care and enabling people to stay at home (Scottish Government, 2010a). Also published was a delayed discharge report. *The carers strategy for Scotland 2010–2015* (Scottish Government, 2010b) and *The young carers strategy for Scotland 2010–2015* (Scottish Government, 2010c) aimed to give more support to unpaid carers. More significant were two statutory based initiatives. In 2011, a Social Care (Self-directed Support) (Scotland) Bill was introduced to implement a Scottish Government paper – *Self-directed support: A national strategy for Scotland* (Scottish Government, 2010d). This initiative seeks to ensure that adults, including carers, are given more choice and control over meeting their social care needs. Self-directed support must be offered by local authorities to those assessed as requiring community care services through direct payments, users directing the available support or traditional local authority-arranged support. In 2012, a major report was published for consultation on the integration of adult health and social care in Scotland (Scottish Government, 2012a). The aim was to improve existing integration for all adult health and social care services through bringing together the accountability of the statutory partners with a vision of a statutory underpinning, and integrated budgets, clear accountability, consistency of outcomes and also better outcomes. Health and social care partnerships would be the joint and equal responsibility of health boards and local authorities.

Northern Ireland demonstrates a picture of relatively few strategies dedicated specifically to adult social care. The lengthy review of public administration in Northern Ireland (Review of Public Administration (RPA), 2005) was focused on delivery and structures but comments on social care were largely confined to maintaining support for the principle of the structural integration of health and social care in the reform of structures in 2006–07. In 2010, a major consultation document was published entitled *A 10 year strategy for social work in Northern Ireland 2010–2020* (DHSSPS, 2010). However, this document was almost totally focused on issues relating to the requirements of the social work profession, issues of governance, leadership and public perceptions and invited only limited comment on issues of protection, prevention and designing services around the needs of people. A final report – *Improving and safeguarding social wellbeing: A strategy for social work in Northern Ireland 2012–2022* – was published (DHSSPS, 2012a). This strategy was confined closely to social work as a profession rather than wider social care aspects. The report had a focus on building leadership and trust, strengthening the capacity of the social work workforce and improving social work services. The last of these headings was used to encourage more flexibility in integrated working and what is called person–centred approaches and in management tasks.

A more significant independent review of health and social care was commissioned and carried out in a short period of time in 2011 (DHSSPS, 2011a). This review had an overarching purpose to recommend a change of direction from acute health services to care in the community. This would mean a considerable shift in resources from services in hospitals to services in the home or community. Consequently, social care would have to be developed and resourced as a key component in implementing this transformation. Anticipated benefits were seen in terms of care closer to home, more prevention and reablement, promoting independence and safeguarding the most vulnerable. As in Wales, the report also included children's care. The report and subsequent debates tended to be dominated by health issues, particularly the reconfiguration of acute hospitals. Somewhat surprisingly, given the long-established integrated structures for health and social care in Northern Ireland, a major proposal in *Transforming your care* (DHSSPS, 2011a) was for 17 integrated care partnerships across Northern Ireland to join together the full range of health and social care services, including GPs. There was little discussion of budgetary or governance arrangements or what in the existing structures presented barriers to integration. The review did, however, note the limited progress in Northern Ireland with personalisation, including direct payments, and also drew attention to the need for a debate on the issue of the costs of care for older people. The value and principles of personalisation and user involvement, key to transformation agendas in Great Britain, were not fully developed in the review document and given little attention in the implementation document (DHSSPS, 2012b). A separate document 'Who cares: the future of adult care and support in Northern Ireland' was brief and focused mainly on cost effectiveness (DHSSPS, 2012c). There was no proposal to introduce new legislation akin to that proposed in England, Scotland and Wales to put social care entitlements in a new statutory framework.

Boxes 14 to 17 list the key policy developments in England, Wales, Scotland and Northern Ireland, respectively.

Box 14: Adult social care policy timeline (England), 1997–2012

Year	Policy/legislation	Main provision/developments
1998	Policy document *Modernising Social Services*	Set out Labour government 'third way' for social care and identified separate national objectives for adult services
2006	White Paper *Our Health, Our Say: A new direction for community services*	Set out a vision of community services taking centre stage and of a more personalised approach to the delivery of social care
2007	Concordant *Putting People First: A shared vision and commitment to the transformation of adult social care*	Set out an agreement between central and local government in England to implement a new vision of adult social care over a ten-year period
2009	Green Paper *Shaping the Future of Care Together*	Result of a national engagement process which identified key challenges for adult social care and set out an aspiration for a national care system for England
2010	White Paper *Building the National Care Services*	Set out six founding principles and six pillars of a national care service including universality within a framework of national entitlements and personalised care and support
2010	Policy document *A Vision for Adult Social Care: Capable communities and active citizens*	Set out Coalition government's agenda for reform of social care in England with emphasis on personalisation and direct payments
2011	Report of Dilnot Commission independent inquiry on a funding system for care and support in adult social care	Recommendations included capping individual lifetime contributions and increasing the means-testing threshold
2011	Law Commission report on social care law	Advocated the adoption of an overarching principle that adult social care must promote and contribute to the wellbeing of individuals. Recommendations included a new national eligibility framework for users and caring

---

2011	Strategy document *Caring for Our Future: Shared ambitions for care and support*	Key areas covered included: quality of care and quality of the social care workforce, personalisation, prevention and integration
2012	White Paper *Caring for Our Future: reforming care and support*	Was to bring together key recommendations from Dilnot Commission, Law Commission and the Vision for Adult Social Care. Set out a number of core principles including personalisation, independent living and safeguarding
2012	Draft Care and Support Bill	Aimed to consolidate an adult social care statute informed by the recommendations of the Law Commission report on social care law (2011). Places a number of duties on local authorities including to carry out assessments. Proposes introduction of national threshold for eligibility.

Box 15: Main policy developments: Wales

Year	Policy/legislation	Main provision/developments
2007	Strategy document *Fulfilled lives, supportive communities: a strategy for social services over the next decade*	Set out Welsh government approach to social care based on welfare, social justice and inclusion
2010	*From Vision to Action: The report of the independent commission on social services in Wales*	Public engagement exercise. Proposals emphasised preventative services built around service users, families and carers
2011	*Sustainable social services for Wales: A framework for action*	The strategy rejected retrenchment approach and set out priorities for action linked to renewal and innovation with focus on user involvement
2012	Social Services (Wales) Bill	Seen as an attempt to set a national care system for Wales. Proposed eligibility thresholds, a national contract for care homes and regionalised commissioning arrangements

Box 16: Main policy developments: Scotland

Year	Policy/legislation	Main provision/developments
2006	*Changing lives* (report of 21st-century social work review)	Mostly focused on social work but did discuss broader issues including increasing demand for social services, integration and delivery principles
2007	Adult Support and Protection (Scotland) Act	Major legislation setting out provision for adult care and support
2010	*Reshaping care for older people*	Programme of public engagement. Set out approach based on shift from hospital to community and home care
2010	*Self-directed support: A national strategy for Scotland*	Set out proposals for initiatives to promote user and carer choice and control. Proposed a requirement on local authorities to offer provision to those assessed as requiring community care
2012	*Integration on adult health and social care in Scotland* (consultation report)	Major report aiming to improve integration for all adult health and social care services. Set out a vision of statutory underpinning for integration and integrated budgets

Box 17: Main policy developments: Northern Ireland

Year	Policy/legislation	Main provision/developments
2005	*Review of Public Administration* (Consultation)	Document setting out proposals for reform of public administration. Expressed support for continuation of integrated structure for health and social care in NI
2011	*Transforming Your Care: A review of health and social care in NI* (Independent review of health and social care)	Commissioned review (included adult and children's care) recommended a shift from acute to community services. Acknowledged this would mean major shift in resources from hospitals to community services. Concepts such as personalisation and user involvement were not fully developed in the report.
2012	*Improving and safeguarding social well-being: A strategy for social work in NI*	Focused on social work as a profession rather than broader social care issues. Emphasis on improving social work services and capacity of social work workforce
2012	*Who cares? The future of adult social care and support in NI* (policy document)	Strong focus on cost effectiveness in adult social care. Some, although limited, discussion of personalisation and user involvement. No proposal to put social care entitlements on a statutory footing

Identifiable shortcomings

Much of the focus in recent government reports, research papers and evaluations and commentaries by academics and practitioners has addressed perceived shortcomings in the system of adult social care. These are summarised in Box 18.

Box 18: Perceived shortcomings in adult social care

- Inadequate funding of services. In 2012, the House of Commons Health Committee (2012a, para 57) stated that 'we consider the current social care system is inadequately funded'. There has been talk of a crisis in the current funding arrangements, with reductions in local authority budgets in Great Britain, requirements to make unprecedented efficiencies, and an end to ringfencing the social care budget (House of Commons Health Committee, 2012a, para 21). The Local Government Association in England has continued to comment on a current and growing funding crisis in adult social care, with cuts of 7.7% for top-tier councils in England for 2011/12 and 6.8% for 2012/13 (Local Government Association, 2012).
- The special critical financial issue of funding the cost of residential and long-term care and what the nature of state support should be. The unfairness of means testing, especially for people with modest means, and the scale of unmet need, as more people are excluded from eligibility criteria. Some people have faced disposing of their assets and savings to meet the potentially unlimited costs.
- The lack of joined-up approaches with limited health and social care integration and inadequate linking up, for example, on assessments, and dealing with people with

multiple needs. Fragmentation also inhibits cooperation between different sectors, local authorities, the NHS, the voluntary sector and the independent sector.

- Variation in provision of social care services across Great Britain and between local authorities.
- Variation in the quality of care and safeguarding, with inadequate inspection and regulatory processes over providers and provision.
- A lack of follow-through in the implementation of strategies, for example, extending direct payments, reablement strategies, safeguarding measures and the implementation of assessments.
- Increasing demands on carers, with insufficient support and lack of entitlement to support.
- Age discrimination, with inadequate equality impact evaluations, and new or changes in policies that disadvantage older people. A House of Commons inquiry (House of Commons Health Committee, 2010, para 161) found that many of the shortcomings in social care appeared to relate to a persistent ageism, both overt and covert, pervading the whole system, with care not focused on the individual user.
- A lack of information and advice. A lack of information and advice about what support and services are available has been identified as a problem, with too many people unaware of the options available to them.
- It has been argued that the social care system primarily focuses on existing social care needs, rather than seeking to prevent needs developing in the first place (House of Commons Health Committee, 2010, para 110), with the system too often only reacting to a crisis (DH, 2012a, p 15).

The identification of such shortcomings has led to a debate about the need for major change in adult social care and a transformation or new vision in social care. This debate has been carried on by both the last Labour government and the new Coalition government, by the devolved administrations, by academic analysis, by practitioner bodies and by voluntary organisations and research and policy institutes. It is possible to summarise the main themes of this debate as it has evolved since 2005/06.

Issues of debate

A number of issues are subject to ongoing debate and development, which are summarised in Box 19.

Box 19: Issues of debate
- Integration
- Personalisation
- User participation
- The shift to home-based care, prevention and reablement

- Costs of long-term residential care
- Providers
- Safeguarding and quality of care
- Workforce issues
- Equality, diversity and minority ethnic groups
- Reduced resources.

Integration

The integration of social care with health has become a dominant theme for government planning and strategy. There is a widespread consensus that it is necessary to break down the barriers between health and social care. Close cooperation and working together has been accepted as a means of securing easier access for users, coordinated or even seamless care and better outcomes as well as reducing dependency on acute care. There has been much debate on the options and alternative mechanisms to promote more integration between local authority social care and the NHS. A major theme has been the value of more structural integration vis-à-vis more partnership working. There has also been a range of variables suggested for promoting integration: leadership, management processes, funding, team building and flexible multidisciplinary working. There are further dimensions to integration, covering the relationship between adult social care and children's services and the linkages of adult social care with other services, particularly with housing.

It is also the case that the approach to integration differs between the four countries of the UK, with Scotland moving to legislate for more structured partnerships and Northern Ireland having integrated structures. Progress with integration has remained patchy in England (Audit Commission, 2011). In all four countries, the continuing rise in demand, reduced resources and structural reform has kept the issue of integration at the top of the adult social care agenda. The House of Commons Health Committee (2012a) has supported integration as a very powerful tool to improve outcomes for people. The 2012 White Paper in England sees the transformation it envisages as promoted by innovation and integrated working between health and social care (DH, 2012a, p 58). The structural reforms in England, with the establishment of clinical commissioning groups replacing primary care trusts (PCTs) and new health and wellbeing boards in local government to lead integration, will present challenges for the direction of integration. Furthermore, a continuing debate exists on the effectiveness of integration and different organisational models.

Personalisation

Personalisation has become another top of the agenda issue for adult social care. The term was used in the past in a low-key sense, meaning only person-centred planning or tailoring support to individual need, that services should fit people rather than people fitting services. Subsequently, the meaning of the term shifted to refer to more choice and control over services (SCIE, 2009a). However, the use of the term was to develop further to become closely associated with direct payments, individual and personalised budgets and self-directed support. With direct payments, individuals would have control over the financial resources for aspects of their care and choice over the nature and provider of the care. Direct payments are a cash payment made in place of regular social services, with the individual making the arrangements for support. The introduction of direct payments throughout the UK was followed by pilot studies of individual budgets in England, involving wider sources of funding and a range of services. Direct payments have been called the first step on the road to personalisation but self-directed support has also become synonymous with personalisation (Payne, 2012). There has been a debate about methods to increase the numbers of people using direct payments and a discussion of the evidence base. Research and evaluations have demonstrated the popularity, value and achievements of direct payments and the development of innovative arrangements and support (Leece and Bornat, 2006; Glasby and Littlechild, 2009; Glendinning et al, 2009). There has been a focus on giving support to people using direct payments as well as some criticisms of the scheme as not everyone may wish to take on the organisational tasks involved. In England, the Department of Health's vision paper (DH, 2010a) supported extending the roll-out of personal budgets to give people and their carers more control and purchasing power and for greater use in such areas as respite care. The White Paper *Caring for our future* (DH, 2012a) places personalisation and people in charge of their own care at the heart of the discussion and recommendations. So personalisation remains at the centre of discussion on the transformation of adult social care in England. In contrast, debates on the issue in Scotland, Wales and Northern Ireland have shown less support for personalisation. The Welsh Assembly Government, in preparing a future strategy for adult social care, actually rejected personalisation as too closely associated with market-led consumer care (Welsh Assembly Government, 2011).

User participation

User participation in adult social care has been a third major agenda item. This covers the involvement and participation of service users in the formulation of policies, in consultation mechanisms, in shaping and participating in the delivery and administration of services and in the monitoring and evaluation of provision. User participation has moved from low-level formats of consultation to more significant forms of participation through ideas of co-production of services to more radical forms of delegation of authority to users (Bochel et al, 2008). User involvement in adult social care can be said to be at a more advanced level than in any other public service. The practice of user involvement has been extended in social care into areas such as research, training and education. There have also been developments in the support for user participation through the growth of user organisations, the extension of principles of participation to both users and carers and new initiatives in the practice of advocacy. There is a general consensus on the value of user and public participation, through more local responsiveness, more public accountability, the empowerment of users and resultant improvements in the standards and quality of services. User involvement has developed to a greater degree in some areas of social care than others, particularly in mental health. A debate continues on the likely impact of restructuring in England. Will the localism and Big Society agendas promote participation, how will participation fare in the new structure with such new bodies as Healthwatch and will more localised and diffuse commissioning present barriers to effective user participation?

The shift to home-based care, prevention and reablement

There has been a continuing change over recent years to provision to enable people to live at home. The number of residential care services fell by 10% between 2004 and 2010, while the number of domiciliary agencies increased by over a third (CQC, 2011, p 8). A trend away from an emphasis on acute hospital-based care and institutional care to home and community-based care has come to the fore. This marks a shift in provision and resources in the direction of adult social care. The UK government's White Paper *Caring for our future* (DH, 2012a) seeks to promote independence and prevention and postpone and minimise people's need for formal care and support. In Scotland, the government has stated that fewer resources will be directed towards institutional care and more resources will be directed towards community provision and capacity building (Self-directed Support [Scotland] Bill 2012). In Northern Ireland, a shift from hospital-based services to community-based services and care and better prevention is central to the transformation strategy for health and social care (DHSSPS, 2011a). In Wales, early intervention, prevention, maintaining people's independence, flexible services and alignment with the NHS are part of transformational change (Welsh Assembly Government, 2011, p 18), although the Welsh vision is not so specific about a shift from health to social care. Despite this planning there have been warnings that in England shortfalls in local authority spending may lead to more demand on NHS services (NHS Confederation, 2012a). Preventative social care has developed as a more recent idea and a transformation from the traditional crisis intervention. New ways of investing in prevention are emerging but it is not yet a priority area and difficulties arise in targeting those who may benefit and in measuring success (DH, 2012d). This shift in emphasis is also demonstrated in the development of reablement as a short intensive service to help people regain better functioning and independence in their homes.

Costs of long-term residential care

This is an issue that for periods has attracted major attention from politicians, government departments in the four countries of the UK, the public, the media and commentators. Rising demand and the rising costs have produced elements of crisis. There have been two significant developments in this area. First was the agenda set by the Scottish Government in introducing free personal and nursing care covering those in residential and domiciliary settings, a policy that England, Wales and Northern Ireland felt unable to copy. The second major development was the recommendations of the Dilnot inquiry in England (Dilnot Commission, 2011), which included a proposal for a cap on the costs to an individual and their families for residential care and examined other proposals on determining what the contribution of users should be. This has produced an ongoing discussion as the UK government seeks to formulate a new policy.

There is also a wider issue of the nature of charges for other forms of adult social care. It has been estimated that for older people 20% of gross expenditure is recouped in client contributions (House of Commons Health Committee, 2010, para 31). While it may be the case that most people get some help with social care needs in England, some 120,000 people pay privately for places in care homes and 150,000 purchase community support privately.

Providers

The question of who should provide adult social care is a further issue that has attracted much comment and has been at times a divisive party political issue. Traditionally, adult social care was provided by the state, mainly through local government. There has been a steady growth in outsourcing and commissioning services from the independent sector, the voluntary sector and the private sector. In the case of residential care, the state has largely moved out of the provider role, replaced by private sector provision. There are again some differences between the four countries of the UK. More recently, domiciliary services have increasingly been outsourced to the independent sector with local authorities acting as commissioners of services. In England local authorities no longer deliver many services themselves. Elsewhere there is a more mixed scenario of local authorities acting as direct providers of services and commissioners. The provider sector itself presents a mix of statutory, voluntary and private bodies but also partnerships and increasingly social enterprises. The UK government has moved to legally require local authorities to use services that promote diversity in the social care market but also to take measures against provider failure.

Safeguarding and quality of care

Safeguards against the risk of abuse especially to vulnerable older people and people with learning disabilities have been receiving attention from policy makers for some time, but a number of incidents that received media attention have made the issue a priority. Structural measures have been put in place over a period of time to provide stronger statutory protection against the risk of abuse or neglect. Adult safeguarding boards have been set up, based in local authorities but multi-agency in nature and in 2012 this became a statutory requirement. In fact, Scotland had earlier taken legislative action to establish a statutory framework for adult protection.

Closely related to safeguarding procedures are the issues of quality control and dealing with complaints. The quality of social care has been regulated in a number of ways. There has been a debate about the effectiveness of the public body in England, the CQC, in carrying out its remit to uphold standards for adult social care and carry out inspections and inquiries. Assessing the performance of local councils in England in providing adult social care has also been carried out by other forms of evaluation, particularly by the National Audit Office. Devolution has also had a major impact on inspection and regulation, and Scotland, Wales and Northern Ireland all have their own structures and arrangements separately from England. Procedures for dealing with individual complaints exist within all the statutory provider bodies. There are also mechanisms for taking complaints to regulatory bodies or Ombudsmen.

Governments have also given much attention to adult social care outcomes. An Adult Social Care Outcomes Framework was launched in 2011 and updated for 2012/13 (DH, 2012e). The document that presents the framework sets out for England principles for measuring outcomes and performance in relation to impacts on quality of life, people's independence and experience of care and support. In Wales, the Social Services (Wales) Bill (Welsh Government, 2012a) also sets out a national outcomes framework, designed to reflect the principle of wellbeing and the Bill specifies powers and resources to measure performance and ensure national outcomes.

Workforce issues

Issues relating to the social care and social work workforce have received considerable attention in recent years although being a somewhat low-profile issue for government and the public. Issues of training, registration, initial and post-qualifying awards have been the subject of policy development. There have also been more fundamental analyses about the future role of social work and about the future nature of the social care workforce. Changes in the workforce are seen as a consequence of changes in the approach to social care through personalisation, integration, the role of service users as well as the whole public reform agenda. Interestingly, all four governments in the UK embarked on separate reviews of the roles and tasks of social work. The findings and recommendations of these exercises were not too divergent but the outcome has been rather different in terms of structural and policy changes in England, compared to the other three countries. Workforce developments implemented or under discussion include personal assistants, social care apprenticeships and direct payments officers.

Equality, diversity and minority ethnic groups

The growth of an equality agenda, concern about discrimination and racism and the growth in immigrant populations have been a significant policy area for adult social care. The topic tends to arise in two main contexts. The first context is the impact of equality legislation and duties, particularly the Equality Act 2010, which imposes duties to eliminate discrimination and promote equality of opportunity between people with protected characteristics, including age, gender, disability, race, ethnicity and sexual orientation. The requirements for equality impact assessments have influenced the content of policies, strategies and implementation plans. The second context is the study of high levels of need and disadvantage in minority ethnic communities and evidence about this and involvement of minority ethnic groups in adult social care (Vickers et al, 2012).

Reduced resources

A key contemporary issue for the delivery of adult social care is the reduction of available resources for adult social care. Table 2 sets out expenditure per capita on personal social services and on health and personal social services by country of the UK. Per capita expenditure in England on social care is lower than in the other countries of the UK, with Scotland having the highest per capita spend. Expenditure is appreciably lower in Northern Ireland than in Scotland and Wales but the differences reduces when health expenditure is included. England remains with the lowest expenditure per capita when social and health care are aggregated. These figures mainly reflect the working of the Barnett Formula for allocating funding to the devolved administrations and not just need or decisions made by the devolved governments.

Table 2: Expenditure per capita on personal social services by country of the UK (£) (2010/11)

	Personal Social Services	Health and Personal Social Services
Northern Ireland	512	2,618
Scotland	625	2,697
England	487	2,387
Wales	617	2,634

Source: O'Neill et al (2012)

The Audit Commission (2011, p 3) has noted that financial pressures combined with demographic change have created 'tough times for adult social care'. The UK government's position is that extra money – £1 billion – has been made available and the NHS has made more money – another £1 billion – available for social care but the general funding grant for local government has been cut by 26% and ringfencing for social care grants has been removed. Councils are expected by central government to maintain the level of services through efficiencies and value-for-money exercises. However, it has been suggested that since the 2010 Spending Review settlement, the social care sector has had to make unprecedented levels of efficiency savings (House of Commons Health Committee, 2012a, para 1). A survey by the UK Home Care Association (2012) presented a dominant view of independent providers believing that commissioners valued low price above quality, as shown in Table 3.

Table 3: Providers' perceptions of whether councils/trusts value low price or quality of services

	England	Scotland	Wales	Northern Ireland
Low price	76	60	69	53
Equal priority	18	30	23	47
Quality	7	9	8	0

Source: UK Home Care Association (2012)

The government's intentions for adult social care provision do not seem to be reflected in the actual actions of many local councils in England. Some of these consequences have been seen in the following.

Reduced social care budgets

In both 2010/11 and 2011/12 there was a one per cent rise in cash terms but a decrease of one per cent in real terms. When adjusted for funding transfers from the NHS, expenditure fell by between 2 and 7 per cent in real terms. In the years 2007/08 and 2009/10 expenditure had risen by 5 per cent each year; between 2006/07 and 2011/12 expenditure increased by 3 per cent in real terms and over the ten years from 2001/2002 it increased by 33 per cent in real terms.

It has been reported that 63% of local authorities were reducing their social care budgets by an average of 6.6% between 2010/11 and 2011/12 (House of Commons Health Committee, 2012a). Most local authorities were planning to reduce expenditure on care home placements, long-term support in the community and preventative services but increase expenditure in reablement services, mainly because of a one-off £70 million government fund. Local councils in Wales face a cut of £3 million in the adult social services budget.

Table 4: Gross expenditure by councils in England with adult social care responsibilities (2007/08 to 2011/12)

Year	Gross expenditure (billion)
2007/08	15.3
2008/09	16.1
2009/10	16.8
2010/11	17.0
2011/12	17.2

Source: Health and Social Care Information Centre, 2012

Changes in entitlement and assessment

Local councils have the discretion to determine eligibility for services but, after 2003, people were assessed according to a set of four standard threshold criteria, in the Fair Access to Care scheme. These were:

- critical – where life is in danger or serious abuse or neglect has or will occur or there is an inability to carry out vital personal care or domestic routines;
- substantial – where a person is unable to carry out the majority of personal care or domestic routines, there are no social support systems and abuse or neglect is likely;
- moderate – where a person is unable to carry out several personal care or domestic routines and several support systems cannot be sustained;
- low – where a person is unable to carry out one or two personal care or domestic routines or a few social support roles cannot be met.

Local authorities still have the discretion to prioritise their eligibility criteria according to their available resources and there has been criticism that with reduced budgets many councils are now only using or responding to the 'critical' criteria.

Cuts in services

There have been criticisms of local councils for imposing cuts in services, for example, day centres, or not implementing the outcomes of assessments for care packages. Attention has focused on the setting by councils of short time slots for the care of people in their own homes. A survey revealed that 73% of homecare visits in England were 30 minutes or shorter, the figure being 42% in Scotland and Wales and 87% in Northern Ireland (UKHCA, 2012), with many councils operating with a minimum period of 15 minutes seen as threatening safety and dignity. Data presented in Table 5 show the substantial number of short visits.

Table 5: Homecare: average visit duration by country (% of visits)

Duration of visit (minutes)	England	Scotland	Wales	Northern Ireland
15 or fewer	10	11	4	28
15–30	63	31	38	59
31–45	11	24	19	6
45–60	10	22	27	3
60+	6	12	12	4

Source: UK Home Care Association (2012)

Increase in charges

Many local authorities in England and Wales have increased their charges for services. It has been reported that 35% of councils had increased their maximum personal charge for social care, 38% had increased their charges for residential care and 49% had increased their charges for non-residential care items, such as the hourly rate for home helps. Some councils had acted to increase their income through improved income collection, recovery of debt and benefits advice (House of Commons Health Committee, 2012a, annex).

Savings and efficiencies

Most councils have engaged in efficiency savings, through such measures as improved procurement or reducing payments to private sector providers, reducing staffing levels, increased personalisation and primary prevention services and making back-office efficiencies (Audit Commission, 2011). It has become a debatable issue as to whether there are adverse effects as a result in the standards of services or outcomes for users. A report in 2011 from a human rights perspective has made criticisms of the impact of outsourcing of home care contracts to private bidders on the levels of services (EHRC, 2011).

Conclusions

- Since 2005, adult social care has been subject to intense debate and scrutiny and a number of policy developments have been published by the UK government.
- The devolved administrations have published separate policy documents although common items and similarities can be found in policy papers, particularly in relation to personalisation, integration and support for independent living.
- A number of items are at the centre of contemporary debate. These include funding of services, safeguarding and regulation.

Sources

Key policy documents produced by the UK and devolved governments and by independent inquiries are listed in the chapter. Reports by the Association of the Directors of Adult Social Services and the Local Government Association are a useful source of information and commentary on contemporary developments. The Social Care Institute for Excellence (SCIE) has produced a substantial volume of material, including briefing papers on contemporary issues including personalisation, integration and user involvement.

Questions

- What are the main areas of similarity in the major adult social care documents produced since 2005 by the Labour and Coalition governments in the UK?

- How has the Law Commission report on social care influenced social care policy?

- What are the key differences and similarities in the legislative proposals to develop adult social care as produced by the UK, Scottish and Welsh governments?

- What are the main financial issues addressed in recent UK government policies and proposals?

FOUR

Governance of adult social care

Overview

This chapter examines the governance arrangements for the delivery of adult social care in the UK. These operate on a multi-level basis and the key levels can be identified as government departments and ministers, local authorities, public bodies or quangos and partnerships. Also included is parliamentary influence. The arrangements for the devolved administrations are also briefly described. The governance arrangements cover policy making, strategy, finance, commissioning, guidance, delivery and monitoring.

Government departments and ministers

Responsibility for adult social care rests with Whitehall and the devolved administrations. The location of adult social care within a Whitehall department has been strongly established as falling largely in a department of health. This is the position with the Coalition government and was also the position with the previous Labour government. The responsibility of the Department of Health for adult social care relates only to England. The devolved administrations have their own arrangements and form of central administration for adult social care. In Scotland, responsibility rests mainly in a Health and Social Care Integration Directorate under the health theme in central administration. In Wales, it is a responsibility of a Department of Health, Social Services and Children, before 2011 a Department for Health and Social Services, and in Northern Ireland, it is a responsibility of a Department of Health, Social Services and Public Safety.

The alignment of social care with health can be seen as recognising the importance of a close relationship with health. At the same time, this alignment has raised issues and concerns about social care occupying a minor position compared to the priority given to health, with health matters dominating the departmental agendas. The removal of children's care services from the Department of Health functions in England to the department responsible for schools and families may actually have acted to enhance the position of adult social care. Within the Department of Health there is a Social Care Local Government and Care Partnership Directorate, which provides professional advice and leadership on all aspects of social care policy. The Secretary of State for Health in the UK government is the political head of the Department of Health and has overall responsibility for adult social care, again for England only. There are four junior ministerial portfolios in the Department of Health and one, with the rank of

Minister of State, is the Minister for Care Services. This portfolio covers most of adult social care although the current minister has some responsibilities involving health, for example, for personal health budgets, end-of-life care and long-term health conditions. A second Minister of State covers health only and two parliamentary under-secretary posts cover public health and quality issues.

Each devolved administration has a senior minister covering health and social care. These are, in Scotland, a Secretary for Health and Wellbeing whose specific responsibilities for social care are spelt out, in Wales, a Minister for Health and Social Services and in Northern Ireland, a Minister for Health and Social Services and Public Safety. Scotland does not have a specific junior minister for social care but has a junior minister for local communities and public health who has some overlapping responsibilities. In Wales, there was a junior minister for social services, but since 2011 this role has been combined with responsibility for child protection services. While the Minister for Health and Social Services has overall responsibility, it is the Deputy Minister for Children and Social Services who has day-to-day responsibility for all social care. The single minister in Northern Ireland has a portfolio including health, public health, adult social care and children's social care.

Functions of departments

The overall role of government departments can be described as:

- formulating policy;
- preparing legislation;
- defining strategy;
- allocating funding;
- setting standards;
- monitoring delivery and performance.

At times there may be a new or special emphasis, for example, on restructuring, efficiency drives, new strategies or policy initiatives. The Department of Health (2012a) describes the scope of social care functions, which relates to traditional areas – older people, physical disability, learning disability and mental health – but also refers to more detailed specifications reflecting contemporary concerns – long-term care reform, dementia, autism and safeguarding vulnerable people. Areas that overlap with health may be flagged up, indicating that services may fall more into the social care ambit, for example, end-of-life care and long-term conditions. A particular focus of current activity may also be indicated in departmental narratives on their priorities in relation to social care, for example, personalisation. The devolved administrations tend to be less specific in listing aims but the Welsh Government has specified adult social services as covering the traditional categories of older people and people with learning disabilities, physical disabilities, sensory disabilities or mental health problems but also alcohol and drug misusers, people with HIV/AIDS and people with a terminal illness. The Scottish Government outlines ministerial functions as older people, mental health, learning disability, community care, carers, substance misuse and the work of Social Care and Social Work Improvement Scotland. Specific areas of policy initiatives by the administration in social care are care and support, including delayed discharge, free personal care, unpaid carers, national care standards and self-directed support. Overall, the position of adult social care is addressed in accounts of ministers' roles, departmental organisation and senior professional posts.

In Wales, although the Department of Health uses a subtitle of 'Public health, adult social care and the NHS', the department does not give major separate recognition to adult social care in organisational terms. The department has eight directors-general below the permanent secretary but only one post is clearly identifiable as covering adult social care. There is a director-general post for Social Care, Local Government and Care Partnerships. None of the responsibilities of the six chief professional officers relates to social work or social care. A departmental board forms the strategic and operational leadership of the department and consists of the ministerial team, the leading civil servants and non-executive members. An executive board of civil servants supports the permanent secretary as principal accounting officer. The Scottish central administration is organised into some 42 directorates and although one Health and Social Care Integration Directorate covers social care services for adults and support for carers as well as mental health, it has other responsibilities, including primary healthcare, dentistry and the integration of health and social care. The Scottish directorates are organised around six themes in terms of civil service organisation, each headed by a director-general and one such post is Director-General Health & Social Care and Chief Executive of the NHS in Scotland. Some of the other six directorates under the Health and Social Care strategic objective have functions relating to adult care, including health and social care integration, health and healthcare improvement, and workforce and performance.

The structure in Wales resembles the model of the ministerial department with a coterminosity between the minister and the departmental structure for health and social services. The Department for Health, Social Services and Children is one of seven headed by a director-general. The Welsh Government's responsibilities are for funding, setting the policy and reviewing, inspecting and regulating social services, and they also cover care, advice, grants and voluntary care.

The single Northern Ireland department is organised into six key business groups and two directorates, which include a Social Services Inspectorate and an Office of Social Services.

Local government

The delivery of adult social care has developed in Great Britain as a responsibility of local government. From the 1970s this was as part of a single integrated department of social services or social work as a consequence of the Seebohm

Report (Great Britain Ministry of Housing and Local Government, 1968). Seebohm's vision was of a powerful organisation responsible for a full range of social services and where new needs could be identified and planned for (Gibb, 2001). The Seebohm departments in local government brought together children's services and services for vulnerable adult groups with generalist social workers. The Local Authority (Social Services) Act 1970 implemented Seebohm's proposals in top-tier local authorities within two-tier systems of county and district authorities or in unitary authorities (Hill, 2000). Social services and social work departments maintained their role and identity through periods of local government reorganisation and the expansion of social service functions, the growth of the social work profession and the development of new forms of social care (Adams, 1996). Local government restructuring led to a range of different types of local authorities becoming responsible for social care (see Table 6). While some of these structures are well established, the process for the formation of unitary authorities has been slowly continuing over a lengthy period.

Local authorities' role, post Seebohm, in unified social services covered a similar range of functions for children, families, older people, mental health, physical disability and learning disability, with a strong emphasis on direct statutory provision of services. The model of a comprehensive authority was to survive policy developments such as community care. The commitment to care in the community actually enhanced the role of local authorities. The Griffiths Report in 1988 (Griffiths, 1988) recommended that all services other than hospital provision should be commissioned by local authorities, which would be the lead authority for care in the community approaches. The following legislation – the NHS and Community Care Act 1990 – fully implemented by 1994, produced a major shift towards increasing the responsibilities of local authorities and resources were transferred from social security.

Table 6: Local authorities and social care

Local authority	Number
England	
County boroughs	34
Unitary authorities	47
Metropolitan boroughs	36
London boroughs	33
Scotland	
District councils	33
Wales	
District councils	22

The coming to power of a new Labour government with a modernisation agenda was to have a significant impact on local government social services. The White Paper *Modernising social services* (DH, 1998a) set an agenda for stronger accountability, more efficiency, accessibility and a new regulatory framework for social care. While advocating breaking down the barriers between social services and the NHS and working towards a new spirit of flexible partnerships, the White Paper concluded that major structural reorganisation was not a solution to the problems identified. In 1998, the consultative paper *Partnership in action* (DH, 1998b) set out the government's plans to make partnership working between health and social care a reality by removing barriers in the existing system and introducing new incentives for joint working at planning, commissioning and service delivery levels. It was stated clearly that health and social services must work together but it was not the intention to introduce major structural changes that could threaten separate local authority social services departments. Consequently, it seemed that despite the agenda of change, the basic administrative structure of social service departments would endure largely intact. The pursuit of greater integration and the intention to end the institutional barriers between health and social services produced in 2000 a more radical proposal for new integrated care trusts in England (DH, 2000). The prospect of such a radical restructuring would have had major implications for social services departments, but ultimately very few care trusts were set up (see below).

A major internal restructuring within local government was to take place, which did impact on social care but this was generated by decisions on the delivery of children's services in England. Following a number of inquiries, which highlighted deficiencies in the coordination of services for children, the government put in place a strategy for strengthening collaboration and creating clear accountability for children's services. Children's trusts emerged as the mechanism to enable local authorities with relevant partners to integrate the planning, commissioning and provision of children's services. The establishment of children's trusts meant the joining together of children's social services from the social services departments in local authorities with all the services of education departments in local authorities, headed by a new powerful director of children's services. The actual configuration of children's services has varied in local authorities but this process did mean that social services departments were left in local authorities only with responsibilities for adult social care. This has been described as a process that led to the disintegration of the comprehensive social services departments that had existed from 1970. This development only took place in England, not in Scotland, Wales or Northern Ireland. Generally, distinct adult social care departments emerged but some local authorities took the opportunity to create wider community service departments (Petch, 2008).

Adult social care falls within the statutory remit of the 152 local councils with adult social services responsibilities. Within local government, most of the funding for social care comes from central government, through the Revenue Support Grant, which takes account of the social characteristics of each area, including the levels of deprivation and the numbers of older people (House of Commons Health Committee, 2010, para 19). A substantial proportion of the funding is raised by councils themselves, through Council Tax and charges. Subject to some central government restrictions, local councils have discretion on the amount to be spent on social care. There are relatively few statutory obligations that have to be met and there is also discretion over eligibility for services. Overall, around 12% of local government expenditure goes on adult social care. Recent years have also seen the erosion of a near state monopoly of service provision, with a change from the direct provision of services to an enabling role for local authorities, purchasing services from statutory, voluntary or private providers. This enabling role has continued to expand with developments such as direct payments. The Community Care (Direct Payments) Act 1991 gave local authorities the power to offer people a cash payment in lieu of direct statutory services. With the new Coalition government, pressure has grown on local authorities to outsource most of their adult social care services.

Local government delivery of adult social care

Each local authority in England has a director of adult social services (DASS) in post. The post-holder has to be given the necessary authority to provide professional leadership. The DASS is directly accountable to the chief executive of the local authority and is comparable in terms of senior authority with the director of children's services. A joint appointment of a person to a DASS post and a post in the NHS is possible. The post of DASS usually covers the following responsibilities:

- accountable for assessing local needs and delivery of a full range of adult social services;
- providing professional leadership, including workforce planning;
- leading the implementation of standards;
- managing the necessary cultural changes;
- delivering an integrated whole-systems approach;
- promoting social inclusion and wellbeing and support for people with high levels of need;
- tackling inequalities;
- improving preventative services (DH, 2012e).

Wales has a system of 22 adult social service heads although the titles can vary between assistant director of adult services and senior manager of adult services and even head of integrated services. Until 2001, all local authorities in England and Wales had a committee system for taking policy decisions. After this the majority of councils adopted a new system of leader and cabinet membership, with one cabinet member having social care within their remit, usually as part of care and health or health and wellbeing. Scotland has configuration in council departments around social care, housing and health. The Social Services (Wales) Bill 2011 noted the importance of directors of social services having clear accountability arrangements to councillors and all staff engaged in delivering social service functions. The Bill proposed strengthening local accountability by requiring that director appointments comply with specific competences to ensure they can lead new models for social services (Welsh Assembly Government, 2011, p 50).

Most local authorities have similar listings of adult services that they plan, commission and deliver and these normally cover the following categories:

- the assessment process for social care needs, followed by a support plan;
- home care, including meals on wheels, flexible care and support to increase independence and reablement care at home;
- residential care, nursing home care and intermediate care;
- day care and facilities;
- housing support, working with housing departments, to provide extra care, adaptations and equipment;
- specific services for vulnerable groups, covering learning disability, physical disability, mental health, dementia, HIV patients and support for carers through assessment and services;
- information and guidance particularly on direct payments.

In most local authorities it is the practice to provide detailed information on costs and payments for home care and residential care and the nature of financial assessment procedures. In England, councils often provide assurances that they will not make a profit on the provision of care services, that costs are set at a reasonable level and never exceed full cost and that costs may be waived in the case of hardship. Some councils do not impose any charges, for example in the case of some special initiatives such as reablement services there may be no costs. There are no charges for personal social care in Scotland for people over the age of 65 in residential care or at home, although some councils extend free services to younger groups. Domiciliary care is provided without charges in Northern Ireland. In Wales, some 22% of recipients make payments for residential care and there is a cap of £50 per week.

It is common for local authorities to publish their adult social care strategy. They may also market their more innovative policies and initiatives. Councils may focus on reablement services, for example, Staffordshire County Council has launched Living Independently Staffordshire, a service that aims to give people more choice and more support to live independently following illness or injury, whether leaving hospital, or simply starting on the road to recovery. Access strategies have also been an area for initiatives, setting up a single point of access to care and information, and with a single assessment process. Partnership strategies with carers' groups or voluntary groups also are popular. With local authorities moving from a direct provision to a commissioning role, many councils have formed partnerships with the voluntary, community and private sectors, for example the Manchester Learning Disability Partnership.

Representative associations

A number of national organisations carry out a lobbying and developmental role for adult social care. The most significant are associations of senior managers in social care and local government-related organisations. In England, ADASS has a major task of promoting adult social care and also providing a forum for discussion and policy development. ADASS has set up six priority workstreams covering contemporary themes, including long-term care, local government/ GP commissioning, responding to a reduction in resources and a vision for adult social care over the next five years. In addition, there is a range of policy networks relating to the different vulnerable groups and key themes such as personalisation, safeguarding and workforce development. A large programme promoted by ADASS and some other network bodies has been 'Towards Excellence in Adult Social Care', which seeks to help councils improve their performance in adult social care. The aim is to develop key elements to produce a coherent approach to sector-led improvement and work has been carried out with councils previously judged adequate for adult social care by the CQC.

The Association for Directors of Social Services (ADSS) Cymru is a Welsh group of statutory directors and senior managers and represents the interests of social services in Wales. There is also a group of all-Wales adult social services heads, incorporated under the umbrella of ADSS Cymru. This group of the 22 heads of adult social services for each local authority in Wales meets regularly to discuss operational strategies, provides peer support and produces joint pieces of work on topics such as examples of good practice.

In Scotland, the Association of Directors of Social Work (ADSW) is the professional association of senior social workers in Scotland and has over 150 members, representing all 32 local authorities. The organisation promotes the interests of those working in social work and social care, lobbies Parliament, assists in policy implementation, develops best practice and interacts with the media. ADSW has warned against a costly reorganisation with regard to integration in Scotland without being sure that it will lead to improved outcomes for people.

The various local government associations in each country have also taken an interest in lobbying/campaigning on issues in adult social care. The Local Government Association (LGA), covering England, has long argued for the reform of the care and support system, has campaigned for improvements in individuals' experience of adult social care services, has campaigned for more resources to meet rising demands and has sought to maintain a clear role for local government in providing adult social care. The Convention of Scottish Local Authorities (COSLA) has a representative role and issues guidance to all local councils on a range of social care matters, for example, guidance on non–residential charging policy for social care. The Welsh Local Government Association (WLGA) is part of a strong partnership arrangement with the Welsh Government and is able to represent social care services' interests in that context. SOLACE is an organisation of local authority chief executives from throughout the UK and regularly comments on adult social care as part of its health and social care network. The organisation promotes conferences and training on such topics as integration, leading in transition in adult social care and social care reform.

Use of quangos and public bodies

The use of non-departmental public bodies, arm's length bodies and other quangos (quasi-autonomous non-governmental organisations) has been more limited in Great Britain in relation to social care than in relation to health. Such bodies are a form of governance and public administration, which lie outside government departments and the civil service and outside local government. Most of the quangos that have responsibilities in adult social care have responsibilities for the whole of England, Scotland, Wales or Northern Ireland and are not organised on a more localised basis. Some bodies relate to the whole of Great Britain or the UK. Quangos normally operate with a board appointed by a minister and government department, employ their own staff, are funded by the department and are accountable to the department. National public bodies with responsibilities covering social care are mainly involved in regulatory, inspection and research activities.

In 2010, the new Coalition government conducted a major review of quangos, with the intention of making major reductions in the number of quangos and delivering substantial savings. This review process examined the work of 18 bodies, identified as 'arm's length' bodies in the health sector. The outcome was a strategy of abolitions and mergers, aimed at reducing the number from 18 to 8 or 10 (DH, 2010c). Only five of these bodies had a clear social care role. The General Social Care Council (GSCC) set standards for and regulated the social care workforce in England, as an executive non-departmental public body. The review proposed the abolition of the GSCC and the transfer of its functions to the Health Professions Council. The CQC was created in 2008 to regulate the quality of health and social care and from 2009 it brought together the work of the Commission for Social Care Inspection, the Healthcare Commission and the Mental Health Commission. The review recommended the retention of the CQC with some additional functions. Also retained was the Information Centre for Health and Social Care, which coordinates and streamlines the collection and sharing of data about health and adult social care. Two other research related bodies – the Alcohol Education and Research Council and the National Treatment Agency for Substance Misuse – were to be abolished.

Quangos dealing with regulation, training and inspection for adult social care are organised separately in each country of the UK. In Scotland, the Scottish Social Services Council is responsible for registering people who work in social services and regulating their education and training. The Care Council for Wales performs a similar role in regulating the social care profession in Wales and setting standards for skills, training and behaviour. The Northern Ireland Social Care Council is similarly responsible for registration, education and training. These bodies along with the GSCC for England all follow the quango model of governance with a nine- to 12-person board, appointed by an appointments commission or panel on behalf of the Secretary of State for Health for England and the respective ministers for health and social care in the three devolved administrations. There are no plans to abolish the care councils in Scotland, Wales or Northern Ireland, unlike England, where the Health and Social Care Act 2012 transfers the regulatory function for social workers from the GSCC to the Health and Care Professions Council (formerly the Health Professions Council). The Health and Care Professions Council has the statutory responsibility for approving and monitoring education programmes but some aspects of education and training will fall to the new professional body, The College of Social Work. There has been some concern at the effective representation of social work interests in the existing board model of Health and Care Professions Council, as the council or board consists of 20 members representing some 10 health/medical-related professions.

Scotland, Wales and Northern Ireland also have separate arrangements for inspection and improvement. The precise configuration of functions differs somewhat but again the quango model is mainly used. The CQC for England is largely mirrored in Northern Ireland with a Regulation and Quality Improvement Authority (RQIA) for health and social care, which also acts as a mental health commission. Differences relate to the Northern Ireland body covering child protection services and the body for England covering some health-related functions. Both bodies are non-departmental public bodies with appointed boards and their own staff and separate identities. Scotland has a Social Care and Social Work Improvement Scotland body, usually referred to as the Care Inspectorate in Scotland. This body is also a quango with ten members appointed by Scottish ministers. Its role has distinctive features in being separate from the equivalent health body, Healthcare Improvement. Social Care and Social Work Improvement Scotland regulates, inspects and supports improvement of child protection as well as adult care and social work, similar in this respect to the Northern Ireland RQIA but different from the CQC. The Care and Social Services Inspectorate Wales is similar to the Social Care and Social Work Improvement Scotland as a body responsible for regulating, inspecting and giving advice on social care and social services, although including early years settings. However, the Welsh body is not a quango but lies within a Welsh Government department and there are a number of safeguards to ensure its independence.

The improvement function through research, the analysis of best practice and the dissemination of knowledge and learning materials has been augmented by a number of other organisations that formally are not quangos but are closely related to the governance function for adult social care throughout the UK. SCIE produces a range of materials, e-learning resources, practical guides, research reports and a good practice database and conducts events and seminars. Formally, SCIE has the status of an independent charity governed by a board of trustees but is funded by the Department of Health, the Department for Education, the Department for Health, Social Services and Public Safety in Northern Ireland and the Welsh Government. Wales has a separate organisation – the Social Services Improvement Agency – to promote and support improvement in social care. Formally, this agency is a partnership based in local government but works closely with SCIE. For local authorities in Wales, the Social Services Improvement Agency is seen as the first port of call. The new body for England, The College of Social Work, established to develop the profession and work with the regulatory framework for social work in England, also has a more unique non-governmental status, as a not-for-profit company, with a membership-elected board.

Table 7 lists the regulatory and inspection public bodies in the UK.

Table 7: Regulatory and inspection public bodies in the UK

Care councils – registration, education and standards	Format
Health and Care Professions Council – England	quango
Scottish Social Services Council	quango
Care Council for Wales	quango
Northern Ireland Social Care Council	quango
Inspection and improvement	**Format**
CQC – England	quango
Social Care and Social Work Improvement Scotland	quango
Care and Social Services Inspectorate Wales	quango
Northern Ireland Regulation and Quality Improvement Authority	quango

Care trusts

The proposals in the 2000 NHS Plan to facilitate the establishment of a new organisation, a care trust, to better integrate health and social care held out the prospect of a restructuring of local authorities' social care departments. The proposal seemed to open the way for new, single, multi-purpose organisations to commission and be responsible for all local health and social care (DH, 2000, p 73). A care trust would be a statutory body with its own governance board, as a distinct organisation from its parent bodies, the local authority and the NHS body. The intention was that the scope of the trusts would be wide, with an amalgamation of the social services of existing local authority departments with those of PCTs or NHS trusts. At first the government proposed to give itself powers to impose care trust arrangements and it appeared that all adult social care services might be transferred to care trusts within five years (Hudson and Henwood, 2002). Care trusts would be NHS organisations to which local authorities could delegate functions to provide integrated local health and social care. Thus, they were based on an NHS model of governance with an appointed board of executive and non-executive members, including local authority representatives, and would employ their own or seconded staff. Care trusts would be a form of quango or health public body, akin to PCTs or NHS trusts. They had the potential to revolutionise the way in which social care was delivered (Glasby and Peck, 2005) and represented a major threat to the traditional role of local authorities.

Much concern was expressed by local authorities and local government representative organisations at the impact of such a radical reorganisation (Glasby and Peck, 2005) and about an NHS takeover of adult social care. This led to the removal of the compulsory element from the NHS and Social Care Act 2001 and consequently the first trusts were established on a voluntary basis by local agreement. A care trust could cover more than one local authority. By 2004, only four trusts were in existence and the numbers were never to grow beyond 10 at any one time. Of those established few, really only three care trusts covered a comprehensive range of social care.

North East Lincolnshire NHS Care Trust Plus was a new organisation replacing the former North East Lincolnshire Primary Care Trust, as well as inheriting responsibility for the management of adult social care from North East Lincolnshire Council. Its aim was described as being responsible for commissioning health and adult social care services and managing the community health and adult social care staff who provide services. Northumberland and Torbay Care Trusts also developed, providing a comprehensive range of services. The majority of care trusts developed with their main focus on mental illness.

The positioning of care trusts within the NHS was clearly demonstrated by some care trusts achieving NHS foundation trust status, including Sheffield Health and Social Care Trust and Manchester Mental Health and Social Care Trust. However, there was no major movement towards care trusts and the model was not popular with local authorities as it threatened a loss of responsibilities and local authorities had to turn their attention to establishing children's trusts at this time. The care trust option was not to have a major impact on most local government social services departments. It was described by a minister (Burstow, 2012) as an experiment that never really got out of the lab.

The process of change in the NHS will impact on the operation of the small number of care trusts. Since 2011, PCTs across England have been grouped into clusters for their commissioning functions, pending their intended abolition in 2013. Care trusts have kept their statutory functions in the meantime, separating directly provided services from commissioning responsibilities. The pending abolition of PCTs has raised questions about the continuation of the existing care trusts.

Integrated health and social care quangos in Northern Ireland

Since the 1970s, Northern Ireland has had a distinctive system of structural integration for the delivery of health and social services. The administrative model used has been that of local or sub-national quangos. The original decision was based on a need to reorganise local government, including county council and county borough welfare departments, and the new proposals in 1969 left no role for local government in delivering social services or social care (Heenan and Birrell, 2011). The best framework for the development of personal social services was seen as their coming into a structural relationship with health. By the time of the restoration of devolution, integrated health and social care were organised by four commissioning health and social services boards covering Northern Ireland

and by 18 trusts. Of the trusts, 11 were community health and social services trusts, based on geographically defined areas, and seven were hospital trusts. A reform of the structures in 2006/07 led to a more streamlined structure of larger units but based on the same integrated principles. The new structure had a single health and social care board for the whole of Northern Ireland, replacing the previous four boards. This single board was responsible for commissioning health and social care and was advised by five local non-statutory commissioning groups. Five fully integrated health and social care delivery trusts replaced the 18 trusts, creating a fully integrated structure across adult and children's social care and primary and secondary healthcare. Separate specialist but centralised quangos were set up for patient and client involvement, common business functions and public health. Each integrated board and trust is an employer body for the full range of social care and health professions and operates with its own budgets. Social care is not seen as operating within the NHS and the system is formally described as Health and Social Care to reflect its integrated nature. Each board/ trust consists of a non-executive chair and a membership of executive and non-executive members. The non-executive board members are appointed after open applications and interview. The final appointments are made by the Minister of Health, Social Services and Public Safety but the process is monitored by a Commissioner for Public Appointments. The membership of boards/trusts does not consist of any nominees or local government representatives. Hudson and Henwood (2002, p 163) saw this Northern Ireland model as contributing to the 'political thirst' for integrated structures in Great Britain. However, this delivery model is dominated by quangos and has been criticised as meaning weak user and public involvement and little local accountability or responsiveness (Heenan and Birrell, 2009), with an over-representation in the background of board members of those from a health or business/management background rather than a social care background. The proposal following the *Transforming your care* review (DHSSPS, 2011a) – to establish within the five trusts, 17 health and social care partnerships – suggests difficulty with the operation of the five delivery quangos related to the large size of the quangos, the commissioner–provider distinction and the engagement of GPs and consultants.

Partnerships

Partnership working between different sectors has become an important feature of the delivery of adult social care. It has been dominated by a range of partnership working between local authority social services and NHS trusts, mainly PCTs. There is no agreed model or type of partnership. The nature of the partnership can have a number of different forms, ranging from sharing good practice, cooperation, collaboration, working together and joint arrangements, to more formal or deep partnerships, which can be based on written agreements and protocols or even have a statutory foundation. Normally, social care partnerships have involved public sector bodies but they may extend to include the voluntary and private sectors or there may be separate partnership arrangements with voluntary and private sector organisations. The whole ethos and development of partnership were prompted by New Labour through its ideas on partnership working and joined-up working (Glendinning et al, 2002). The actual main mechanism for producing partnerships was through the section 75 flexibilities provisions of the NHS Act 2000 covering joint provision, joint commissioning and pooled budgets. The majority of councils with responsibilities for adult social care have used section 75, primarily pooled budgets, to develop partnerships with PCTs and care trusts, rather than acute trusts (Goldman, 2010). It has been noted (Ham and Oldham, 2009) that these partnerships started in a policy vacuum but, apart from the flexibilities measures, this proved to be an advantage in that it created opportunities for creative development. Thus, partnership working between local authorities and the NHS trusts has developed with the following main arrangements:

- pooled budgets with the authorities transferring monies and resources into a common pool, which is managed by one of the authorities on behalf of the other;
- joint commissioning in which there is agreement to jointly commission services, usually by one body becoming the lead commissioner;
- joint provision of services, which can be a joint operation or agreement that responsibility is transferred to one body;
- integrated teams operating on a multi-professional basis;
- staff secondments to facilitate joint working;
- joint management of collaborative provision and where a team, section or project leader may be drawn from social care or health;
- joint posts at a senior level, where there may be a joint post of local council chief executive and PCT chief executive;
- a single assessment process;
- complete delegation with one body taking over full responsibility;
- co-location of services, which means housing local council and NHS staff in the same building/offices, having a single point of referral and a single line manager (Syson and Bond, 2010).

Governance arrangements tend to operate through local partnership boards, with a cross-membership of local authority members and NHS trust members. The membership can also contain representatives of managers, clinicians, voluntary bodies and user organisations. There may be a separate management committee or more locally organised forms of management. Tucker (2010) suggests that the best approach is local, clearly important for coordination.

The operation of partnership working was improved after 2005 by a review of PCT boundaries to align them with local authorities, which helped drive greater joint working. Alternative configurations could work, for example, Trafford Borough Council's partnership with two hospital trusts (Connor and Kissen,

2010). However, overall views on partnership arrangements remained mixed. An Audit Commission (2011) review found that partnership working between councils and the NHS was variable, poorly coordinated and insufficiently focused on outcomes. Williams and Sullivan (2010) pointed out that failed partnerships are very damaging. The local authority/NHS barrier can present organisational problems of leadership, working with elected politicians and differences in culture and values, and generate inter-agency disputes about the financial arrangements. On the other hand, partnerships have been seen as a mechanism for a whole-systems approach of integrated care for older people across organisational boundaries (Wilding, 2010). Partnerships have brought integrated service delivery without major organisational change.

In Scotland, community care partnerships have been the key mechanism for providing integrated health and social care. A special Joint Futures initiative had developed ways of improving joint working based on local partnership agreements between the NHS and local government (Bruce and Forbes, 2005). The initiative was driven forward by a form of national partnership involving the Scottish Government, NHS Scotland and the COSLA (Hendry, 2010). Use was also made of legislation: the Community Care and Health (Scotland) Act 2002 and the Local Government in Scotland Act 2003 on community planning. The original guidance on community health partnerships (Scottish Executive, 2004) described basically a health-based model with some linkage to local authority social services. This resulted in the NHS and local authorities examining potential alternative models to closely integrate health and social care (Evans and Forbes, 2009). This produced the growth of either partially integrated partnerships, perhaps covering only some aspects of adult care, or integrated partnerships, with the local authority and the NHS Board delegating operational management and service delivery powers to the community health partnerships with there being dual accountability and governance structures. These community health partnerships were usually recast as community health and social care partnerships (Evans and Forbes, 2009, p 75). These partnerships have developed with differences in governance, accountability arrangements, role, functions and size.

There were 40 community health partnerships with at least one in each council area, operating with the 32 local councils and the 14 comprehensive health boards. Separate primary and acute care trusts were abolished in 2004. In 2011, the Audit Commission (2011) in Scotland reported 36 community health partnerships. Its report criticised the cluttered partnership arrangements, which had led to a lack of clarity or duplication in roles, for example, local councils and NHS boards did not always have agreements in place covering services that the council had delegated to the community health partnership. A study the previous year (Scottish Government, 2010e) had stressed the importance of organisational arrangements and strengthening joint working arrangements with local authorities.

All community health partnerships are committees of NHS boards. In December 2011, the Scottish Secretary for Health announced plans to reform the integration of health and social care (Sturgeon, 2011). Community health partnerships would be replaced by statutory health and social care partnerships, which would be the joint and equal responsibility of the NHS and the local authority and would also work in partnership with the third and independent sectors (Scottish Government, 2012b, para 2.6). The health and social care partnerships would be accountable to the leader of the local council and the Cabinet Secretary for Health. The health board and local authority will be required to devolve budgets made up from primary and community health, adult social care and some acute hospital spend to the health and social care partnership. Voting members of the health and social care partnership committee will be made up of an equal number of health board non-executive directors and local elected members. The NHS chair and the local authority leader will form a 'community of governance' overseeing the effectiveness of the partnership (Scottish Government, 2012b, para 4.9). The partnerships will be accountable to ministers, local authorities and health boards for nationally agreed outcomes. There will also be a single, jointly appointed, senior accountable officer in each partnership.

Local government-led partnerships

The development of safeguarding boards, to protect vulnerable adults receiving care, has been a further example of partnership working but clearly led by local government. These boards have operated as partnerships in order to involve those organisations involved in adult safeguarding. They have operated under statutory advice but the establishment of such partnerships was not mandatory originally. Most local authorities set up inter-agency partnerships and developed preventive systems for vulnerable adults based on cooperation and the planning and implementation of joint prevention strategies. Despite the Department of Health guidance on how groups should operate – *No secrets* guidance on the development and implementation of multi-agency policies and processes (DH and Home Office, 2000) – there was considerable variation in structures and partnership relationships. The safeguarding boards that were set up usually had a range of members, drawn from commissioning bodies, health providers, regulatory bodies, supported housing, care groups, advocacy groups, the voluntary and private sectors and the police. For example, the Birmingham Safeguarding Adults Board had 13 member organisations. The local authority had the lead role and coordinated the work and could set up a sub-committee structure. In 2011, it was announced that it would become a legal requirement for all local authorities to have a safeguarding adults board. This followed a recommendation from the Law Commission's report on adult social care (Law Commission, 2011). The recommendation was largely copied from the Adult Support and Protection (Scotland) Act 2007, which had placed a duty on each local council in Scotland to establish an adult protection committee and specified that certain bodies must nominate a representative to be a committee member. The mandatory structure for England will be based on the partnership principle, with the main partnership bodies representing – NHS bodies, the police and the voluntary sector – and there will also be members representing the local community.

Health and wellbeing boards will be a new and important form of local government-led partnership in the delivery of social care. Under the reform of health and social care in England, these boards will be the mechanism for health and social care bodies to work together, replacing the local government–PCT relationship. A health and wellbeing board will be established for each top-tier and unitary authority. The general purpose of the boards will be to foster collaboration and joined-up services and bring together clinical commissioning groups and councils. They will drive local commissioning of integrated services but also public health and undertake a joint strategic needs assessment. The Health and Social Care Bill 2011 mandates a minimum membership of:

- one local elected representative;
- a representative of each local clinical commissioning group;
- the local authority directors for adult social services and children's services;
- a representative of the local HealthWatch organisation;
- the director of public health.

Local boards will be able to expand their membership to include a wide range of perspectives and representatives and there will be a statutory duty to involve local people. Out of 152 local authorities, 138 already have emerging health and wellbeing boards in shadow form. Health and wellbeing boards will be established as committees of local authorities. It is also envisaged that they may develop opportunities for greater working across tiers of local government (NHS Confederation, 2012b). As a partnership the members of the boards will be formally accountable to different parts of the system. A national learning network for health and wellbeing boards has been established to support health and wellbeing board members to develop knowledge and behaviours that will enable them to work effectively to deliver their shared purpose.

Parliamentary scrutiny

An important mechanism of scrutiny over the delivery of social care is exercised by the House of Commons through the select committee system. This is undertaken by two main bodies in the House of Commons: the Health Select Committee and the Public Accounts Committee. With devolution, responsibilities as they cover adult social care are restricted to England. The Scottish Parliament and the Welsh and Northern Ireland Assemblies have set up similar scrutiny arrangements. The House of Commons Health Select Committee has a remit to examine policy proposals, identify policy deficiencies, and scrutinise and monitor the performance, administration and planning of the Department of Health and associated public bodies. The members of the committee decide on the topics for inquiry and they take evidence, can commission advice and produce detailed reports with recommendations to government for changes. The committee has had a strong interest in developments in social care and has produced two major reports (House of Commons Health Committee, 2010, 2012a). The later report made very strong recommendations on the need to promote and give priority to integration. A further report was also produced, analysing expenditure on social care and identifying a funding gap (House of Commons Health Committee, 2012b). The government does not have to accept the recommendations of the committee but does publish a response and committees can return to issues as well as inquiries acting as a forum for public debate. The devolved Parliament and Assemblies have not prioritised social care issues and they can hold short as well as full inquiries. In Scotland, the Health and Sport Committee has been examining the integration of health and social care and the regulation of care for older people. The Health and Social Care Committee in Wales has examined residential care for older people and community mental health services.

Public Accounts Committees have a high status in parliamentary procedures and have the task of scrutinising expenditure by the government and its agencies, to check for efficiency, effectiveness and value for money and the topics for investigation may be fairly detailed. Adult social care has not attracted major attention. The House of Commons Public Accounts Committee has been examining user choice and providers' role in care markets. The public accounts function is again devolved. The Scottish Parliament has a Public Audit Committee, which has examined community health partnerships and transport for health and social care. The Welsh Public Accounts Committee has been examining delayed transfers of care and the Northern Ireland Public Accounts Committee has reported on the quality of care in homes for older people and domiciliary care for older people. Public accounts inquiries do produce formal responses from departments and may lead to departments changing their financial procedures and possibly accepting policy changes. The House of Commons has also an all-party Parliamentary Group on Social Care. This brings together members of the House of Commons and House of Lords from all parties with an interest in social care. It has no formal role in the policy process. The main activities may involve hearing from prominent speakers, for example, Andrew Dilnot, chair of the Commission on Funding of Care and Support, or the group may hold an inquiry into particular social care issues. A number of other all-party groups may have overlapping interests, and there are similar groupings in the devolved bodies relating to such matters as disability, dementia and older people.

Local government housing-related support

The focus on community care approaches meant that close attention had to be paid to housing provision. Sharkey (2000, p 46) expressed the clear view that 'without appropriate housing community care cannot work'. There was a need for close cooperation between local authority housing and social care departments. Local authorities had direct social housing responsibilities but also responsibilities for housing adaptations and repair and renovation grants in all housing sectors. Also required was close collaboration with housing associations, which had developed originally catering mainly for special needs housing, largely for older people, but then assumed functions from local authorities in Great Britain for all new-build social housing and the management of much of existing social housing stock. With one third of all social housing tenants over the age of 60, housing had a major role in community care provision. The importance attached to the value and objective of living independently had a significant housing dimension. The housing needs of vulnerable groups other than older people became widely recognised, particularly for people with mental health problems and people with learning disabilities (McDonald, 2006, p 159).

The most common form of specialist housing has been various types of sheltered accommodation. This now comes in various design, layout and size patterns and in different tenures – social housing, owner-occupied or private renting – and where social housing is provided by housing associations. The main characteristic is the linkage with social care, through an on-site or off-site warden, with varying degrees of social support. Surprisingly, Wright et al (2010) found an absence of a daily meal in six new schemes and restricted night cover. Recent developments have included extra-care housing, offering people with high levels of care and support needs the opportunity to live in their own home. Although Extra Care is the most common term for housing with care developments, Care Plus, 'very sheltered housing' and 'assisted living' are other terms used. These refer to a style of housing and care that falls between sheltered housing and residential care homes. Wright et al (2010) found in the absence of a national definition of extra care, that schemes were idiosyncratic. They tended to suit older people who need a high level of personal support but who are otherwise able to live independently. Such provision consists of clusters of independent living units with 24-hour on-site staffing and caters mainly for frail older people, including some especially built for people with dementia. Although there have been problems attracting people with high dependency, Extra Care housing is trying to offer a different model of care, one that older people support: to remain as independent as possible. Extra Care housing tends to be provided by charity providers and private companies but generally in partnership with social services, which provides the care needed. A variation may be small units of shared accommodation with on-site support suitable for younger people with disabilities. Major initiatives have also taken place to bring large numbers of homes to mobility standards. Home improvement agencies can help older people and others to make changes and adaptations to their homes, which allow them to stay there.

In the past, the importance of housing-related social care was totally accepted by government but there was an element of confusion over the use of housing and social care budgets. This led to a major initiative, developed from 1999 but introduced in 2003 – the Supporting People programme. This was a programme of housing-related support for vulnerable groups. It aimed to provide a better quality of life to people in these groups, to allow them to live more independently and to enable them to participate fully in the social and economic life of the community. It had an important objective of preventing problems that could lead to hospitalisation, institutional care and homelessness and also of facilitating a smooth transition to independent living. A key element was that Supporting People brought together several funding streams, including support through Housing Benefit, into a single budget. The programme was delivered locally by local authorities, some 150 in England, with the aid of a Supporting People grant from the government. A list of seven funding streams was included, which included one funding stream for Scotland and one for Wales. Northern Ireland had the same scheme but this was administered by the Northern Ireland Housing Executive. The actual services were based on commissioning and partnership working involving health, housing associations, probation, voluntary bodies and care agencies. Once fully operating there were around one million people receiving help under the programme at any one time and there were some 6,000 providers of housing-related support in England. There was not a definitive list of people requiring support but the main groups mentioned in documentation were people who:

- were frail due to age;
- had mental health problems or a learning disability or were experiencing psychological trauma;
- were leaving institutions, including ex-offenders released from prison;
- had a physical or sensory disability;
- had alcohol or drug problems;
- were chronically ill;
- were at risk of domestic violence;
- were vulnerable due to their age, including teenage parents;
- had HIV/AIDS;
- were homeless or sleeping rough (House of Commons Communities and Local Government Committee, 2009, para 1).

The primary purpose of Supporting People was to develop and sustain an individual's capacity to live independently in their accommodation. There was no statutory definition of supported housing services. However, examples of support services included:

- visiting with support services for older people in their own homes;
- enabling individuals to access the correct benefits;
- ensuring that people had the correct skills to live independently and maintain a tenancy;
- warden services within sheltered housing schemes;
- help for people leaving institutions or who had been homeless, to set up home;
- advice on home improvements so that existing accommodation continued to meet their needs.

Flexibility was important with no prescriptive list of what housing support should mean. Floating support became important, with support workers able to visit people to help with specific tasks. Short-term support was free for up to two years and then charges were applicable only to people receiving long-term services who could afford to pay.

Although the programme only commenced in 2003, a year later the government commissioned an independent review, which noted the high costs and concern that local authorities were taking the opportunity to transfer to the Supporting People budget the costs of services previously funded by housing, social care or community budgets (RSM Robson Rhodes, 2004). However, the Audit Commission (2007) found that four years on from its launch the programme had delivered real improvements on the ground and in 2007 the government was able to claim there was a great deal to celebrate in the success of the programme (DCLG, 2007). A new Supporting People strategy was launched based on four themes:

- keeping people who need services at the heart of the programme;
- enhancing partnership working;
- delivering in the new local government landscape;
- increasing efficiency and reducing bureaucracy.

Voluntary organisations were providing some two thirds of the services and receiving £31 billion annually from local authorities. It also appeared that, by 2009, value for money had improved through better commissioning and procurement of services. Four local authorities in England were awarded Beacon status for work in developing efficient Supporting People local partnerships. The work of Supporting People became focused on four main groups in terms of expenditure – people with a learning disability, homeless people, older people and people with a mental illness – as shown in Table 8.

Table 8: Expenditure on groups

Group	%
People with a learning disability	22
Homeless people	21
Older people	19
People with a mental illness	17
People experiencing domestic violence	7
People with an addiction	5
People with a physical and/or sensory impairment	2
Ex-offenders	2
People from minority ethnic groups/refugees	0.5

Source: Northern Ireland Housing Executive (2009)

Despite the increase in support, some concerns remained about the programme. The government had only loosely defined housing-related support and this resulted in variation in types and amounts of support in different areas (Fyson et al, 2007). With expenditure cuts, some local authorities restricted services and tasks or hours of support. In 2008, it was announced that the ringfence would be removed from 2009 and that local authorities would have the flexibility to spend the money as they saw fit. This raised concerns that funding would be redirected to other services. As part of the 2010 Spending Review, the new government announced that there would be a 3% cut in the Supporting People budget and the Supporting People grant was subsumed into a Formula Grant from April 2011 (House of Commons Library, 2012, p 21). The government continued to urge councils that the Supporting People allocations should only be spent on related programmes. The *Caring for our future* strategy proposed new duties to be placed on local authorities to ensure that adult social care and housing departments work together, for example, regarding adaptations and to develop new housing options.

Conclusions

- It appears unlikely that the structures of government will change very much. Central government organisation of adult social care at ministerial and departmental levels in both UK and devolved governments is closely linked to health but largely recognises adult social care as a separate identity.
- Local government has a key role in commissioning and provision in Great Britain and also a key role in partnerships with NHS bodies and with the voluntary sector. Local government also provides the main forum for organising housing support services with social care, either within council structures or in Parliament with housing organisations.
- In 2012, the Minister for Health stated that there would be no drive to merge health and social care organisations across England into a grand design (Burstow, 2012). It will be left to health and wellbeing boards to push forward integration of health and social care, mainly through commissioning arrangements.
- In Scotland it was announced in 2011 that the government had decided not to create a statutory organisation separate from the NHS and local authorities, which would create further barriers to integration (Sturgeon, 2011).

There are views that, faced with cuts in available funding, integration of health and social care is essential (The King's Fund, 2010). This still means that the two systems remain separate in Great Britain based in different forms of governance, although there may be a question as to whether new forms of local integration may emerge (NHS Confederation, 2010). It is clear that the new GP consortia will have to work in partnership with local councils, which may mean groupings of GP consortia and some problems with a lack of coterminosity. The main tasks will include joint commissioning. At least, local council social care departments will have a role in assisting consortia to make the transition to partnership working (Goldman and Carrier, 2010).

Sources

Glasby and Peck (2005) provide a useful analysis of care trusts. Analysis of developments and debates about partnership between health and social care can be found in Glasby and Dickenson (2008), Ham and Oldham (2009) and Syson and Bond (2010). Evans and Forbes (2009) provide a comparative perspective on partnerships in England and Scotland. The governance of the integrated structure of health and social care in Northern Ireland is covered in Heenan and Birrell (2011).

Questions

- What have been the key changes in the role of local authorities with regard to social care?

- Why has the administrative experiment with care trusts had limited appeal?

- What role have quangos played in administering and delivering social care?

- Why has partnership working became a major feature of social care provision?

FIVE

Personalisation in adult social care

Overview

This chapter discusses the development of the personalisation agenda and the way in which it has moved to influence thinking on and the direction of adult social care policy. It looks at:

- the key ideas and concepts associated with the term 'personalisation' and how it aims to put users at the centre of the care process;
- the origins of personalisation, its links to the disability and user movements and its influence in policy developments;
- how personalisation is operationalised in adult social care and in the implementation of direct payments and personal budgets;
- the impact of personalisation policies on users and carers;
- the future of personalisation in a context of major structural change in social care, healthcare and in the context of reductions in public expenditure.

The term 'personalisation' is a relatively recent one but many of the ideas important to it have a longer history. In particular, independent living and services tailored to the needs of the user have their origins in the disability and user movements, which evolved in the 1970s. Advocating a social model of disability, these movements campaigned for independent living, empowerment and choice because of dissatisfaction with the traditional delivery of social care, which treated people as passive recipients of care who were expected to fit into existing services (Bynoe et al, 1991; Campbell and Oliver, 1996). The social model of disability sees people as disabled not by their impairment but by the disadvantages and restrictions caused by societies that take no account of those who have physical, sensory or mental impairments (Oliver and Barnes, 1998). The philosophy of independent living is based on the idea that people should have the same choice and control as other citizens. Beresford et al (2011, p 45) summarise independent living as being 'a rights based philosophy based on the achievement of disabled people's full human and civil rights', pointing out that it is about 'ensuring service users have the support they need to live their lives on as equal terms as possible'. Importantly though, as the authors also stress, while independent living replaces the idea of 'care' with that of 'support', it is not about people managing on their own. Rather, independent living requires the right kind of support when people need it, which they do not have to rely on family members to provide.

'Personalisation' is now used to refer to broader person–centred approaches and the concept is applied to day and residential services and domiciliary settings. It is generally explained as being about viewing need and provision from the perspective of the user and increasing choice and control. Rather than people having a service provided to them, they have a say about the services that would work best for them (Leadbeater, 2004). Through the receipt of cash payments such as direct payments or personal budgets, individuals can purchase services for themselves.

A number of terms are associated with personalisation, as shown in Box 20.

Box 20: Terms associated with personalisation

Person-centred care. This is about people having choice and control over the services they use. Services should be focused on the individual's needs rather than the needs of systems or organisations.

Independent living. This is one of the goals of personalisation and does not mean doing things alone. It is about the individual having a say about what they need in order to have access to work, leisure and go about their daily life.

Self-directed support. This is the term used by the Scottish Government. It originates from the *In Control* project, which had pioneered self-directed support for people with learning disabilities. It is about the support and the financial resources required by the individual, with that support being controlled by the individual.

Direct payment. This refers to a cash payment that the individual can receive in order to buy their own care rather than having the care they are assessed as needing provided to them by the local authority or, in Northern Ireland, by the health and social care trust.

Personal budget. This is the term used to describe the budget available for an individual's services based on an assessment of their needs. It can be taken by the individual as a direct payment or it can be managed by the local authority (with the individual having control over how it is used) or managed by another third party provider.

Development of 'personalisation' policy in adult social care

Means (2012, p 318) explored the extent to which the current policy and debates about personalisation represent a complete break with the past and argued that 'most "new starts" and "brave new worlds" have much deeper roots than governments often want to admit'. Certainly policy ideas about individual choice can be seen in discussions about the introduction of the community care legislation in 1990. The White Paper on community care (DH, 1989) stressed choice and service provision linked to individual needs but the predominant vision was of the user as a 'consumer' of services within a social care market. The subsequent NHS and Community Care Act 1990 led to individual needs assessment and care management and a mixed economy of care.

Contemporary policy ideas about the application of personalisation in social care were introduced in a Green Paper on adult social care (DH, 2005), which set out aspirations for transforming social care to achieve greater control and flexibility for users. This was followed through in subsequent policy documents and a focus on personalisation was evident in *Putting people first: A shared vision and commitment to the transformation of adult social care* (DH, 2007). This was a concordat between central and local government departments and the independent sector and it set out ideas for a personalised adult social care system and the values guiding what was described as the transformation of social care:

> The time has now come to … replace paternalistic, reactive care of variable quality with a mainstream system focussed on prevention, early intervention, enablement, and high quality personally tailored services. In the future, we want people to have maximum choice, control and power over the support services they receive. (DH, 2007, p 2)

In this vision, person-centred planning and self-directed support would become mainstream and define individually tailored support packages. In another policy paper the following year, there was a stated intention to extend the ability to make choices and to have control beyond those living in their own homes to all care settings, including residential care (DH, 2008a). A Labour government 2010 White Paper, *Building the national care service* (DH, 2010b), set out plans for a long-term vision of personalised care and support. Building on developments linked to individual budgets, it put forward plans for all users to have access to a personal budget – a clearly identified amount of money available to the individual – who would then have more choice and control over how their needs are met. This budget could be held by the local authority or passed to the individual to control by way of a cash direct payment.

These personal budgets built on the experience of direct payments, introduced in 1996, which had given some recipients of services the right to apply for a budget, which they could use to purchase their own support. Initially, eligibility was restricted to disabled people but this was subsequently extended to other groups. There was also experience of providing cash payments to users through the Independent Living Fund, which was set up in 1988. Established as a Department for Work and Pensions non-departmental public body, it was to support a shift from residential to community care by operating a discretional trust fund to which disabled people could apply for cash payments. The 2005 Green Paper on adult social care (DH, 2005) had included proposals to pilot a new initiative – independent budgets – which would be held by the local authority on behalf of the user and which would be used to pay for services tailored to individual need.

These were piloted in 13 local authorities in England between 2005 and 2007. The model for these independent budgets had been strongly influenced by the work of the *In Control* project, which as mentioned earlier had pioneered self-directed support for people with learning disabilities (Glendinning et al, 2008).

The Coalition government endorsed the personalisation agenda and in *A vision for adult social care* (DH, 2010a) stated that it was putting personalised service and outcomes centre stage. While it was acknowledged that personal budgets would not automatically mean that services would be personalised, they were, it was argued, an important factor in improving outcomes and quality of life and the government proposed that everyone eligible for ongoing social care should be provided with a personal budget by April 2013.

A list of key policy documents in England that have impacted on personalisation policy is presented in Box 21.

Box 21: Key policy documents in England impacting on personalisation policy

2001   *Valuing people: A new strategy for learning disability for the 21st century*

2005   *Independence, wellbeing and choice: Our vision for the future of social care for adults in England* (Green Paper)

2006   *Our health, our say: A new direction for community services* (White Paper)

2007   *Putting people first: A shared vision and commitment to the transformation of adult social care*

2008   *Transforming social care* (local authority circular)

2010   *Building the national care service*

2010   *A vision for social care: Capable communities and active citizens*

2011   *Social care* (Audit Commission Report)

2012   *Caring for our future: Reforming care and support* (White Paper)

Personalisation and devolution

While ideas associated with the concept of 'personalisation' can be found in social care policies in each of the four countries of the UK, the personalisation agenda has been pursued with more vigour in England. In Scotland, the term 'self-directed support' has been used by the Scottish Government to encompass greater choice and independence on the part of users. A 2010 Scottish Government 10-year strategy on self-directed support referred to making it the mainstream mechanism for the delivery of social care (Scottish Government, 2010d). It described self-directed support as 'the support individuals and families have after making an informed choice on how the individual budget is used to meet the outcomes they have agreed. SDS [self-directed support] means giving people choice and control' (Scottish Government, 2010d, p 7). Its recommendations included the need for new legislation to address barriers to the uptake of direct payments and the promotion of independent budgets to all older and disabled users who want one while stressing that this would be 'available to everyone but imposed on no-one' (Scottish Government, 2010d, p 2).

The 2012 Social Care (Self-Directed Support) (Scotland) Bill imposes *duties* on local authorities to increase options available to users and requires local authorities to have regard to three principles – involvement, informed choice and collaboration. The Bill stipulates the forms of support that must be offered by local authorities. Similar to the type of support offered in England, these can be summarised as:

- direct payments to users to purchase their own provision;
- directing the available resource – where the user selects the support that they wish, using the budget available to them but the provision is arranged by the local authority – with a principle here that the resource should follow the individual and their wishes;
- local authority-'arranged' support – where the authority arranges support on the user's behalf to meet their needs – the traditional method of service delivery;
- a mix of the above options for aspects of the individual's care (Payne, 2012, p 9).

In Wales, a number of policy documents have included discussion of personalisation of adult care services. A 2007 strategy for social services (Welsh Assembly Government, 2007) referred to a vision rooted in a social model of disability and in a rights-based approach that promotes choice and equality. In 2011, a policy paper entitled *Sustainable social services for Wales* (Welsh Assembly Government, 2011) was published in response to an independent commission report on social services and social care (Independent Commission on Social Services in Wales, 2010), which had advocated a much stronger voice and greater control for users and carers. Under a heading 'Citizen centred services' in the paper, it was suggested that the Welsh approach would not follow the consumerist approach being adopted in England, noting that 'the label personalisation has become too closely associated with a market led model of consumer choice but we are taken with the Commission's approach to stronger citizen control' (Welsh Assembly Government, 2011, para 3.16). The Social Services (Wales) Bill (Welsh Government, 2012a, para 2.7.1) reiterates this position. The Bill does, however, contain proposals to seek the powers to enable Welsh ministers to make regulations relating to direct payments. It is envisaged that these could be used to allow ministers to prescribe the clients and circumstances under which direct payments may be used (and cover both individuals receiving social care services and carers). Such powers could also potentially be used to allow direct payments to be extended to allow the purchase of residential accommodation (2012a, para 2.7.12).

In Northern Ireland, there are references to personalisation within a number of policy documents but there is no explicit policy or targets. A regional strategy published in 2004 (DHSSPS, 2004) included a reference to people taking control of their own care. A 2010 document on the Spending Review (DHSSPS, 2010, para 6b) talked about patient- and user-centred care but also suggested that one of the ways by which the unit cost of social care could be reduced is through individual budgets. A major review of health and social care services in Northern Ireland, *Transforming your care* (DHSSPS, 2012b), had as one of its stated principles 'placing the individual at the centre of any model' (2012b, p 37). Personalised budgets were briefly discussed in the document but the focus was mainly on promoting the use of direct payments, with no concrete proposals regarding broader approaches to personalisation. A discussion document on the future of adult care and support (DHSSPS, 2012c) noted the piloting of personal budgets but contained no details on how personalisation should be understood and the impact on users and the workforce. Nor was there reference in the document to the values or principles that should underpin future social care provision or proposals for future policy.

Personalisation in practice

In this section we will be looking at personalisation in practice. The Social Care Institute for Excellence (SCIE, 2010a) summarises the meaning of personalisation, as presented in Box 22.

Box 22: What personalisation means
- tailoring support to individual need;
- ensuring people have access to information, advocacy and support to make informed decisions;
- finding new ways of collaborative working so that people can be actively engaged in the design, delivery and evaluation of services;
- having leadership and organisational systems that enable staff to work in person-centred ways;
- embedding intervention, reablement and prevention;
- ensuring a 'total system response' whereby all citizens have access to universal community services and resources (Carr, 2010).

Participants (users, carers, policy makers and practitioners) at a SCIE seminar talked about what personalisation meant to them. Their points included:

- freedom, choice and control – being an individual and being able to make your own decisions;
- the focus is on the person rather than the service – delivering quality of life and happiness and enabling you to live on your own terms;
- being valued as a person;
- keeping people in the mainstream and in the community, being included/ integrated and being citizens on equal terms;
- 'nobody tells you what to do';
- liberation – including being able to take risks and make mistakes;
- being listened to and heard (SCIE, 2011, p 6).

The move to personalised care in England was supported by a three-year £520 million Transforming Social Care grant to cover the period from 2008 to 2011. Local authorities were also given targets for the number of users receiving personal budgets and were required to set up at least one user-led organisation in each authority. In practice, personalisation has been operationalised largely through mechanisms such as direct payments and personal budgets.

The first legislation on direct payments was introduced in the UK in 1996, largely as a result of campaigning by disabled people's organisations (Oliver and Sapey, 1999). This gave local authorities in Great Britain and health and social care trusts in Northern Ireland the power to make cash payments to adults who could then use these payments to purchase their own support. For the most part, direct payments were used to employ personal assistants. In doing so, the holder of the direct payment became an employer and had to work within the statutory conditions associated with that position. A number of conditions were attached to direct payments. Close co-resident recipients could not be employed and, as noted earlier, initially eligibility to apply for a direct payment was restricted to disabled people. From 2000, direct payments were extended to other client groups and in 2001 local authorities in England were obliged to offer direct payments to all those eligible for social care services and assessed as capable of managing direct payments (DH, 2001a). This was rolled out across the UK from 2003/04.

The uptake of direct payments has varied considerably between user groups, between English regions and between the countries of the UK. A UK-wide study (Riddell et al, 2006) found that the highest take-up was in England, where there was a strong policy emphasis on direct payments. In Scotland and Wales, lower uptake of direct payments was linked to a defence of collective provision. Take-up was lowest in Northern Ireland. Of the 59 local authorities in the study with direct payment uptake above the mean average, only one was in Northern Ireland. This could perhaps be linked to the absence of any real policy debate about direct payments in Northern Ireland and the small number of independent organisations providing advice and support to users. Figure 2 shows the uptake of direct services by client group for England.

Figure 2: Adult direct payments by service user group (England)

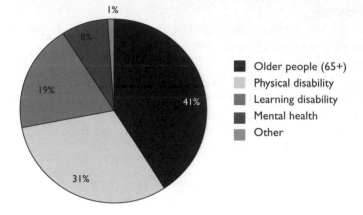

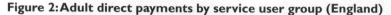

Source: Health and Social Care Information Centre (2012)

Assessments of the impact of direct payments have identified positive outcomes, including greater user satisfaction and better continuity of care (Hasler et al, 1999; Glasby and Littlechild, 2006), but since their introduction questions have also been raised about the extent to which they are appropriate to all users. Concerns have included criticism that they represent a move towards privatisation and that they threaten the future of collective provision. Other issues, include restrictions in terms of what direct payments could be used for (resulting in them being used mainly to employ personal assistants), lack of government commitment to funding support services over the long term and the implications for the working conditions of personal assistants, as will be discussed in Chapter Six (Leece, 2006; Pearson et al, 2006). However, direct payments have been a major impetus behind the development of personal budgets.

The initial prospect of individual budgets offering greater scope due to the fact that they could be used for a more diverse range of support seemed not to be entirely borne out by the findings of the national evaluation of the individual budgets pilots in England (Glendinning et al, 2008). There was evidence that individual budgets resulted in many users feeling more in control of their lives and more satisfied than those receiving conventional social care services, with mental health service users in particular identifying improvements in their quality of life. However, over half of users in the study still spent their budgets on traditional mainstream services and personal assistants. Concerns about the adequacy of the budget to pay for much beyond personal care and a desire for the security associated with continuity of existing care appeared to have been contributing factors to this. Having said that, even within mainstream services it appeared that there was better scope for people to exercise more choice and control than previously – such as being able to use personal assistants for a wider range of activities and the use of individual budgets for leisure activities. An important aspect of the pilot of individual budgets was the potential arising from the integration of funding from a range of different funding streams, including local authority social care funding, Disabled Facilities Grants, Supporting People (for housing-related support), Access to Work and the Independent Living Fund. Despite the centrality of this to the success of the project, the evaluation pointed to many difficulties with this aspect of the pilot, which the evaluators attributed to 'legislative and administrative barriers that required action by central government' (Glendinning et al, 2008, p 245). The fact that the personal budgets developed since the pilot of independent budgets, and discussed below, have tended to be based mostly on local authority social care funding may be indicative of the challenges of addressing such difficulties.

Personal budgets

Since 2009, government has used the term 'personal budget' rather than individual budget. People who are assessed or have been self-assessed as being eligible for services are told how much money is available for these services. In England, several forms of resource allocation system (mostly point–based systems) have been used to determine the size of personal budgets. The allocation is upfront and can be a full or a partial contribution to the care costs. The budget can also be topped up by users to pay for additional support. Personal budgets can be taken via a direct payment, be put into an account managed by the local authority according to the views of the user or the direct payment can be placed with a third party (such as a provider) or a mixture of these.

If a budget is managed the amount available for services should be known to the user and they should have choice and control over the services provided (Putting People First Consortium, 2010). The user should have knowledge of how much has been spent and on what, and a support plan should be worked out and agreed by the local authority. The document *A vision for adult social care* (DH, 2010a) contained a goal that everyone eligible for non-residential personal care should have a personal budget by April 2013. This was reaffirmed in the 2012 White Paper on adult social care (DH, 2012a), which also proposes a requirement on local authorities to extend the use of direct payments through the commissioning of independent advice and support services for users. Also included in the White Paper is the intention to extend eligibility to personal budgets to people living in residential care.

The number of people in receipt of a personal budget in England increased significantly between 2010/11 and 2011/12 (see Table 9). In March 2011, there were around 338,000 personal budget holders across England, twice that of the previous year, representing one third of eligible people and, by 2012, 52% of those entitled to personal budgets were using them (ADASS, 2011, 2012).

The differences in uptake geographically, and across different client groups, are still an issue. A number of reasons have been put forward to account for this, including: a lack of clarity on the part of some users, especially older people, about personal budgets, including confusion about how their budget had been calculated; and the persistence of judgements about the suitability of direct payments for

Table 9: Number of personal budgets (England) (2008/09 to 2011/12)

Year	Number of personal budgets
2011/12	432,349
2010/11	312,911
2009/10	168,000
2008/09	93,000

Source: ADASS Personal Budget Survey, March 2012

some groups of users. An example of this is evidence of older people being steered towards managed budgets as a 'better' option than direct payments. This is put down to some professionals and carers having reservations about older people's ability to cope with direct payments (SCIE, 2011). A similar issue has been raised with regard to the relatively small number of people with a learning disability who are recipients of personal budgets, with questions about whether adequate consideration has been given to the complexities of personal budgets for people with learning disabilities or to the level of support for these users, their families and carers and staff working with them (Abbott and Marriott, 2012).

As Vickers et al (2012) show, there has been little consideration of the needs and experiences of people from black and minority ethnic groups in discussions about personalisation or in research on the topic. However, there is evidence of lower engagement with direct payments and personal budgets and a lack of information and knowledge about the processes and systems (Needham and Carr, 2009). Research by SCIE looking at how direct budgets could work for black and minority ethnic people concluded that:

- assessment processes were not taking account of black and minority ethnic service users' backgrounds and requirements;
- people who used services were unaware of how to access important information on direct payments;
- there were difficulties in recruiting personal assistants who could meet the cultural, linguistic and religious requirements of black and minority ethnic people;
- there was a lack of resources for local schemes (Carr and Robbins, 2009, p 17).

The experience of direct payments suggests that unless staff are well informed and confident about systems and processes, they will be reluctant to encourage users to opt to receive a cash budget to buy their own care. A similar problem applies in relation to personal budgets, with staff not understanding the 'nuts and bolts' of personalisation and personal budgets and therefore not being confident enough to advise users. To some, one of the biggest risks of personalisation would be that essentially little changes in what users opt for or can realistically choose – in other words that people buy the services they always had (Glasby and Littlechild, 2009). While there was a marked increase in the number of users with personal budgets between 2010 and 2012, uptake of direct payments did not increase. This is concerning given the evidence that users with direct payment experience have better outcomes than those with managed budgets (ADASS, 2011; Callaghan et al, 2011).

An additional issue has been raised by ADASS (2012). Concerned about whether local authorities, worried about meeting the 2013 personal budget targets set by government, are moving people onto local authority-managed budgets without offering them genuine choice and control, it has called for a review of personal budgets for older people. It has also raised the broader issue of whether the target that all eligible users of services in England should have a budget by April 2013 is practical or wise.

Among personal budget holders there seems to be evidence of positive impact in a number of areas, including feeling more in control of their lives, being able to access more appropriate and tailored support and a better quality of life. This can be seen in how some people have chosen to spend their personal budgets. One study looking at the experiences of older people, people with mental health problems and their carers found that one of the greatest challenges was reassuring people who were concerned about spending their personal budget on the 'right' thing. With appropriate support, users could develop plans that were specific to their needs and wishes (Newbronner et al, 2011). See Box 23 for examples of how people in the study used their personal budgets.

Box 23: Examples of how some people with mental health problems, older people and their carers have used personal budgets

- Purchasing one-off items to enable them to pursue a hobby.
- Buying computers that they used to help them keep in touch with friends and family.
- Using the personal budget for social activities such as buying a football season ticket or attending a gym.
- Paying for domestic tasks such as cleaning and gardening.
- Paying for transport, especially taxis.
- Some older people and their carers were using their personal budgets to pay for a mix of services such as residential respite and day services, although this was very dependent on the level of the budget
- One carer had purchased Sky Sports for her husband who had dementia, as he had always been a keen sports fan and while he was watching television she could get on with jobs in the home or simply have some time to herself,

Source: Newbronner et al (2011, p 44)

The 2011 National Personal Budget Survey (Hatton and Waters, 2011) of 2,000 users and carers found that the vast majority of personal budget holders felt that their views had been taken into account in the drawing up of their support plan and that they had got the support they needed when they needed it. The picture was not entirely positive, however, with considerable variation between councils and examples of difficulties at different stages of the process. The authors concluded that a number of factors were related to positive outcomes, as shown in Box 24.

Box 24: Factors linked to positive outcomes for personal budget holders

- How personal budgets are managed is robustly linked to outcomes for personal budget holders. People with direct payments paid directly to them reported more positive outcomes and people with personal budgets managed by the council reported less positive outcomes.

- Personal budget holders and carers need to be kept informed of essential aspects of the personal budget. People who did not know how their personal budget was managed or did not know the amount of their personal budget reported less positive outcomes.

- The support planning process for the personal budget is critical. Personal budget holders and carers who felt that their views were more fully included in the support plan were more likely to report positive outcomes across the board.

- Positive outcomes are related to duration of use. People who had been using their personal budgets for longer reported increasingly positive outcomes.

- A greater weekly amount of personal budget support was robustly associated with more positive outcomes.

Source: Hatton and Waters (2011, p 40)

Research by SCIE (2011) found that access to advice and advocacy services is agreed to be fundamental to the successful working of personal budgets. Much of this work has been undertaken by third sector organisations, some by user-led organisations. Users who have the support of such organisations have been shown to be more likely to go beyond standard services and access what has been referred to as 'mainstream' activities, that is, leisure services, using budgets for kitchen equipment more suited to their needs and so on (Harlock, 2009; Needham, 2011). User organisations have also expanded their role as provider organisations, including as social enterprises, and some of the most innovative forms of provision that have been developed have been pioneered by them.

Personal health budgets

Building on the experience of social care personal budgets, personal health budgets for people with long-term conditions have been piloted across half of PCTs in England. The pilot commenced in 2010 and a final evaluation was published in 2012 (Forder et al). This concluded that there was evidence that personal budgets were cost effective and supported a wider roll-out. Introduced as part of the Darzi review of the NHS (DH, 2008b), personal health budgets have been described as 'a cornerstone of government policy to improve the responsiveness and flexibility of health services in England and … part of a much broader agenda to "personalize" the care delivered by the NHS, which includes giving patients more choice and control' (NHS Confederation and National Health Development Unit, 2011). The UK Coalition government is keen to press ahead with the initiative and in September 2012 announced that, subject to the evaluation of the pilot programme, up to £1.5 million would be made available to support early roll-out in the period from October 2012 to March 2013. In October 2011, the-then Secretary of State for Health, Andrew Lansley, had said that by April 2014 everyone in receipt of NHS Continuing Healthcare would have a right to ask for a personal health budget, including a direct payment, a development that it was argued would further the integration of health and social care services. A 2012 discussion paper elaborated on this proposal (DH, 2012f).

The Department of Health guidance (DH, 2010g) on personal health budgets states that:

- NHS values still hold – no one will pay their own money to get services they need or be denied essential treatment as a result of having a personal health budget.
- Having a personal health budget does not entitle someone to more services, more expensive services, or preferential access to NHS services.
- Services should be safe and effective. Using them should be a positive experience.
- Personal health budgets should help people get a service from the NHS that best suits them.
- You should have as much control over decisions as is appropriate. Organisations should work in partnership with you and with each other.

With regard to the interface between health and social care, the interim report of the national personal health budget pilot study (Davidson et al, 2012) did not find that personal health budget holders reported problems managing their health budgets alongside any social care provision they were receiving. More problematic was a number of issues highlighted by some carers supporting people with very complex conditions where they were also receiving substantial social care personal budgets or a social care funding contribution to an NHS Continuing Healthcare funding package. These brought into sharp focus the difficulties of trying to combine funding streams, with the risk of users experiencing serious problems and delays with primary care trusts and local authorities with regard to their level of contribution or if there were significantly different management issues.

An earlier report by the NHS Confederation (2011a) on the experiences of mental health users and their carers of personal health budgets suggested that views were divided about the benefits of personal health budgets. Arguing that the kind of improvements they wanted to see in their services required organisational culture change and better person-centred planning, some respondents questioned whether, if these things happened, there would be a need for personal health budgets. There could perhaps be optimism about the potential of personal health budgets to support people with continuing health needs to be able to live independently outside of residential care. However, the indications are that a number of implementation problems have to be addressed.

Commissioning of adult social care services

Traditionally, commissioning has been a process largely of local authorities allocating block contracts to private or voluntary sector organisations. Personalisation suggests a fundamental shift in this approach towards smaller-scale purchasing, including individual service users taking on a commissioning role and contracting directly with provider organisations or personal assistants. It also means commissioners purchasing a much wider range of services, from advocacy or support services to leisure services, aids and adaptations and holidays, in line with the philosophy of services being tailored to the specific needs of users (Needham, 2011).

SCIE (2010b) sees new contractual models for commissioning, including:

- framework contracts and approved provider lists – people managing their own budget can draw on a range of approved services;
- person-centred contracting – anonymised information from individual support plans is used in 'mini tenders' and people and families are involved in evaluating bids;
- joint commissioning with partners;
- service users as commissioners.

While it is the individual commissioning of services that has attracted much attention, there are clearly challenges and uncertainties associated with users being able to successfully negotiate the social care market. User choice depends on the presence of a number of providers and the availability of services in local areas. There is an expectation on local authorities to know local markets and shape and manage these by encouraging alternative providers into the market. *Putting people first* (DH, 2007) expected all local authorities by 2011 to have a commissioning strategy to stimulate the development of high-quality services and encourage independent sector participation and innovation – including new social enterprises. There are examples of innovation, with some projects ensuring that the wider social, economic and environmental impacts of services are considered and such projects are often based on consortia of local organisations. However, this has proved challenging for many local authorities, which have acknowledged the slow progress in finding viable alternative services. Needham (2010, p 21) draws on interview data with policy makers, frontline staff, trades union representatives, providers and users to group the difficulties for commissioners into the themes outlined in Box 25.

Box 25: Challenges for commissioners of adult social care services

- Understanding the market at the local and regional levels – challenges include mapping local markets and lack of skills required to shape the market.

- Supporting providers to meet demand – challenges include the need for providers to assume new roles such as care management and support planning and less security for providers in the new commissioning environment.

- Decommissioning – challenges are presented by the difficulty of taking money out of traditional services and transferring it to new services provided by other organisations or directly to individual users. There may also be a lack of agreement about what services should be 'decommissioned'.

- Costing and pricing – challenges are presented by a lack of information about cost of services and the difficulty of ensuring that support plans adequately reflect the costs of services, which may act as a disincentive for people to take their budget as a direct payment.

- Developing the workforce – challenges are presented by the need for significant workforce change, including concerns about the further fragmentation and deskilling of an already vulnerable workforce.

Source: Needham (2010, pp 20-7)

In addition, an as yet unknown factor is the impact that cuts in local authority budgets might have on local authorities' commissioning practices, possibly making them more hesitant about offering a choice of suppliers to users as they attempt to constrain costs. In a survey of local authority officers and political representatives working in social care conducted by the Local Government Information Unit and Mears Group, a provider of home care and support services, three quarters of respondents disagreed that the systems and processes in their local authority were sufficient to manage adult social care in the future. More than 90% said that resource pressure was making them reconsider how they provided social care (Lucas, 2012).

Successive policy papers (DH, 2007, 2008b, 2010a, 2012a) have suggested an expectation from government that commissioning would be undertaken jointly with the NHS authorities and other statutory agencies to ensure more integrated provision and better user outcomes (including prevention and early intervention strategies) and that it would achieve economies of scale. However, progress and outcomes in relation to joint commissioning have been patchy, leading the Audit Commission (2009) to conclude that the financing arrangements rather than the outcome of improved integration and better user outcomes have been the focus of attention. More recent research, including the national evaluation of the personal health budgets, shows continuing difficulties (Davidson et al, 2012). However, as discussed earlier, the challenges of commissioning services on the basis of shared budgets are not inconsiderable and the Audit Commission also accepted that fundamental differences in entitlement to NHS services (free at the point of delivery) and social care services (which are means tested) create practical difficulties in the pooling of budgets.

The 2012 White Paper on adult social care (DH, 2012a) places new duties on local authorities to shape markets, promote a diversity of providers and improve the quality of provision. The establishment of new clinical commissioning groups in England, as a result of measures in the Health and Social Care Act 2012 (DH, 2012a), puts in place a different commissioning landscape. These new arrangements may present opportunities for better integration of health, social care and other provision. The development of a joint health and wellbeing strategy at the local level through health and wellbeing boards is being seen by government as 'an opportunity to agree the commissioning decisions across the NHS/local authority interface' (NHS Commissioning Board, 2012, p 4). However, there is some concern that the size and bureaucracy associated with these new commissioning frameworks may adversely impact on joint working with local authorities or that innovation may be stifled by a structure of commissioning that is too removed from localities (Hay, 2012). In February 2012, the House of Commons Health Committee (2012a, para 11), in the report of its inquiry into social care, included in its proposals a recommendation that adult care, housing and health should be brought under a single commissioner in each area to improve support for older people and help address the funding crisis in social care. It argued that successive governments' commitments to integration had failed to address the fragmentation of services and the 'silo mentality' among service providers and that real progress could only be made by bringing the commissioning of health, housing and adult social care together. Criticism of the proposals included the committee's focus on commissioning as being integrated 'around a local authority or a clinical commissioning group', failing to take into account the increasing volume of services being commissioned by individual users (Henwood, 2012).

Participants at a seminar organised by SCIE (2012a) identified specific measures that need to be taken by national and local government, policy makers, service providers and practitioners to achieve improvements in personalisation.

These included:

- the need for a holistic approach that addresses all aspects of people's live, supported with overarching legislation based on a shared vision on what personalisation should mean;
- the need for a pooling and coordination of resource, bringing together current funding from a range of government departments – it was suggested that the Office for Disability Issues in the Department for Work and Pensions could take on a coordination role for this new approach to budgeting for personalisation;
- the need for better and closer collaboration between national and local policy makers and service providers;
- the need to develop clear and independent evidence of what is and is not working in relation to personalisation;

- the need to develop co-production with service user and carer organisations on the basis of equality, mutual respect for expertise and power sharing.
  Source: SCIE (2012a, p 15)

The future of personalisation

Few would disagree with the principles at the heart of personalisation and the outcomes associated with it, such as greater autonomy and choice for users. There are, however, deeply held opposing views about personalisation as it has developed in the UK. This is particularly the case with regard to personal budgets and the increased outsourcing of provision. Opponents claim that personalisation as it is conceived in the UK is over-individualistic with its emphasis on individuals holding budgets, poses a threat to collective provision and could result in greater inequality (Henwood and Grove, 2006; Ferguson, 2007; Roulstone and Morgan, 2009). Ferguson (2012, p 57) suggests that 'there is no true meaning of personalisation any more than there is a "true" meaning of empowerment or participation or choice. Rather, these are contested concepts, terrains of political struggle and debate on which different social forces seek to impose their preferred meaning'.

The extent to which the personalisation agenda has provided users with greater independence and control has been discussed above and a number of other issues relating to personalisation are covered elsewhere in the book, for example, the implications for unpaid carers (Chapter Seven), the implications for the paid workforce (Chapter Eight) and the debate about safeguarding and regulation (Chapter Ten). Whether or not the rolling out of personal budgets is seen as a good thing is strongly contested. Supporters of the potential of personal budgets see them as a vital factor in achieving a better quality of life for users of services and their carers. Critics object in principle to what they regard as increasing privatisation and the imposition of market principles on social care, which in the long term will result in a diminishing social care sector where users and carers will be more vulnerable. This is illustrated by Needham's (2011) discussion of the controversial closure of day centres. While advocates of personalisation often support the closing down of what they regard as communal provision that is not person centred, as Needham shows, there is evidence of support for day centres with many users, including those with personal budgets, opting to continue to use them.

The extension of 'personalisation policies' at a time of substantial cuts in public sector expenditure, including major reductions in local authority budgets, and as radical social security reforms will significantly impact on people with disabilities, has given rise to much debate. Even formerly strong supporters of personalisation (see Duffy, 2012, for example) caution against a focus on targets rather than entitlements. As local authorities have to make efficiency savings, the focus on higher-level needs in adult care may mean that some users will risk having budgets cut or choices restricted as local authorities rationalise commissioning arrangements. Or, if the eligibility threshold is increased, people will be assessed when they are already in a vulnerable or crisis position and not in a good position to be making choices. Duffy (2012) sees the failure to place entitlement at the heart of the model of personalisation as leading to a range of problems:

- The rationing process (known as the resource allocation system) is often too bureaucratic and too complex and yet ambiguous.
- The resource allocation system is also being used to make cuts in ways that seem unreasonable and are possibly illegal.
- The planning process has become more burdensome, with disabled people and families forced to get their own plans through a panel of managers.
- Expensive monitoring systems take away real flexibility and damage independence.
- Little effort has been made to redesign systems to make them more workable for service users or social workers.
- Some people are assigned budgets.

Other observers have discussed how personalisation or self-directed support policies, introduced at a time when services are experiencing cuts, are associated in people's minds with reduced services and increased costs for users (Rummery et al, 2012). The *Community Care* Personalisation Survey of social care professionals (UNISON and The College of Social Workers, 2012) reports a quarter of those surveyed seeing decreases in the value of personal budgets over the previous year, with half saying that personal budgets were not of sufficient value to allow people to meet their needs. The proposal to abolish the Independent Living Fund (which operates across the UK and is a discretionary fund that can make cash payments to disabled people with high-level needs to help them fund the support required for independent living) in 2015 and devolve its budget to local authorities (DWP, 2012) has given rise to concerns that existing fund users, who have high-level needs, would not continue to receive the same level of support (Mithran, 2012; Morris, 2012).

Although there are concerns that expenditure cuts and bureaucracy linked to personal budgets are undermining the implementation of personalisation, there is also optimism that there is still potential for the personalisation agenda to benefit most users. There are those who argue that there has been too much emphasis on individual funding rather than a more 'collectively organised personalisation' (Tizard, 2010) and that what is needed is a rethinking or refocusing on the conceptual underpinnings of personalisation.

Conclusions

- The personalisation agenda has had a major influence on the development of adult social care policy. However, there is divergence between the countries of the UK in terms of the nature and pace of personalisation policy, with more rapid and substantive changes in England, which has seen the rolling out of personal budgets and new commissioning framework structures. Scotland and Wales have embraced rather different models of personalisation, while policy debates have yet to take place in Northern Ireland.
- The policy focus on personalisation has undoubtedly resulted in more users being able to access better-tailored and more innovative provision, with service users holding a personal budget reporting higher levels of satisfaction than those relying on traditional services.
- There may, however, be challenges in retaining the innovation that can be associated with smaller, time-limited initiatives or pilot projects (Parr and Nixon, 2009). There continues to be low take-up of personal budgets among some groups and clear evidence that they are not having sufficient impact on outcomes for older people (ADASS, 2012).
- There is also a concern that some users have been more isolated due to living 'independently' as opposed to receiving more collective provision.
- Much of the critique of personalisation has centred on the individualistic approach being adopted. This, it is argued, contributes to seeing personalisation in its narrowest sense – an individual with support needs rather than a person who is part of a family and a community (Fox, 2012).

Sources

Texts on the politics of disability provide a useful foundation for understanding the ideas and concepts linked to personalisation. In particular see Campbell and Oliver (1996), Oliver and Barnes (1998) and Bynoe et al (1991). The Social Care Institute for Excellence (SCIE, 2010) *Personalisation: A rough guide* is a useful starting point for information on contemporary ideas and developments. Glasby and Littlechild (2006 and 2009) are good sources on the working of direct payments. Critical perspectives on contemporary personalisation policy can be found in Ferguson (2007 and 2012) and Duffy (2012).

Questions

- To what extent do current policy ideas about personalisation represent a break from or continuity with the past?

- How has policy on personalisation differed or been similar in the countries of the UK and is there evidence of different models of personalisation emerging?

- How will the greater focus on personalisation impact on the social care workforce and on unpaid carers?

- What are the arguments that greater personalisation will lead to a more individualistic approach to social care?

SIX

Integration of health and social care

Overview

This chapter traces the development of the policy of increasing integration between health and adult social care and explains its contemporary importance. The nature and organisation of integrated working is set out covering partnership working, care trusts and more structurally integrated arrangements and the introduction of new frameworks. The main strategies and factors that promote integration are analysed, including pooled budgets, joint commissioning and integrated teams. An assessment is made of the performance of integration on the basis of existing results and evaluation.

Development of policy and strategies

It is possible to trace the growth of collaboration between health and personal social services through the 1970s and 1980s. The stark division between health and personal social services was readily identifiable in structural and professional manifestations and as the cause of difficulties with delivery to meet health and social service needs. While support for integration grew, some of the uncertainty about the way forward was indicated even by the use of different terminology with imprecise meanings. These terms included cooperation, collaboration, joint working, partnerships and integration. Traditionally, widespread examples of cooperative practices and close working could be found in adult services. The development of community care initiatives brought the need for policies on collaboration to be put onto the government agenda. Difficulties and fragmentation in community care was seen as caused by a lack of inter-agency cooperation (Hudson and Henwood, 2002). The NHS and Community Care Act 1990 had opted for making community care a responsibility of social service authorities but there remained a struggle over the respective responsibilities of health and local government with the introduction of quasi-markets, particularly over responsibilities for the long-term care of older people (Lewis, 2001). The issue of the barrier between social services and health was to be more specifically addressed in key policy papers of the incoming Labour government in 1997 and then the Coalition government, which came to power in 2010 (see Box 26).

Box 26: Key policy documents addressing barriers between health and social care

- *Modernising social services* (DH, 1998a) clearly articulated the message about cooperative working. The paper noted that the NHS is a crucial partner in almost all social services work. Reference was made to bringing down the 'Berlin Wall' that can divide health and social services. One key aspect of the strategy was that collaboration could be pursued without any major administrative restructuring.

- *Partnership in action* (DH, 1998b) brought forward proposals focusing on partnership working between the NHS and social care.

- The Health Act 1999 included provisions to make joint working easier. Section 31 enacted what was to become known as the Health Act flexibilities, which removed obstacles by introducing pooled budgets, allowed one body to be the lead commissioner and allowed local authorities and health bodies to merge their services to deliver more integrated provision. Other sections of the Act permitted the transfer of funds between local authorities and the NHS to finance joint working.

- *The NHS Plan* (DH, 2000) recognised that a major blockage to people receiving the best care were the old divisions between health and social care, which had to be overcome. *The NHS Plan* declared that fundamental reforms were necessary and made a radical proposal for care trusts as an administrative innovation. These would be NHS bodies but with social care responsibilities delegated to them. There was a suggestion that if financial incentives to promote collaboration failed, care trusts could be made compulsory. In practice, close working between social services departments and PCTs was to develop on a largely voluntary basis with strong Department of Health support.

- *High quality care for all* (DH, 2008b) called for every PCT to commission comprehensive wellbeing and prevention services in partnership with local authorities, to meet the needs of the local population.

- *Shaping the future of care together* (DH, 2009a) – this Green Paper again emphasised more joined-up working.

- *A vision for adult social care* (DH, 2010a) – the new Coalition government quickly published this policy document, which listed the first of three government commitments as to 'break down barriers between health and social care funding to incentivise preventative action' (DH, 2010a, p 6).

- *Caring for our future* (DH, 2012a) confirmed the commitment to integrated care.

The House of Commons Health Committee fully endorsed the importance of integration when it conducted an inquiry into the issues facing the future of social care in advance of a major government White Paper for 2012. A well-funded, fully integrated system was seen as essential to provide high-quality support and care (House of Commons Health Committee, 2012a, para 3). The UK government in its response to the committee's recommendations noted that a stronger but flexible legal framework will be put in place to support and encourage integration (Health and Social Care Act 2012). The White Paper *Caring for our future* (DH, 2012a) reiterated a commitment to integrated care that was coordinated, continuous and person–centred. In examining policies on integration and integrated provision, it is important to distinguish between organisational or structural integration and integrated practice (Petch, 2012).

Acceptance of the rationale for collaboration

The rationale for the promotion of collaborative and integrated working between health and social care has become widely accepted and popular and widely supported by practitioners, professionals, users and administrators. The rationale as expressed covers a number of dimensions.

First, in relation to people's needs, they do not fit neatly into two categories or into two services. As Glasby (2007, p 66) notes, 'it was assumed that it was possible to distinguish between people who are sick and have needs met by the NHS and people who have social care needs and fall under the remit of local authority services'. The division can be a source of confusion for people who do not necessarily regard themselves as having clearly one type of need – either health or social care. Patients and users may fall awkwardly between the two systems.

Second, the institutional separation can lead to problems. Each has its own priorities, funding regimes, planning procedures and separate identities. The division can lead to boundary disputes and to obstacles to collaboration, both professionally and structurally, and to continuing cultural differences in attitudes and work practices. This makes more difficult the flexibility needed for cooperation.

Third, there is a recognition that an integrated system will deliver improved outcomes in supporting people's independence and preventing hospital admissions and in assisting carers.

Fourth, the principle of joint working between different professions and agencies has become more acceptable and the benefits of multi-professional and multi-agency working recognised. Support for joint working has developed in all the main health and social care professions and in particular the value has been recognised of close working relationships between social work and social care and the medical and health professions.

Fifth, there has been an increasing awareness of the importance of integrated working and delivery for new and growing needs; with the rise in numbers with long-term conditions, dementia and the frail elderly; for people with multiple disabilities; and for key service issues, hospital discharges, intermediate care, reablement and carers' needs. With these developments has been a recognition that some of what was regarded as healthcare has shifted to social care.

Sixth, there has been an increasing acceptance of and importance attached to the view that integrated approaches have the potential to make significant savings and provide good value. This can be achieved through the more efficient use of resources and elimination of waste, and thus integration has become a major tool for producing more efficient delivery (House of Commons Health Committee, 2012a, para 4).

The nature of integrated working

Attempts have been made to categorise the nature and scope of collaborative working. Analysis has been carried out on the depth and breadth of the relationship between health and social care in terms of structures and coverage. Glasby (2005) suggested a continuum of depth of involvement and breadth of the relationship. In analysing Glasby's diagrammatic presentation, Dickenson (2006) also noted that partnership working can have different purposes. These typologies are based heavily on existing systems in England and it is possible to present a more comprehensive categorisation over a number of dimensions.

The breadth of the working arrangements across health and social care can include quite a variation of combinations and can be listed as presented in Box 27.

Box 27: Breadth of working relationships across health and social care

- All health and social care.
- Some areas of health and all social care.
- Some areas of health and adult social care.
- Some areas of health and some areas of adult social care.
- Only one or two service areas included, for example, mental health.

It is useful to extend the concept of 'breadth' to possible wider remits with a range of services and these can be listed as including:

- children's services;
- housing, mainly social housing;
- voluntary sector services and independent sector services;
- community services;
- urban regeneration and rural development schemes.

Another dimension to the categorisation can be made on the basis of the purpose of the joined-up working. This is described as differentiating types of partnership by the type of commitment (Glasby and Dickenson, 2008). The following typology can be drawn up:

- mainstream service based;
- project based;
- problem based;
- innovative or experimental;
- priority driven;
- legally driven or required.

The organisational nature of the relationship between health and social care can be set out as follows:

- integration of health and social care bodies in a single structure;
- merger of parts of existing organisations;
- formal partnership between separate organisations;
- network of separate organisations;
- mechanisms for collaboration and cooperation between health and social care bodies;
- methods to achieve coordination between health and social care bodies.

Examples of all these structures can be found in the UK for health and social care. It can be argued that there are four main broad categories:

- full structural integration;
- partial structural integration;
- partnerships, that is, a working structural arrangement between, as Dowling et al (2004) describe them, 'otherwise independent bodies';
- collaborative working outside a specific formal structure.

Care trusts

A formal integrated form of structure was proposed in *The NHS Plan* (DH, 2000, p 73). A new organisational format of a care trust was envisaged, which would be based on a new level of PCT/care trust, and would be a single, multi-purpose, legal body to commission and be responsible for all health and social care. The new organisations could build on existing partnership arrangements but had a unique framework to better integrate health and social care and can be seen as a high state of integration. The benefits of care trusts were expressed in terms of bringing together existing systems to work more effectively:

- a single strategic approach;
- continuity of care;
- improvements in equality for service users;
- more focus on the needs of clients and users;
- a one-stop shop approach;
- easier integrated information;
- the facilitation of complex care packages (DH, 2002).

The PCT model was regarded as ideal for consideration for the governance of care trusts and care trusts would be in the NHS, but local authorities would delegate services to care trusts, not transfer functions. This meant that governance arrangements would reflect the shared responsibilities of the partners. It was also accepted that no one model would fit all circumstances and flexibility was needed to respond to different local situations and boundary issues. Care trusts were formed from PCTs or NHS trusts and local government functions under the Health and Social Care Act 2001, which set out the necessary legal framework and the governance arrangements, including representation of local councillors and users on boards. The framework was based on a partnership of equals (DH, 2002). Although *The NHS Plan* had referred to the possibility of compulsory care trusts, they emerged on a voluntary basis where there was agreement at the local level. Care trusts were not intended to replace other forms of partnership. It was not specified which client groups care trusts would focus on or whether they should focus on all groups. It seemed likely that they would focus on older people and people with a mental health problem. Care trusts could be provider bodies or combine provision and commissioning. The first care trusts came into existence in 2002 but the response to the facility was very low and no more than 10 care trusts at any one time came into existence in England. The number of trusts has continued at this level.

Restructuring to establish care trusts did not prove a popular choice. Hudson (2002) suggested a number of reasons for the unpopularity of the idea at that time, in terms of the absence of an evidence base, dilemmas over financial boundaries, different cultures and values, and concerns over democratic accountability. Local authorities were reluctant to lose their social care responsibilities to what could be interpreted as an NHS takeover, as officially care trusts would be NHS bodies. There was also concern at possible consequences of underfunding of social care while local authorities would not have direct control but would still remain accountable. The impact of reorganisation was a further deterrent, especially when at the same time local authorities found that they had to undertake a compulsory reorganisation under the 'Every Child Matters' agenda to set up children's trusts. There was also trades union opposition to change and the transfer of staff, especially given doubts about the long-term viability of care trusts. By 2003, only eight care trusts had been established followed only by a few more, including Solihull in 2006. In 2011, only nine care trusts continued to operate and were faced with likely disappearance after the abolition of PCTs. Some moves to create trusts broke down owing to disagreements over management structures, finance and accountability (Baggott, 2004, p 289).

Care trusts that were established varied in their remit, but most had a strong emphasis on mental health. Camden and Islington Mental Health and Social Care Trust deals solely with mental health. Manchester, Sheffield and Sandwell Mental Health and Social Care Trusts deal with mental health and learning disability. A few have developed comprehensive services. Solihull NHS Care Trust covers adult social services and North-East Lincolnshire, described, since 2007, as a Care Trust Plus, involves all adult social care commissioning and provision transferred from the local authority. Northumberland Care Trust has a very comprehensive range of functions, providing directly a wide range of primary, community and intermediate healthcare services and care services for older people, people with mental health problems, people with physical disabilities, people with learning disabilities and many other social care services on behalf of Northumberland County Council, including day care and home care. The number of staff employed ranges from only 100 to 1,500.

Given the small number of care trusts it is difficult to evaluate their success and there have been no comprehensive assessments. An early study gave a positive assessment of the initiative (DH, 2002). Some care trusts have received good star ratings and Torbay Care Trust won awards. Torbay Care Trust, created in 2005 and contracted to provide all social care functions, offset concerns at a NHS takeover (Thistlethwaite, 2011) and achieved local success. Some care trusts have not performed so well. A few care trusts, for example, Sandwell, have sought and obtained NHS Foundation Trust status. Glasby and Peck (2005) reported concerns over the limited focus of care trusts, the possibility of domination by NHS targets and that they were hard work to establish. However, they were viewed as more accessible and flexible, even if respondents could not identify anything that marks care trusts out from other forms of partnership. Care trusts were the most integrated form of health and social care organisation in England. However, the low number of care trusts indicates a failure for the concept as a model for the promotion of integration. A strong view developed that the objectives of partnership working between health and social care could be achieved without major organisational change. It was not the organisational form that made the difference but the behaviour within organisations (House of Commons Select Committee, 2012a, para 49). Forms of partnership and use of the Health Act flexibilities could bring about improved cooperation and progress integration. The idea of care trusts has not been completely abandoned with the NHS reorganisation, and the Health and Social Care Act 2012 supports the care trust model in the reformed system. NHS foundation trusts, clinical commissioning groups and local authorities can form care trusts in the future (Health and Social Care Act 2012, section 200).

Partnership working and flexibilities in England

With the lack of development of care trusts in England the main mechanism for taking forward the integration agenda in England and Wales has been through partnerships and use of the flexibilities provisions. The main characteristics of this partnership working, which is mainly between PCTs and local authorities, can be listed and describes as pooled budgets, lead commissioning, integrated teams, co-location, leadership and joint management and posts.

Pooled budgets

Pooled budgets are one of the most popular of the core flexibilities mechanisms and require health bodies' and local authorities' adult social care to put an agreed proportion of their respective budgets into a mutually accessible joint budget. As Lewis (2002, p 319) had noted 'the financial dimensions of the health/social care boundary must be targeted first'. Pooled budgets work best and have maximum impact when used as intended in a flexible manner. The obvious use is for joint projects, including joint capital projects, but the implication is that once money is pooled there is no requirement to spend the budget in the same proportion as contributed. NHS money could be used for home care provision by the local authority, if agreed and such decisions were justified as a better use of financial resources. Pooled budgets have also been seen as reducing transaction costs, bureaucracy and overheads, producing a streamlined payment service, reducing duplication and producing economies of scale. Partnerships may be able to redeploy into the pooled budget additional and external sources of money and commit funding to developing innovative services (Hafford–Letchfield, 2009, p 52). Such budgets require robust management and normally one of the partnership bodies manages the single pooled budget. Pooled budgets tend to be concentrated in some service areas, particularly learning disability, mental health and community equipment. A national evaluation by the Audit Commission (2009) found the use of pooled budgets had little impact on per capita spend or delayed transfers and the effect on efficiency or quality of care was unclear.

Lead commissioning

The second core flexibility and a major characteristic of partnership working is a system of lead commissioning. One body in the partnership takes responsibility for purchasing both health and social care, with the authority delegated from the other partner. Joint commissioning is normally combined with pooled budgets and agreed aims or programmes. The designation of one lead body means that in practice the NHS body can be commissioning nursing and home care services, while the local authority may be commissioning services for older people with mental health problems or commissioning nursing and occupational therapy for people with learning disabilities. Historically, social care has operated in a more decentralised setting than health. New organisational approaches can also be developed, for example, in terms of locality-based commissioning: one trust – North-East Lincolnshire – decided on four localities each with 40,000 people (Ham, 2009, p 7). As well, commissioning can be built around service themes such as diabetes or stroke rehabilitation or it can be aimed at more preventive activity. More localised commissioning also allows for involvement by local people. The importance of joint commissioning has been stressed at this time of tight fiscal constraints and population-level priority setting seems to target resources where need and capacity are greatest (Williams et al, 2010).

Integrated teams

The establishment of integrated delivery teams has been a major characteristic of partnership working. Integrated teams can take different formats but the most important characteristics are their multidisciplinary nature, their coverage, their composition and their organisational accountability. Joint operational teams of social workers, nurses and therapists are the basis for an integrated team with a single management system. The teams usually work on a geographical locality basis but may operate across the whole partnership.

The services and activities covered show a degree of similarity within adult social care, mental health services but particularly community mental health teams for young people and for older people. Specific integrated teams for older people usually have a specific focus: people with dementia or frail older people. Learning disability and physical disability are other common bases for integrated teams, often including carers as well. The coverage of integrated teams may extend beyond these groups and services. With local authority involvement in Great Britain, housing and accommodation services may be included for a particular team, while in Northern Ireland child protection may be included in trust services. Aspects of children and family services may be included in an integrated team's remit or work. A partnership operating integrated teams may also include voluntary or independent sector bodies in, for example, joint addiction teams. Integrated teams are usually associated with formal partnerships, using the flexibilities legislation in England and Wales or formal partnerships or integrated structures in Scotland and Northern Ireland. Teams can be set up on a more informal and ad-hoc basis throughout health and social care bodies. A review of research (Cameron et al, 2012, p 5) found few examples of organisational models being used for team working.

It has been widely recognised that inter-professional team working faces formidable barriers (Hudson, 2006) and it is not always easy to promote team working between staff from different professional backgrounds (Ham, 2009, p 11). Respect and trusting relationships have to be worked at; identifying what professions have in common and understanding each profession's role are all important. Hudson (2006, p 17) notes the importance of shared values in outcomes, of innovative practice and of parity of esteem, and states that one of the most tangible signs of a functioning team is that previous professional affinities are now seen as less significant than new team-based affinities. Also important is the balance of power within integrated teams and the particular relationship between medicine and social work. Lymbery (2006) has argued that it may be easier for professions that occupy similar structural positions such as social work and community nursing to work out joint working that is complementary and not competitive.

In relation to more innovative practice, social work has made a particular contribution through, for example, a more holistic approach, social models of health and disability and the commitment to anti-oppressive practice. It has been suggested that through their values social workers have brought a powerful organisational and strategic role in multidisciplinary teams (Herod and Lymbery, 2002). Research on integrated specialist mental health teams and user, carer and staff perceptions was carried out by Freeman and Peck (2006). This study found mixed responses. Integrated specialist teams could find the experience unsettling with regard to the blurring of professional roles as a result of multidisciplinary working practices, but multiple professional perspectives may be explored, providing learning across professional boundaries. Users and carers referred more to practical benefits, especially the ability of staff to liaise with other services, for example, the introduction of GP-led commissioning may endanger the balance needed in integrated teams. A study by Tucker et al (2009, p 345) found two thirds of old-age psychiatrists reported key connections with social work staff members of multidisciplinary community mental health teams. Ham (2009, p 10) stresses the significance of a primary motivation to integrate arising from a concern to ensure that people using services experience benefits. Integrated teams do face difficulties with accountability arrangements. This includes their accounting for statutory duties to their parent organisations, budgeting arrangements and maintaining separate professional lines of accountability.

Co-location

Co-location is one of the more practical characteristics of joint working and means that a partnership or integrated structure would ideally be located in one building, displaying a physical unity. A management team may also ideally share accommodation, rooms and reception areas. Co-location also accords with a one-stop shop access and presentation to users. Practical suggestions have also been made about the desirability of a location in the centre of a community or in proximity to other cognate services. Other benefits of co-location have been claimed in terms of encouraging staff to form better working relationships and have more informal contact, knowledge transfer (Syson and Bond, 2010) and sharing and learning from different professional views. Hudson (2006, p 21) suggests that it also allows them to be more creative. It can be anticipated that co-location will also encourage quicker and easier communication, although some studies have reported co-location causing greater informality, which undermined professional practice (Cameron et al, 2012, p 12).

Leadership

There is a body of management research and theory on leadership that has been adopted to suggest that collaborative leadership requires some special qualities and different approaches and practices to those needed for single organisations. Collaborative leadership in health and social care has been seen as focusing on a commitment to partnership working, for the good of the users, seeing commonalities and common interests and making connections, sharing a vision, sharing power and trust and building resources (McKimm and Held, 2009).

The leadership of partnership organisations depends not just on administrative managers and professionals but also on the health board members and the elected members of councils. The mix of elected and non-elected members runs along a spectrum, from the composition in England and Wales of appointed quango members and local councillors, in Scotland where it is proposed that health bodies will consist mainly of elected members as well as local councillors and in Northern Ireland where there is almost a total absence of elected members on boards and trusts. Commitment from the top can be seen as different from but as important as leadership skills in helping joint working (Gleave et al, 2010).

Work in Wales has suggested the importance of developing networks between the two sectors to understand each other's worlds and keep 'resisters' to a minimum (Jones et al, 2004). A later analysis in Wales has suggested no less than six principles for leadership for collaboration, covering:

- facilitating effective interpersonal relationships between diverse people and organisations;
- understanding multiple relationships and connections between organisations;
- appreciating different perspectives, cultures and aspirations of different agencies and professions;
- an ability for innovation and experimentation and sharing of ideas;
- promoting a learning environment for reflection and knowledge transfer;
- favouring a more dispersed, empowering and facilitative leadership (Williams and Sullivan, 2010, p 9).

A further study in Wales (Williams, P., 2012) argues that the leadership role for learning and knowledge needs to focus on four areas: promoting common purpose, developing a collaborative culture, facilitating multidisciplinary teamwork and developing learning and knowledge strategies. An additional perspective is that in delivering care for groups most likely to benefit from integrated provision, such as frail older people, it is necessary to create high-performance professional teams and leaders with a strong ethic of care (Cornwell, 2012). This would mean higher status, qualifications and care progression than exists at present.

Joint management and posts

It has been suggested that the argument that leadership is an essential component in inter-agency partnerships has been overstated (Dickenson and Peck, 2008). Perhaps more importantly, it has also been suggested that there has been an overemphasis on the roles of senior managers in partnership working rather than on all individuals developing relationships between health and social care partners. This view would stress the importance of middle and junior managers working across the boundaries of their professions and organisations and that a range of professionals can provide leadership around the value of integration. In considering this, Phillips (2009) claims that most successful partnerships have occurred when genuine communities of practice have developed, established through mutual engagement, joint enterprise and shared techniques. The concept of 'communities of practice' has been criticised as based on commonality and conformity rather than diversity and wide-ranging multi-professional learning (Miers, 2010). While there may be some different views on the characteristics of promoting collective ownership of partnership working and models of leadership there is acceptance of the need to avoid poor decision-making,, in particular through taking decisions and business back to their own organisation. The leadership of partnership organisations depends not just on administrative managers and professionals but also on the health board members and the elected members of councils. The mix differs throughout the UK from the composition in England and Wales of elected local councillors for social care and appointed non-executive members on the boards of health bodies. In Scotland, as well as elected local council members it is now proposed that health boards will consist of nominated councillors but also directly elected members. Northern Ireland is different in that health and social care boards are quangos and consist totally of ministerial appointees.

Research has shown the value of broad perspectives, based on the role of senior managers occupying joint posts between local authorities and PCTs (NHS Confederation, 2010). These were normally combinations of a chief executive of a council and the local PCT at the highest form of joint post, or posts might link a chief executive of a PCT and a director of adult social care services, or a chief executive of a care trust and a director of other council services. This research showed a recognition that such joint posts carried unique challenges and success was dependent on them negotiating complex systems of public and personal accountabilities and networks. Opinions were expressed that a perfect organisational format for joint appointments had not developed and particular joint working structures should not be centrally mandated. Factors identified as making senior joint posts work were a focus on improving outcomes, the value of local determination and wide support from their organisations. There was less consensus on the best style of leadership for someone managing health and local authority services, particularly between having to be fluent in two 'languages' or creating a new 'language'. Significant problems were also identified, including the mismatch in the hierarchies of councils and PCTs and resistance to joint working from middle management (NHS Confederation, 2010, p 3). The existence of barriers to joint working has been important at times and can explain the relatively limited number of senior joint posts that have emerged, with as few as 10 in operation in England by 2011.

Health and social care partnerships in Scotland

Scotland has developed its own partnership model, although based on much the same principles as in England. Similar community care initiatives had resulted in major joint programmes between health and social care and joint working around the closure of mental hospitals and long-stay learning disability hospitals. Immediately after devolution in 1999, a *Joint Futures* initiative was set up to deliver improved social care, particularly for older people, by providing for more joined-up activity (McTavish and Mackie, 2003). The essence of Joint Futures was the establishment of formal partnerships between NHS boards and local authorities.

The devolved government in Scotland had already taken action in 2002 on a major reorganisation to form unified health boards. The Scottish rationale had echoes of the NHS plan in undertaking to remove barriers to joint working and planning between health and social care. Joint Futures partnerships between the new health boards and the local authority social work departments were given a strong lead from the centre aligning budgets, planning shared assessment and jointly managed services (Bruce and Forbes, 2005). Joint Futures led to the setting up of a Local Partnership Agreement and it was anticipated that coverage would extend to areas other than older people (Scottish Executive, 2006). Joint Futures became a step towards a new type of partnership body. The Scottish Executive's 2003 paper *Partnership for care and delivering for health* suggested a clear focus for closer working relationship between primary and secondary health care and social care. Health and social care integration was to be achieved through new community health partnerships (CHPs).

Each NHS board had to submit a scheme of establishment and CHPs had to link clinical and care teams and work in partnership with local authorities and other bodies (Freeman and Moore, 2008). It was intended that CHPs would create better results for the communities they serve by being aligned with local authority counterparts. A number of the 22 health boards had several CHPs in their area. There were 39 in total, with the majority coterminus with local authorities. A study (Scottish Government, 2010e) found variation in the structures of each CHP but close relationships with other bodies was the key to how they conducted their work. Achievements included improving partnership working, linking health and social care, responding to local news, improved access and availability for the service user, and the reduction of services. Further work was suggested to strengthen structures and governance and affect CHPs as facilitators.

The partnership arrangements between the Scottish unified health boards and local authorities allowed a more focused approach to local service delivery. This has been seen as assisted by national partnership working between the NHS and local government through national guidance and performance management and the ending of initial local authority suspicion. Each CHP has a committee to drive forward improvements strategically and a small management committee to handle operational aspects. Although the original Scottish government guidelines had proposed CHPs as sub-committees of the NHS board and delivering mainly primary and community health services, discretion was given in the development of the form of partnership. This has resulted in the emergence of alternative integrative models. Evans and Forbes (2009) identify three models: a 'health only CHP', which may only link health to community planning; a 'partially integrated CHP', with only some services, for example mental health, integrated at a local level; and an 'integrated CHP', in which an NHS board and local authority develop joint management arrangements, and health and social care responsibilities are merged in one organisation. This does not mean a unified, independent, integrated organisation. The parent bodies retain statutory responsibilities, the CHP has dual accountability and governance structures to reflect this arrangement and there is no change of employer (Evans and Forbes, 2009, p 75). The majority of CHP partnerships have been renamed community health and social care partnerships – some 25 out of 40. It can be noted that not all of these cover or give the same priority to all aspects of adult social care. Mental health, learning disability, addiction services and older people are the most common but there is much local variation. A number of problems have been identified: duplication and lack of coordination, unclear governance arrangements and limited progress on joint funding of services (Petch, 2012, p 32). The Scottish Government and its statutory and non-statutory partners agreed that better integration is required if we are to ensure the ongoing provision of high-quality, appropriate, sustainable services. In 2012, the Scottish Government launched proposals to enhance integrated health and social care, meaning services that are planned and delivered seamlessly. It sought to address features of the existing structures that acted as barriers to better integration, including professional territories, an unequal delegation of authority, unintegrated budgets and poor clinical engagement. The new proposal is for a framework based on statutory health and social care partnerships. They will be required to integrate budgets for joint strategic commissioning and delivery of services. Health and social care partnerships will be the joint and equal responsibility of health boards and local authorities.

The integrated structure of health and social care in Northern Ireland

Northern Ireland continues to have the most structurally integrated and comprehensive model of integration in the UK. This integration structure of health and social care has been in existence since 1972 but was not at that time based on any detailed analysis of principles in support of integration but was put forward as part of a reform process to remove major services including welfare services from existing local government. The outcome was an integrated administrative structure of boards and sub-districts. The decision was based on little discussion of the merits of integration, and the government Green Paper (HMSO, 1969) at the time only contained brief references to the need for coordination and joint planning and the best framework for the continued development of personal social services would be found in their coming into some form of partnership with health services. Organisational changes were made to the structure with the adoption of the community care agenda and the purchaser/provider split. By the time of devolution the structure consisted of four health and social service boards with a planning and purchasing role and 18 separate delivery trusts. Seven of these were basically hospital trusts based on acute general hospitals while the other 11 were community health and social service trusts directly providing a comprehensive range of primary and community health services and social work services with some of these trusts also responding for hospitals in their areas. The introduction of devolution coincided with a review of health structures, which was merged into a wider review of the devolved system of public administration.

The outcome of this review was not finalised until 2009 but both the UK Direct Rule administration (2002–07) and the Northern Ireland devolved administration supported the proposition that the integrated system of health and personal services was one of the strengths of the system and any changes to structures should not work against the integrated services approach (Review of Public Administration [RPA], 2005). The final restructuring created a single new health and social care board, replacing the four existing boards, which would be responsible for all health and social care, and advised by five local commissioning groups. Five health and social care delivery trusts came into operation fully integrated across primary, secondary and social care. The main features of this fully integrated structure in each board or trust are:

- a single employer and single budget;
- integrated programmes of care;
- integrated management;
- integrated teams;
- a 'single strategic approach'.

There has been some questioning of problems in identifying how well the Northern Ireland system operates. Hudson and Henwood (2002, p 163) suggested that the Northern Ireland experience showed that structural integration did not guarantee well-coordinated practice on the ground, while Field and Peck (2003) argued that community care did not operate in a seamless joined-up service but suffered from similar difficulties as in Great Britain. Managers and directors of programmes of care have identified more positive aspects of the operation of the structure in the ease of distribution of resources, better use of communication, collective team working, access for users, single organisational aims and values, a single employer and the facilitation of smooth hospital discharge (Heenan and Birrell, 2006). The fully integrated structure means that integration is totally mainstreamed and seen as a core and essential part of normal procedures and operations. It does not mean that professional differences necessarily disappear and health provision, particularly acute healthcare, can be in a dominant position in terms of funding, service priorities and board membership. Questions remain as to whether the full potential of the integrated structure has been realised (Heenan and Birrell, 2009). An independent review of health and social care (DHSSPS, 2011a) suggested enhancing integration through integrated care partnerships, based around hubs of GP practices. The Department of Health, Social Services and Public Safety's implementation plan (DHSSPS, 2012b) suggests that GPs should have a lead role, given that Northern Ireland has fully integrated structures. This partnership idea seems confused and has a background of an attempt to increase clinical engagement and counter the large size of the existing integrated trusts.

Integrated approaches in Wales

The Welsh range of practices has largely followed experience in England but there are some organisational differences. Welsh local authorities have maintained a unified adult and children's social services structure. When the NHS in Wales was reorganised into seven local health boards and three NHS trusts, it created a lack of coterminosity with the 22 local authorities, which required more diverse partnership structures. Integrated modes of partnership working between primary health and social care bodies have been significant. The Gwent Frailty Programme demonstrates the response to the existing structure in promoting integration. It is a partnership between one health board and five local authorities and the local voluntary sector. Five integrated community response teams were established in each local authority area to provide urgent assessment, rapid response to health issues and emergency social care, reablement and other services (Burgess, 2012, p 10). The Welsh Assembly Government (2011) White Paper *Sustainable social services for Wales: A framework* for action sets out policy on integration, expecting more efficient and effective delivery through greater collaboration and using resources in a more joined-up way. The distinctive Welsh principle is stressed that 'we will galvanise the strength that comes from social services being at the heart of local government, drawing on its community leadership duties and its wide range of services and capitalising on the benefits of our unique Welsh approach of integrated family based services' (Welsh Assembly Government, 2011, p 7). The Welsh Social Services Bill 2012 provides a legal framework that will drive closer formal partnership working and increase the pace of development. The powers will also allow ministers to mandate the creation of partnerships and define the role of partners (Welsh Government, 2012a, p 52).

Integrated provision and themes

The value of integrated approaches and partnership working has been most clearly demonstrated in a number of specific areas of provision: hospital discharge, a unified assessment process, intermediate care and reablement.

Hospital discharge

The process of discharging patients from hospital has been seen as providing a critical indicator of how well partnership is working between health and social care agencies and epitomises the challenges that beset partnership working (Henwood, 2006). When arrangements work well it can be seen as a seamless transition from hospital to community care. Where it does not work well, there are damaging delays and conflict over the responsibilities and actions of health agencies and social services departments. Hospital discharge has often given rise to difficulties. The term 'discharge' has been criticised as implying an end to one agency's responsibility, rather than a transition in care or an element in a care pathway. Glasby (2004) described hospital discharge as causing problems of inter-agency tension, fragmentation and negative outcomes for service users. He identified poor practice, which included:

- inadequate information sharing;
- inadequate assessment and planning for discharge;
- inadequate consultation with patients and carers;
- the continuing use of the pejorative term 'bed blocking';
- overall failures in inter-professional working.

Evidence from Scotland showed that the principal reason for delayed discharge was that half of cases were waiting for a care place (Audit Scotland, 2012). The solution tried in Scotland was based not on financial incentives but on more integrated practice. In England, the Community Care (Delayed Discharges) Act 2003 introduced a financial penalty on local authority social services departments if they were unable to provide appropriate services within a prescribed timetable. The provision was superimposed on existing legislation and meant that upon notification of likely discharge, social services had three days to make an assessment and arrange services, otherwise the NHS could cross-charge social services with a financial penalty. This scheme appeared to attach blame to social services and not to health bodies and this was seen as divisive and endangering the inter-professional relationship at the bias of the nature of the discharge process (Lymbery, 2006). This blunt instrument did lead to much criticism – that failures were not always the responsibility of social care, that it encouraged a negative blame culture (Henwood, 2006, p 403) and that it introduced new, burdensome bureaucratic practices. Subsequently, there was evidence of consequences from quicker discharges such as increases in readmissions, inadequate rehabilitation and people being discharged from hospital directly into residential care (Henwood, 2006, p 404). A report by the Commission for Social Care Inspection (CSCI, 2004) noted particular issues for delayed financial penalties. These were:

- creating tensions and recriminations between local hospitals and social services;
- encouraging premature discharge;
- being administratively burdensome;
- being regarded as an income-generation scheme;
- diverting money away from hard-pressed social services.

The system also paid little attention to the views of users, subjecting them to a revolving-door policy. However, there was a rather more positive development in that this reimbursement system did not lead to large numbers of fines but did actually provide some incentive for health and local authorities to work closer together on hospital discharges to avoid the negative outcomes.

The integrated structure in Northern Ireland means that a single body is responsible for the discharge, thus avoiding having two agencies debating over responsibilities and costs. This had particular advantages when people with learning disabilities in long-stay hospitals had to be transferred into the community and there was no need to set up joint meetings with local authorities. Research has demonstrated that managers appreciated the ease in moving resources around and spending less on managing the system (Heenan and Birrell, 2006). However, there is also evidence that the full potential of integration was not always realised for producing reductions in the number of delayed discharges (Heenan and Birrell, 2009, p 7). There is some evidence of continuing delays in resettlement into the community from long-stay hospitals. The closure of adult psychiatric beds has not been as rapid as it should have been (Royal College of Psychiatrists, 2009).

Unified assessment process

A single or shared assessment of need across health and social care has been seen as one of the most beneficial outcomes of collaborative working. This partly reflects problems with fragmented systems, duplicating resources; leaving gaps in assessing need, ignoring some risks on systems. As well as addressing such issues, an integrated assessment process facilitates a multidisciplinary assessment with more involved cases (Lymbery, 2006, p 1127). The National Service Framework for Older People (DH, 2001b) took the view that no one professional has the capacity to address issues equally well. At the same time there is an overlap in the capacity and skills in a range of health and social care professions. Since 2003, all adults with mental health and social care needs have been kept apart and there has been a differential ability to make fair access to care services between professional groups. Research on the introduction of a common, standardised, single assessment process for older people's mental health services across health and social care found that it had changed assessment practice in only about a quarter of cases (Tucker et al, 2009). This was despite the widespread acceptance that older people with mental health problems often have a complex and diverse range of needs that require a whole-systems response. The main professionals involved in unified assessments are social workers, community nurses and occupational therapists but not GPs (Challis et al, 2006). One assessment study found district nurses more likely to have the knowledge to conduct housing assessments, while social workers were more equipped to conduct an assessment of needs and a finance-related assessment (Worth, 2001). Frustration for all assessors has been when assessors' determination of needs cannot be met due to resource constraints.

In Scotland, a single shared assessment approach has been proposed as the standard means of determining entitlement to care services and renewed efforts have been made to increase the adoption of shared assessment in adult community care (Miller and Cameron, 2011). In Wales, there has been flexibility in implementation through local discretion, which has made comparisons of performance indicators difficult and limited comparisons across areas (Miller and

Cameron, 2011, p 41). There has been evidence of more consistent application of eligibility criteria and more user-friendly methods in Northern Ireland.

Unified assessment has faced difficulties with financial pressures. Miller and Cameron (2011, p 43) found that the requirement to rationalise needs against costs and an awareness of limited resources represented a significant difference between health and social care services. Health staff have been found more likely to recommend intervention and services (Eccles, 2008) and less accustomed to a gate-keeping role than social workers. The benefits of unified assessment can be listed as: being efficient in removing multiple assessment; involving valuable contributions from different disciplines; improving user and carer involvement; and greater transparency. Criticisms include a lack of essential training; the use of unified assessment for wider needs and services; and obstacles imposed by a complex and unclear legal framework.

Intermediate care

Intermediate care as a strategy was developed in the late 1990s to prevent the need for long-term acute care through rehabilitation programmes. Intermediate care was initially conceived as an alternative to hospital admission and early supported discharge and to assist those facing admission to residential care. Definitions of intermediate care have varied (Melis, 2004) but key objectives are to maximise independence and enable users to live at home or in the community and prevent transfer directly from acute settings to long-term care, and to provide opportunities for further assessment of care needs. Intermediate care was part of a more integrated approach between health and social care and was explicitly intended to dissolve the boundaries between health and social care services (Moore et al, 2007). Included in *The NHS plan* (DH, 2000, p 71) as policy, it was mainly implemented through the National Service Framework for Older People. It was not seen as the responsibility of one agency or professional group although it did largely require robust collaborative arrangements with social work, which was seen as better placed than most other professions to play a key role (Lymbury, 2006). Cross-professional and inter-agency work, particularly cooperation between hospitals, GPs and adult social care, became important and the voluntary sector also had a role. Shared assessment frameworks and shared protocols were developed. A wide range of modes of services came into existence and intermediate care has been a fruitful area for innovation. These can be listed as including:

- rapid response teams for acute care at home;
- supported discharge from hospital with a programme of support;
- residential enablement for short periods;
- day rehabilitation;
- care units;
- hospital at home schemes;
- day hospitals;

- community assessment;
- rehabilitation.

Innovative schemes and coverage have continued to evolve, with a more specialist focus on dementia and stroke rehabilitation, extending hours of access and involving more professional groups such as pharmacies. However, research and evaluation studies have produced criticisms concerning fragmentation, poor integration with other services and risks of isolation (Parker et al, 2011). There have also been criticisms of approaches being too selective and applying strict time limits. Public perceptions may also see the process as just waiting for social services assessment. A study by Moore et al (2007, p 157) found evidence that intermediate care is not a series of partnership arrangements but a more distinct phenomenon, manifested in the operational relationships between services perhaps best described as an integrated service network. Intermediate care with its emphasis on enabling rehabilitation and treatments in community and residential settings has developed as a major area for collaborative and integrated working.

Reablement

Reablement overlaps with intermediate care but its focus on assisting people to regain their abilities is distinctive. Reablement is about helping people learn or re-learn skills they need for daily living, which they have lost through deterioration of their health, ageing or institutionalisation. Reablement is offered mainly to those recovering from illness, frail people and people with disabilities. The focus is on helping people maximise their independence and function better rather than resolving healthcare issues. Reablement is a short, intensive service, from six to 12 weeks, usually delivered in the home with a focus on washing, preparing meals and using stairs. It is seen as a move from traditional home or domiciliary care, which has been task-driven and involves doing things for people. Reablement functions through integrated approaches. In some areas only people who are about to be discharged are referred for reablement, but in other areas people may be referred by a GP or community social services (SCIE, 2012a). No single leading model of delivery exists. Normally reablement workers will visit the person's home, assess abilities and then a multidisciplinary team will activate a reablement plan to support the person to regain functions and activities for independent living. This combines health and social care inputs, with care workers as the bedrock and occupational therapy being important. It is necessary to have a care package in place in some cases after the reablement ends. Research and evaluation is limited to date but Glendinning et al (2010) found reablement to be associated with better home-related quality of life and social care outcomes, compared with traditional home care. A flexible and integrated input from health and social care has to be a key feature of reablement.

Joint working between health and social care has been accepted as particularly important for delivering services to older people as both major consumers of services and as people whose needs and care benefit from a collaborative approach. The UK government has put joined-up provision at the forefront of its policies (Glasby and Littlechild, 2004). The Partnerships for Older People Projects (POPPs) was a government initiative in 2006 aimed at showing how innovative partnership working between local authorities and PCTs could lead to improved outcomes. A review of the 29 pilot sites funded showed that many developed a whole-systems approach to service design and delivery involving different agencies. Schemes included identification of older people at risk of falling, lunch clubs, hospital discharge, crime reduction and access to volunteering and rapid response services. POPPs were led by local authorities and had a main aim of preventing institutional care and covered a wide area of cooperation. The initiative was seen as increasing cost effectiveness, with reduced use of hospital services. Improved relationships with health agencies were generally reported, although there were some difficulties securing the involvement of GPs (DH, 2010d). The NHS Future Forum identified older people as a group who would particularly benefit from integrated approaches to commissioning and delivering services.

Community mental health teams have been a popular and widespread aspect of implementation of integrated working and partnership working This integrated approach has developed into more specialist and more challenging areas, as a mechanism for mental health services for older people with mental health problems (McDonald, 2006), for example, with dementia teams and community mental health teams for young people.

Working in partnership has been a key strategy in developing new and modernised services for people with learning disabilities and fits into the emphasis on the social model, featuring care in the community, supported housing advocacy and personalisation (McDonald, 2006, p 173). Ward (2008) identifies the increasing emphasis on the need for multi-agency working and the need to tackle remaining barriers to effective partnership working, for example, in securing equal access to mainstream health services. Learning disability teams have tended to be based in social services and with flat structures and a lot of joint working (Pollard et al, 2009) based on the importance of person-centred planning.

Problems with integration

Professional differences

Differences in professional attitudes and values can exist between health and social care and there can be different priorities for care and treatment. The two staff groups can create their own boundaries and undermine joint working. Baggott (2004, p 287) argues that it is the cultural barriers between the professional groups and organisations that have caused problems. Different approaches can be identified in health and social care to eligibility, determination, assessment and priorities in respect of community care, noted by Cestari et al (2006) as applying particularly to mental health. Lack of trust between professions can also present problems. Huxley et al (2008) note that health staff may be unfamiliar with social care perspectives and social care can be marginalised within a health paradigm. Resistance to new and different ways of working can also cause difficulties but Ham and Oldham (2009, p 4) suggest this may be more of a problem for managers than for frontline staff. There can even be incidents of lack of trust within the two groups of staff and organisations, for example, within acute hospital trusts or local authority housing departments. Such differences and lack of trust are not surprising, given the limited number and nature of integrated structures and partnerships, with health and social care used to normally operating separately and overall policy and professional agendas that are not aligned. Staff can become preoccupied with change in their professions and practice. Modernisation of care and treatment can lead to new or further differences, which can counterbalance working together. The introduction of direct payments and individual budgets into integrated working and projects may be totally strange to health professionals and present a major challenge to overcome (Ham, 2009, p 4). Given separate professional identities, training and loyalties as well as values and approaches, the issue of professional differences can be seen as a barrier to successful integration and partnership working.

Integrated working has given rise to issues concerning the balance of power between health and social care. The health side and health professionals can dominate partnerships largely because of the higher status given to health professionals and acute services and the perceptions of differences by the public, the media, politicians and other related professions. The relationship may be unbalanced by dominance of the medical model. Social work values and the social model may not be respected by health professionals (Scragg, 2006). At least senior management has to be aware of the possibility of the treatment of social care services as the junior partner and may have to take steps to prevent one profession dominating the other. Priorities given to health issues and policies may also create imbalances. There may be a process of absorbing social care workers into the health system in forms of integrated working, as with some care trusts, which may reduce equity of esteem and Huxley et al (2008) see this as operating in mental health cooperation. Even with structural integration as in Northern Ireland, social services are not always seen as equal partners. This has been demonstrated in terms of social services' vulnerability to funding cuts in a crisis (Heenan and Birrell, 2006, p 60), and the priorities given to health targets and also in the membership of health and social care boards and trusts where there are few people from a social care background and in proposals for integrated care partnerships.

Overall, it has been difficult to maintain equity of status in integrated working but the existence of two separate organisations does help prevent the marginalisation of social care in integrated working. The future enhanced role for GPs in replacing PCTs in England may increase the status differential with social workers but rather paradoxically may increase the status of social care compared to the status of other health professionals.

Human resource issues

Human resources and workforce issues can present difficulties when two or more separate organisations are involved in staffing a partnership or organising joint posts. Ham (2009, p 6) identifies particular issues regarding differences in contracts, pensions and terms and conditions. A number of different models of staffing can be used for partnerships:

- replacing all staff in integrated working arrangements under a single management of one employer, thus social workers could be integrated into a community mental health team under a single management structure but remain employed by the local authority;
- secondment to the other organisations in the partnership, however secondments can cause problems with staff working alongside one another on varying pay rates and under other different terms and conditions (Weeks, 2009);
- transfer of staff within larger-scale integrated arrangements.

Evidence from the UNISON trade union suggests that the majority of section 31 partnerships use secondment arrangements but many of the longer-term and larger-scale providers have instituted staff transfer (Weeks, 2006, p 16). Care trusts have tended to operate with the transfer of staff to the NHS but an exception has to be made in the case of approved social workers because of their specific legal status. The totally integrated structures in Northern Ireland avoid the problems through having a single employer.

Funding difficulties

Pooling funds has often been fraught with difficulties, usually over what has been agreed, extra demands and coping with funding pressures in allocating expenditure. Section 31 partnerships have been prone to this. The UNISON report claimed that local authority partners often felt they that were having to deal with the consequences of NHS funding problems and this caused tension (Weeks, 2006, p 11). Pooled budgets have their own set of challenges. Weatherly et al (2010) point out that pooling of budgets can be a complex process involving alignment of financial frameworks. The Audit Commission (2009) has noted that health and social care bodies have different tax regimes, charges, planning and budgetary timetables and different financial reporting arrangements. The Audit Commission report also argued that short-term, earmarked/targeted grants from central government can be difficult to manage within a pooled budget. There can be unrealistic expectations about one partner's contribution or each contribution loses its identity. There can also be underuse of joint budgets and a surplus in a pooled budget may not be used on services outside the pool. Recent financial constraints have led local authorities to assign individuals to care cores of need (Williams and Sullivan, 2010). Several local authorities now assign individuals to categories of social need and about three quarters of councils now only meet critical or substantial needs (Williams and Sullivan, 2010, p 6). It has been noted that the mechanisms for such denial of services can be prevalent in social care under pressure but are not so obviously available to the NHS (Williams et al, 2010, p 3). In Scotland, the Integrated Resource Framework (IRF) has been developed jointly by the Scottish Government, NHS Scotland and COSLA. This framework seeks to link resources and budgets spent on populations and make integration more effective (Weatherly et al, 2010, p 4). Northern Ireland, unlike Scotland and Wales, has a commissioner-provider model for health but also with the integrated structure for social care. The provider health and social care trust is integrated as are the delivery trusts but in practice the system works as an allocation rather than a commissioning mechanism. The detailed building blocks are integrated programmes of care.

Problem of lack of coterminous boundaries

Collaboration is much facilitated by coterminous boundaries between partners. In England, this has been between local authorities and PCTs. This matching configuration will disappear with the replacement of PCTs by a large number of GP consortia and lead to an end to coterminosity and create planning and delivery problems. A further lack of coterminosity exists in England with different boundaries for NHS hospital trusts. Scotland had largely, but not completely, a system of coterminous local authorities and health bodies within the community partnerships and is proposing to move to a system of health and social care partnerships, coterminous with health boards and local authorities. Wales had coterminosity between local authorises and health boards but this has ended with a reduction to seven health boards from 22. Integrated trusts in Northern Ireland are by definition coterminous for health and social care.

Promotion of integrated working

The Department of Health had adopted a guidance and promotional stance towards integrated and collaborative working. It launched an Integrated Care Network website and adopted a 'how to' approach, making available the lessons of good practice and disseminating research findings, for example, in 2008 publishing an evidence base for integrated care (DH, 2008c). Specific advice could be given on such matters as partnership agreements and objectives and integrated information technology systems (Rosen and Ham, 2008). The NHS Confederation also produced material on the lessons from various initiatives in the country that could be used to help build integrated working (Fulop et al, 2005). In 2008, the Department of Health launched a two-year pilot programme to test and evaluate a range of integrated care. Integrated care pilots were designed to explore different ways in which to deliver care through new integrated models and look beyond traditional boundaries. The programme was focused on 16 pilots, each of which developed an integrated model of care to respond to particular local needs, which included dementia, substance abuse, end-of-life care and care for older people. The provision of training has been identified as a major way to ensure that integrated institutions are understood as well as operational plans and written agreements (Cameron et al, 2012, p 9).

Following the successes in the evaluation of the original partnerships, the programme was expanded in 2010 to identify further innovative initiatives and encourage the sharing of knowledge. The Department of Health had five desired outcomes from the project:

- rapid improvements in the quality of care;
- improved patient and user satisfaction;
- improved partnerships in care provision;
- more efficient use of resources;
- improved relationships between participation organisations (Rosen and Ham, 2008, p 12).

Meanwhile, with the proposed abolition of PCTs in England, the Integrated Care Network website is no longer operated by the Department of Health.

In Scotland, there was a more hands-off approach and a patchwork of guidance. However, in 2004 the Joint Improvement Team (JIT) was established to work directly with local health and social care partnerships across Scotland, including health boards, local authorities, voluntary organisations, service users and carers. JIT provides hands-on support. The scope of JIT is wider than health and social care integration and includes social housing but JIT is part of the Directorate for Health and Social Care Integration within the Scottish Government. The JIT website (www.jitscotland.org.uk) contains a resources toolkit and improvement presentations. There has been a major focus on reshaping the Care for Older People programme. Scotland also has experience of managed clinical networks of multidisciplinary teams of healthcare providers and the concept of 'managed care networks' has extended the principles of clinical networks to health and social care. JIT has developed its work in four main areas: a partnership support programme; action areas; information and advice; and shared learning (Joint Improvement Team, 2011). Throughout the UK, flexibility in work roles has been found to be beneficial and the fully integrated structure in Northern Ireland has facilitated flexibility in work roles (Birrell and Heenan, 2012).

The performance of integration

Assessing the achievements of integration and partnership working over the last decade remains complex. In England, there is no common or agreed structure of partnership working and the wide variation does cause a lack of clarity in defining partnership working and in the use of the term 'integration'. There has also been no overall blueprint or agreement on what the actual achievements of collaborative working should be, although all partnerships and commitments to greater integrated working would find common ground around an aim of improving services. Assessments and research on partnership working in England have had a strong focus on the process involved rather than the outcomes (Dowling et al, 2004). This has related mainly to how partnerships have functioned and on different forms of organisation and has helped to identify the more successful processes and systems. Partnership assessment tools have been devised but again centred on process issues. The Audit Commission (2011, p 18) has noted the use of some high-level indicators of performance but has stated that there are no direct measures of the progress and impact of joint working. Much of the analysis and commentary has examined more theoretical advantages of collaborative working or used the optimistic assertions, enthusiasm and aspirations of discourses in official documents, and such assessments have not been based on research evidence on outcomes. There have been exercises in setting guidelines on successful outcomes or performance measurements officially constructed by national service frameworks or the National Institute for Health and Clinical Excellence. Dowling et al (2004, p 13) summarise outcomes as covering five areas:

- improvements in accessibility;
- more equitable distribution of services;
- improvements in quality, efficiency and effectiveness;
- improvements in the experiences of staff and carers;
- improvements in quality of life and well-being.

Research on outcomes has been limited, whether involving measuring improvements in services through quantitative outputs or the views of managers, practitioners or users. Specific pieces of research have tended not to produce overwhelming evidence of major change following the introduction of partnership working. In 2009, the UK government launched a two-year pilot programme to test and evaluate a range of modes of integrated care. Sixteen integrated care pilots were set up to explore new integrated models. The evaluation found that staff reported improvement in care delivery but this was not reported by users or in reduced costs (Burgess, 2012, p 8).

A study of integrating mental health services for older people in England based on interviews with 318 consultant old-age psychiatrists found measures to facilitate integrated practice poorly developed, with approaching 30% of respondents reporting the presence of fewer than four of 13 markers of integration with social care (Tucker et al, 2009, p 341). No psychiatrist reported the presence of all 13 indicators of integration. A study of the impact of collaborative partnerships on mental health service users and carers between 2002 and 2004 found the attribution of improved outcomes to the partnership arrangements difficult to define (Freeman and Moore, 2008). Reviews of research have also reported patchy evidence. Dickenson (2010) concluded that the case that partnership working improves services for users remains largely unproven. Maslin-Prothero and

Bennion (2010) found few studies on the views of users and main achievements identified were around initial access to services. In England, the joint inspection process of the inspection bodies, the Healthcare Commission and the Commission for Social Care Inspection, has found overall that section 31 partnerships have been shown to have delivered improvements in quality in a range of areas with innovation and flexible service delivery (Weeks, 2006, p 11). Petch (2012) makes the suggestion that the focus in assessing evidence on the effectiveness of integration should be on local systems, cultures and implementation.

There is greater clarity in Scotland, with a single model of community health and social care partnerships, but research on outcomes has lagged behind process analysis. A few research projects have compared aspects of integrated working in Northern Ireland and England. Challis et al (2006) found more evidence of integrated practice in Northern Ireland than in England in care management for older people. Further research by the same group found only slightly more evidence of integrated practice in care management arrangements in mental health services (Reilly et al, 2007). The independent evaluation of integrated care pilots on 16 sites in England considered the impact of better integrated care for older people and found that 54% of staff thought that patient care had improved, 72% of staff reported better communication and 60% of staff thought they worked more closely with team members. A further review of research throughout the UK (Cameron et al, 2012) found the evidence base lagging behind current policy and practice. There was evidence of user satisfaction but limited work on the effectiveness of interventions and of cost effectiveness. Cameron et al (2012) specifically identified difficulties with the evaluation of the outcomes of joint working.

Future of integration

The Coalition government in the UK is producing a radical change in the organisation of the commissioning and delivery of primary healthcare and this may have profound consequences on the future development and role of collaboration, integration and partnerships. This new policy will see PCTs abolished and replaced by GP consortia and GP-led commissioning. This will have a number of clear consequences in that local authority–PCT partnerships will end and that the care trusts will end but may be replaced by clinical commissioning group–local authority care trusts. The scheme will only apply to England, while current arrangements in Scotland, Wales and Northern Ireland will largely continue. It is also clear that there will be a large number of GP consortia, they will be smaller entities geographically and in population terms than the PCTs and they will not have coterminous boundaries with local authorities. There are dangers of the impact of fragmentation on integrated care, with the local authority working with several GP consortia and local hospitals working with several commissioning groupings and with the possibility of different models of enablement in operation (NHS Confederation, 2011b). There are clear legal duties on the NHS Commissioning

Board, clinical commissioning groups and health and wellbeing boards to promote integration in health and social care as a priority in the UK, and with an ageing population living longer it still seems that the future provision and development of health and social care working together will remain essential. This leaves the question of what can be done to foster an improved integrated care approach in the new structure. New health and wellbeing boards of each local authority will be the format for strengthening working relationships between health and social care and encouraging the development of more integrated commissioning of services. The boards will bring together the GP-led clinical commissioning groups and councils to develop a shared understanding of the health and wellbeing needs of the community, under a joint strategic needs assessment, and include recommendations for joint commissioning and integrating services across health and social care. It is realised that the success of this structure may depend on building new constructive relationships and building their capacity and influence (NHS Confederation, 2012b). There are concerns about the dominant position of GPs, who may have not the experience of or commitment to integrated working. The new system may have a strong focus on new models of decentralisation, with greater local authority involvement in commissioning and a more neighbourhood approach involving local communities around GP groupings. It has also been suggested that as budgets are devolved to GP commissioning groups there will be opportunities to align other public services (NHS Confederation, 2012b, p 7). Local authorities are to have a greater involvement in decision making on public health. Future developments will include partnership working with the independent and voluntary sectors, including recovery at home and end-of-life care, and with commissioners requesting integrated services (NHS Confederation, 2012b).

The future development of integrated working will also come under pressure from current financial reductions, with adult social care in general under pressure. This has, however, been seen as an opportunity for different and new models of integration, which may deliver more cost-effective services (NHS Confederation, 2012b, p 2), for example, through greater personalisation. While acknowledging that there may be a natural response for organisations under financial pressure to retreat into their own identity and silos and guard their boundaries and budgets, Glasby et al (2011) suggests that others may conclude that working together is the best possible route to make use of scarce resources and produce better outcomes in care. The House of Commons Health Committee (2012a) has suggested that the issue of a funding cap must be addressed to achieve the level of integration that is required.

Conclusions

- The lack of joined-up care between the NHS and local authority social services has been widely accepted as a continuing problem.

- The integration of health and social care has been a priority for policy development and for models of delivery.
- A number of different organisational forms of integration exist throughout the UK although the partnership model dominates.
- A number of strategies have been key to promoting integrated provision, including pooled budgets, joint commissioning, joint posts and leadership and inter-professional working.
- A number of services have particularly benefited from integrated approaches: hospital discharge, reablement, assessments, intermediary care and community mental health teams.
- Research and evaluation of integrated practices have produced a rather mixed conclusion on achievements and performance.

Sources

Glasby (2006) categorises the scope and nature of collaborative working between health and social care. Hudson (2006), Ward (2008) and Ham (2009) cover the rationale and need for multi-agency working and consider the challenges of inter-professional working and relationships. The role of leadership in promoting integration is covered by McKimm and Held (2009). A Social Care Institute for Excellence publication (Cameron et al, 2012) provides an overview of research findings on factors promoting and hindering integrated working between health and social care.

Questions

- What has it been considered so important to promote integrated working between health and social care and what have been the main methods used to achieve integration?

- In what respects and areas of provision has integrated working led to better outcomes?

- What are the main continuing barriers to successful integrated working?

- Are there lessons to be learnt from examples of fully integrated structures of health and social care?

SEVEN

Unpaid carers and adult social care provision

Overview

As has been the case historically, in the UK most caring is unpaid and provided by families. This chapter examines the issues relating to this population, the current policies for unpaid carers and the implications of recent proposals for adult provision. It discusses the concept of 'choice' and whether the choice agenda with regard to social care extends to unpaid carers. It considers developments with regard to carers' rights and entitlements and examines the financial implications for carers and the debates about whether they should be paid. Complimentarity and tensions in carers' policy and other areas of social policy such as employment policy are explored.

Unpaid care: changing context and main challenges

There is estimated to be 6.4 million people in the UK caring for friends or relatives (Carers UK, 2012). A combination of factors – including population ageing, higher levels of disability, a policy focus on independent living and the personalisation of care, the preference of people to remain in their own homes and the desire to cut public expenditure – means that many, if not most, people can expect to be carers. The number of male carers has grown but approximately 60% of carers are women, and women have a 50:50 chance of providing care by the time they reach the age of 59; men by the time they reach the age of 74 (Parker et al, 2010). While most carers are in the 50–59 age group and one and a half million are over 60, there has been growing attention to the substantial number of young carers. A BBC (2010) investigation suggested that the actual number of young carers in the UK is 700,000, four times more than the official figure.

Caring responsibilities can range from spending a few hours a week helping a person with housework or shopping to intense levels of caring. Census data for 2001 showed that 68% of carers provided care for up to 19 hours per week, 11% for 20–49 hours and 21% for 50 or more hours. More recent data collected for the Northern Ireland Life and Times Survey (Ferguson and Devine, 2011) found that 30% of carers in the survey cared for more than 30 hours per week, with 18% caring for 60 hours per week. Recent debates have also raised the issue of a 'sandwich' generation of multiple carers where some families are caring for three generations, including grandchildren (Carers UK and Employers for Childcare,

2011). The Young Life and Times Survey of 16-year-olds found that one in 10 of the young people who identified themselves as carers cared for 30 or more hours per week. This included tasks of a personal nature such as washing someone or taking them to the toilet (Devine and Lloyd, 2011).

The consequences of caring on individual carers have been well established. These include having to reduce hours worked in paid employment or having to give up paid work altogether, financial problems and vulnerability to poverty, and problems of social isolation and poor health (Parker and Lawton, 1994; Bauld et al, 2000). In 2010, the Northern Ireland Life and Times Survey (NILT, 2010) attempted to identify the difficulties and satisfactions that can come along with the caring role. One in five carers admitted to feeling under pressure most of the time, and another 40% said that they felt under pressure sometimes. Perhaps one of the more difficult feelings for carers to publicly acknowledge is resentment. Only 5% of carers said that they felt resentment most of the time, although 25% said they did sometimes. This means that the majority said that they did not feel resentment at all and three quarters of carers in the survey said they felt happy to be able to help the person they cared for. Certainly, many carers have challenged the idea of care as a burden, pointing to the emotional rewards of caring and the satisfaction of being able to help someone. However, a willingness and desire to care for a relative or friend is not enough to provide resilience against negative outcomes and there has been growing evidence of the importance of timely, adequate and appropriate support.

Recognising unpaid caring

By the 1980s, it had become increasingly evident that policy makers looking at community care were seeing the family as the main provider of care. The 1989 White Paper on care in the community (DH, 1989) placed carers centre stage in terms of the recognition that most care was provided within families. The Northern Ireland White Paper *People first* (DHSSNI, 1990, para 2.4) explicitly acknowledged that the majority of carers were, and would continue to be, women. Feminist writers drew attention to the implications of these assumptions for women. Finch and Groves (1980) argued that community care policies could be counterproductive to the promotion of equal opportunities, given the extent to which they relied on women's unpaid domestic work. This, they pointed out, would have a negative impact on women's ability to participate in the paid labour market. Other writers expounded on the financial, health and social consequences for women (Glendinning, 1992; Twigg and Atkin, 1994). Yet, carers remained largely invisible in policy terms. Baldwin and Parker (1989, p 157) described informal carers as inhabiting 'a strange Alice in Wonderland place where they are the main providers of community care but never the subjects of policy that deals with the provision of care'.

The research focus on carers, the development of a UK carers' movement and effective lobbying and campaigning by those carers' organisations led to increased recognition of the need for greater support for carers and a strengthening of carers' rights. The origins of the movement can be traced back to 1965 when Mary Webster formed the National Council for the Single Woman and her Dependants, followed by the setting up of the Association of Carers in 1981 and the subsequent merger of the two organisations in 1988 with the formation of the National Carers Association (now Carers UK) (Cook, 2007). The work of the movement in making unpaid care a public policy issue and getting carers onto the political map has been fundamental to policy developments and the movement has 'grown in influence, ambition and impact' (Cass and Yeandle, 2009, p 25).

In 1995, carers gained the right to an independent assessment through the Carers (Recognition and Services) Act. Subsequent policy developments include the publication of the first national carers' strategy in 1999, with further strategy documents published in 2008 and 2010 (DH, 1999b, 2008d, 2010e) – each recognising the need to support carers. Post 1998, the introduction of devolution resulted in governments in Scotland, Wales and Northern Ireland developing their own strategies for carers. Current strategies for each of the UK countries are listed in Box 28. There is considerable convergence in terms of the themes and priorities outlined in the strategies, all identifying the importance of carers and the need to maintain a substantial number of carers going into the future as demand for care increases – as illustrated in the Scottish strategy by the explicit acknowledgement that '[p]roviding support to carers makes economic sense by saving resources in the longer term. With appropriate and timely support carers are able to care for longer' (Scottish Government, 2011a, para 2.30).

Box 28: Current strategies for carers

England
Recognised, valued and supported: Next steps for the carers strategy (refreshed carers' strategy) (DH, 2010e)

Scotland
Caring together: The carers strategy for Scotland 2010-2015 (Scottish Government, 2010b)

Getting it right for young carers: The young carers strategy in Scotland 2010–2015 (Scottish Government, 2010c)

Northern Ireland
Caring for carers (DHSSPS, 2006)

Review of the support provision for carers (DSD and DHSSPS, 2009)

> **Wales**
>
> *Carers strategy in Wales* (Welsh Assembly Government, 2000) (a refreshed Carers Strategy (Welsh Assembly Government, 2012) was published for consultation in November 2012).
>
> *Carers Strategies (Wales) Measure (2010)* (Welsh Assembly Government, 2010)

The-then Labour government's 2008 strategy *Carers at the heart of 21st-century families and communities* (DH, 2008d) set out a 10-year vision, stating that by 2018, carers would be 'universally recognised and valued'. It also included commitments that:

- carers will be respected as expert care partners and will have access to the integrated and personalised services they need to support them in their caring role;
- carers will be able to have a life of their own alongside their caring role;
- carers will be supported so that they are not forced into financial hardship by their caring role;
- carers will be supported to stay mentally and physically well and treated with dignity;
- children and young people will be protected from inappropriate caring.

The strategy emphasises the 'normality' of caring and how it will increasingly be 'part of all our lives' (foreword). A core theme is the need to support carers to have the opportunity and assistance to combine caring with paid work. This theme is followed through in the Coalition government's cross-government 2010 refreshed carers' strategy (DH, 2010e), which identifies four key priorities:

- supporting those with caring responsibilities to identify themselves as carers at an early stage, recognising the value of their contribution and involving them from the outset both in designing local care provision and in planning individual care packages;
- personalised support both for carers and those they support, enabling them to have a family and community life;
- supporting carers to remain mentally and physically well;
- enabling those with caring responsibilities to fulfil their educational and employment potential.

Box 29 presents a timeline that shows key policy developments with regard to carers in England since 1995.

Box 29: Timeline of policy support for carers

1995   Carers (Recognition and Services) Act – entitled carers to an independent assessment of their needs, subject to specific criteria

1999   First national carers' strategy – *Caring about carers* – looked at the range of support that carers needed

2000   Carers and Disabled Children Act – gave carers the right to an assessment even if the person they were caring for had refused one. Also gave local authorities the power to provide direct payments to carers

2004   Carers (Equal Opportunities) Act – required local authorities to inform carers of their right to assessment and introduced provision for employment, training and leisure issues to be taken into account in determining services for carers

2006   Work and Families Act – made provision for carers of adults to be given the right to request flexible working arrangements.

2007   Establishment of a Standing Commission on Carers

2008   Children and Young Persons Act – included provision to reduce the number of children and young people taking on inappropriate caring roles

2008   National carers' strategy – *Carers at the heart of 21st-century families and communities* – a 10-year cross-governmental strategy that prioritises 'choice and control' for carers

2010   Refreshed carers' strategy – *Recognised, valued and supported: Next steps for the carers strategy*

Recent policy documents focus on more cooperation and coordination between NHS bodies and local authorities in identifying carers and agreeing plans for carer support. The *Carers Strategies (Wales) Measure 2010* (Welsh Assembly Government, 2010) introduces additional duties through a new legislative requirement on the NHS (as the lead body) and local authorities in Wales to work in partnership to prepare, publish and implement a carers' information strategy. The 2012 Social Services (Wales) Bill (Welsh Assembly Government, 2012a) notes that the Welsh Government is committed to extending the duties contained in the 2010 measure to other local authority functions such as education and housing through secondary legislation (para 2.6.4). The 2012 White Paper on social care in England (DH, 2012a) outlines how the NHS (the NHS Commissioning Board and clinical commissioning groups) is to work with local authorities and carer organisations to identify and support carers.

Assessment of carers' needs

The Carers (Recognition and Services) Act 1995 was seen as a major step forward for carers, giving them new rights to an independent assessment. Under the legislation, individuals providing a 'substantial' amount of care on a regular basis could request an assessment. However, the Act did not require local authorities to provide services to carers although subsequent legislation strengthened this entitlement. The Carers (Equal Opportunities) Act 2004, for example, introduced a requirement for local authorities to inform carers of their right to request a carer's assessment and also added the requirement that the assessment should consider the carer's work, education and leisure wishes. Yet, the number of carers who actually get an independent assessment remains small. The NHS Information Centre (2010) Carers' Survey found that only 6% of identified carers were offered a carer's assessment in 2010/11. Of the carers who had been assessed, 67% said that they had received a service of some kind as a result of the assessment. The numbers of carers being assessed dropped by 3% between 2009/10 and 2010/11, with the numbers receiving a service also declining by 2% (House of Commons Health Committee, 2012a). In Northern Ireland in 2010, the High Court ruled that 41 families with autistic children were wrongly told by their local health and social care trust that their needs could not be assessed because of a lack of resources. The judge found that '[t]he Trust acted in breach of its duty to carry out carers' assessments' (Garboden, 2010, unpaginated).

Victor's (2009) review of studies of interventions directly targeted at carers identifies a number of positive outcomes linked to the statutory carer's assessment. The process of assessment itself appears to be beneficial to carers in that it allows them to be recognised and to have emotional benefits by providing them with the opportunity to discuss their role and to feel valued and supported. However, factors such as the skills of the assessor and their empathy with and knowledge of carers' issues and the availability of resources were linked to better outcomes. Recent proposals have recommended a strengthening of carers' assessment rights. A Law Commission (2011, p 71) report recommended that the duty to assess a carer 'should apply to any carer providing care to another person' and that the existing criteria for assessment – that carers need to be providing a substantial amount of care on a regular basis – should be removed.

Legislative measures to tackle some of the assessment issues were included in the Department of Health White Paper *Caring for our future: Reforming care and support*, which referred to carers having *entitlement* to support and 'a duty on local authorities to provide support for carers equivalent to that for people who use services' (DH, 2012a, p 35). The measures contained in the draft Care and Support Bill (DH, 2012b, clauses 13, pp 17-19), aimed at consolidating adult social care law, would do away with the criteria that a person has to be providing 'substantial' care and the need for carers to request an assessment, making them automatically entitled to one if a local authority considers them to have caring needs as determined by an eligibility framework. Many of the provisions in the

Bill have been welcomed by carers' organisations although concerns have been raised about the impact of the Bill on young carers, who would not be covered by the legislation because it applies only to adult carers – including the absence of obligation on adult services to identify young carers in a household (Clements and Bangs, 2012). This appears not to be the case in the Social Services (Wales) Bill (Welsh Assembly Government, 2012a), which recommends the adoption of a universal definition of carer that would include children and young people who are carers. This Bill also proposes a single duty on local authorities to consolidate their existing duties with regard to carers (para 2.6.7).

Financial aspects of caring

The financial worth of the work carried out by unpaid carers has been estimated at £119 billion a year (Carers UK and University of Leeds, 2011). Pickard (2004) reflects on how such costings were initially discouraged by policy makers. She cites an example from a research project in the early 1980s where no attempt was made to cost the contribution of the informal caring network 'because our research sponsors [the Department of Health and Social Services] requested us not to do so' (Wright et al, 1981, pp 23-4). Despite the amount of money that carers save the Exchequer, a UK-wide survey on the cost of caring (Carers UK, 2012) found that many carers struggled financially, especially in light of increased living costs. This included cutting back on essentials such as food and heating with a third of carers unable to afford their utility bills. The only social security benefit available to carers is the Carer's Allowance. The 2012 rate for this benefit is £58.45 per week. In order to qualify, even for such a small sum, a carer must be caring for at least 35 hours per week and not be earning more than £100 per week. Carers who are over state retirement age are not entitled to claim Carer's Allowance. Many carers who may be entitled to this benefit do not receive it. Take-up figures for Carer's Allowance are not available but the Department for Work and Pensions (Berthoud, 2010) reported that 481,000 carers received the benefit. The majority of claimants were women; most were in the 35–59 age group (about 70%) with 20% aged 18–34. According to a National Audit Office (2009) report, carers often do not apply for the benefit because they do not see themselves as carers; others may not meet the eligibility criteria or are confused by it. Other financial support relates to pension provision. The 2008 carers' strategy (DH, 2008d) introduced a National Insurance carer's credit for carers under pension age providing at least 20 hours care per week, to recognise their need to protect their rights to the state pension and state second pension.

Under the welfare reform measures introduced by the Coalition government there had been some discussion that Carer's Allowance would be wrapped up in the new Universal Credit and means tested. However, following campaigning by Carers UK, Carer's Allowance continues as an independent benefit.

Increasing Carer's Allowance to a level commensurate with lost earnings or even extending it to a broader range of carers would be expensive and this is not something that governments in the UK have shown any inclination to do. There was a failed attempt in the Northern Ireland Assembly in 2008 through a Private Member's Bill to allow carers who became pensioners to continue to receive the Carer's Allowance once the state retirement pension was received. The Department of Social Development advised that the proposal would breach the parity principle (whereby social security benefits in Northern Ireland are kept in line with those in Great Britain) (Gray and Birrell, 2012). Policy discussions on improving the financial circumstances of carers have focused on increasing the number of carers supporting themselves through employment (Himmelweit and Land, 2011).

Carers and employment

Successive governments' labour activation measures mean that many people can expect to combine paid employment and caring. There is evidence that being in paid work brings positive benefits to carers and much of the justification for the focus on enabling carers to combine work and employment in policy is that this is what carers themselves want. Evidence suggests that employment can help reduce social isolation, help the carer retain a sense of their own identity and allow for some to be financially better off (Arksey, 2002a). Yet, combining paid work with unpaid care is far from easy. In the UK, about 4.3 million carers are of working age and around two thirds of working-age carers in the UK are in paid work. It is estimated that 54% of carers give up work to care (Carers UK). Altogether, an estimated one million carers have given up work or reduced their working hours to care (Carers UK and Ipsos MORI, 2009). Ability to stay in or re-enter paid work is related to the nature and intensity of caring (Kotsadam, 2010; Fry et al, 2011) and those providing intensive levels of care and co-resident carers, who are most likely to be women, experience the most adverse effects (Yeandle and Buckner, 2007; Vickerstaff et al, 2009).

Reconciling the demands of paid work and caring poses considerable challenges for individual carers and for policy makers. At the same time as demand for care is growing due to demographic changes, governments are aiming for high employment rates and everyone is expected to work longer in order to address the cost of pensions. In the past it has been left very much to individual carers to try to juggle these responsibilities, in much the same way, in fact, as childcare was traditionally perceived as a private responsibility. Policy measures introduced over the past decade or so have included provision aimed at carers and employment. The Carers (Equal Opportunities Act) 2004 stated that employment, training and leisure issues must be taken into account in determining services for carers and the Work and Families Act 2006 extended the right to request flexible working to carers. The 2008 carers' strategy (DH, 2008d) provided for the setting up of a care partnership manager in every Jobcentre Plus district in England and specialist Jobcentre Plus advisers, access to training and funding for the cost of replacement care during approved training. In 2010, the Coalition government's refreshed carers' strategy noted:

> It is crucial that we place a much higher priority on supporting people of working age with caring responsibilities to remain in work, if they wish to do so. The Government wants to empower carers to fulfil their work potential, to protect their own and their family's current and future financial position and to enjoy the health benefits and self-esteem that paid employment or self-employment can bring. (DH, 2010e, para 2.9)

What is clear is that legislative provision, such as that outlined above, is not sufficient either to significantly increase the number of carers in employment or to address the challenges faced by carers trying to combine caring and paid work. The National Audit Office (2009, p 7) report concluded that '[t]he Department's [Department for Work and Pensions] help to carers who wish to support themselves through combining paid work with their caring responsibilities is not sufficiently effective for carers'. A survey by the Department for Work and Pensions (Vickerstaff et al, 2009) revealed that most employers did not have an explicit policy and that there is considerable variation in workplace support, with many employers lacking knowledge and understanding about what carers need. An additional difficulty is the work-related rules for Carer's Allowance, which discourage carers from entering or remaining in employment or from entering education.

Box 30 contains information on some of the issues that carers themselves feel should be addressed.

Box 30: Carers' views on what helps them to stay in or re-enter employment
- Better support and services for the person they care for, including domiciliary and respite services.
- More flexibility around the delivery of care services.
- A higher earning threshold for Carer's Allowance.
- More awareness on the part of carers about their legal rights.
- Access to jobs with necessary flexibility.
- Flexibility.

Source: Yeandle and Buckner (2007)

Carers wishing to stay in or return to work frequently highlight workplace flexibility as an important factor and governments have placed considerable weight on the role of flexible working as a way of helping carers to stay in employment. This is an area that requires more research but it does appear that there has been only limited growth in availability of flexible work and there is little consistency in practice across occupational settings. The small number of studies to date (see, for example, Henz, 2006; Bryan, 2011) suggest that flexible working makes only a small contribution to reconciling work and care. Bryan (2011, p 24) concluded that 'it is unlikely to have a substantial effect on the amount of care provided and had no impact in situations where carers were providing intensive levels of care'. The impact of the Equality Act 2010, which extended protection against discrimination to carers, including new rights in the workplace, has yet to be established. This legislation replaced existing anti-discrimination laws with a single Act. Under the legislation, carers in England, Scotland and Wales are protected from direct discrimination and harassment at work. The law also provides some protection for carers outside of work such as when they shop for goods or services. Carers can also be protected by virtue of their association with someone who has a protected characteristic (such as a disabled relative). This gives carers in Britain greater protection than the existing legislation in Northern Ireland, where section 75 of the Northern Ireland Act 1998 requires only public authorities to have due regard to promote equality of opportunity of a number of groups, including 'persons with and without dependants' (Equality Commission for Northern Ireland, 2012).

Carers also have some rights under the Disability Discrimination Act 1995 and under sex discrimination legislation. However, as a result of the implementation of the Equality Act 2010, the disability equality legislation in Great Britain has been significantly harmonised and strengthened and this has resulted in somewhat stronger protection for carers.

The implications for policy are strikingly clear. For carers to be able to be in paid employment and sustain caring responsibilities they need to have access to more and better support, employers need to understand and respond to the needs of carers, and policy needs to ensure that carers are financially better off. There is, however, another question – which is whether carers may feel pressurised to be in paid work even though this may add to their stress because either they feel that this is what is expected of them or they feel they have no choice financially.

Should carers be paid?

In allowing payment to be made to family carers, Britain lags behind many European countries. An analysis of 21 European Union countries (Riedel and Kraus, 2011) found that most offer some kind of monetary benefit that is either paid directly to the informal carers or to the care recipient. In some countries the care recipient can decide whether to pay for formal or informal care. However, few pay sufficient amounts to compensate for employment. One argument in favour of payment for care is that this can formalise the contribution of carers and raise the status of caregiving. While this may be one way of improving carers' incomes, there may be implications in terms of relationships – your husband or your wife could become your employer. Carers' organisations report mixed views on the part of carers (Princess Royal Trust for Carers and Crossroads Care, 2011). In the UK, it is possible in some cases for care recipients to use direct payments to pay co-resident carers. Carers can also apply to receive a direct payment. The Household Survey of Carers 2009–10 found that 16% got a direct payment or personal budget (38,400 carers) but there is evidence that, despite there being no legal reason, some local authorities are not allowing carers to use direct payments or personal budgets to purchase replacement care (Princess Royal Trust for Carers and Crossroads Care, 2011). Carers' organisations point out that breaks are what carers most commonly say they would like and the aim of personalisation is to give personal budget holders choice and control. It also appears to contradict the Department of Health (2010d, para 3.1) policy commitment that:

> Personalisation means that all services and support available to carers should be tailored to their specific needs as far as possible … and that universally available services should be flexible in their approaches in order to respond to the variety of ways in which those with caring responsibilities can best be supported.

Studies that have considered the impact of direct payments and individual budgets on carers (Glendinning et al, 2009; Duncan-Turnbull, 2010; Moran et al, 2011), identify the opportunities but also the challenges. They point to the new roles that some carers have to take on and the tension between the policies aimed at supporting carers and those aimed at increasing the independence of users. There is also concern about the adequacy of future financing of direct payment provision and the impact on carers of closure of or reduction in more traditional services as personalisation is rolled out, effectively leaving them with less choice over the caring work they do.

From a cost–effectiveness perspective, there are advantages in governments allowing carers to be paid as it has been demonstrated that they will probably do more than they are paid to do but there is the risk of excessive demands being made on carers. Grootegoed et al (2010), exploring experiences of carers in the Netherlands who receive payment for caring for relatives, found some evidence that payment is considered important to the wellbeing of the caregiver by providing more formal recognition and reward for their care work. Carers also identified advantage in that payment created a more formal contract, which helped to establish a clearer differentiation of care tasks from affection. However, the authors also identified problems in terms of the status and rights of care workers who are also close relatives. They cautioned that the situation in the Netherlands is a kind of 'quasi' employment, with carers not having access to the full labour rights associated with employment but being 'led into a cul de sac of reduced market values and limited employment rights' (Grootegoed et al, 2010, p 486).

Choice

This chapter started by looking at the assumptions that have been made about women and caring. Issues of choice are centrally important to discussions about unpaid care. Questions relating to choice have to be looked at in the context of adult social care policies more generally. Rationing of social care services, including respite services, has been shown to restrict carers' choices as can the lack of appropriate services on offer (Arksey, 2002b) as carers themselves restrict choices because of a perception that statutory services have limited resources. Research on direct payments and personal budgets has shown that choices often have to be negotiated between carers and those they care for and this can give rise to tensions, for example, if a carer needs a break and the person they are caring for does not want to go into respite care or have a replacement carer (Wenger et al, 2002). Arksey and Glendinning (2007, p 172) conclude that:

> [T]he concept and practice of choice is highly problematic for informal carers for two sets of factors – the nature of the relationship between the carer and the recipient of care and a set of broader factors relating to organisational issues such as access to information and the availability of services.

Changes to assessment, such as those outlined earlier (if all carers were assessed and were informed about entitlements), may go some way towards addressing these problems – but this would only be of value if resources were then available to meet the assessed needs. Evidence suggests that the impact of public expenditure cuts could reduce choice for carers or potential carers as paid services come under increasing financial pressure. The UK Home Care Association (UKHCA) study of the commissioning practices of local authorities in light of public expenditure cuts found that 82% of local authorities and health and social care trusts were reducing the number of hours of care they would pay for individual users, and over 75% were reducing the number of care worker visits and reducing the length of visits (UKHCA, 2012). Of homecare visits in England, 73% appeared to be 30 minutes or shorter, 42% in Wales and Scotland and 87% in Northern Ireland. The Welsh paper *Sustainable social services for Wales: A framework for action* (Welsh Assembly Government, 2011, p 6, para 1.11) pointed out that 'retrenchment would see fewer people receiving services, greater expectation that people find their own solutions and increased burden on informal carers'.

The increasing demand for care, coupled with the growing pressure on all adults to work, perhaps suggests that greater reliance on unpaid carers is unsustainable. Pickard (2008) estimates that by 2017 the number of older people needing care will outstrip the number of working-age family members currently available to meet that demand. Issues relating to employment and caring are at the core of government policy but research shows that people already in employment and those with higher wages are less likely to take on caring responsibilities

(Carmichael et al, 2010) and those carers seeking employment often find that opportunities are limited to lo-paid work (Fry et al, 2011), which does little to address their vulnerability to poverty. But, it may also be the case that, especially for women who are working or who are working for low pay, it may be harder in the future to refuse to care.

Conclusions

- This chapter has shown the scale and intensity of unpaid care in the UK.
- The significant contribution made by unpaid carers to the economy is substantial but the financial recompense that carers get is minimal.
- While the policy focus on unpaid carers has increased and there is greater understanding of the challenges and implications of caring, fundamental issues remain unaddressed. These include the extent to which people have genuine choice in their decision about whether or not to take on caring responsibilities.
- The 2010 carers' strategy stated that 'assumptions should not be made about who will provide care and to what extent' (DH, 2010e, para 1.12) but contrary to policies allowing or encouraging people to make active choices about whether to take on a caring role or not, the focus has been on ensuring that caring can be sustained by the introduction of measures aimed at making it easier for carers to combine unpaid caring and paid work.
- The choice to care or not to care has to be looked at in the context of adult care services more generally, including the impact of public expenditure allocations on paid provision.

Sources

Finch and Groves (1980) and Twigg and Atkin (1994) are good sources on the emergence of unpaid care as a policy issue. Carers UK regularly produces factsheets on numbers and profile of carers and publishes research and analysis – see for example the report on the cost of caring (Carers UK, 2012) and research on the value of caring (Carers UK and the University of Leeds, 2011). Issues regarding unpaid carers and employment are discussed by Yeandle and Buckner (2007); Arksey and Glendinning (2007) explore the concept of choice in relation to unpaid care, and Moran et al (2011) the impact of personalisation and personal budgets on carers.

Questions

- To what extent does the policy focus on 'choice' in adult social care extend to unpaid carers?

- Should carers be paid? What issues would proposals to pay carers a wage give rise to?

- To what extent are there contradictions and tensions between policies for unpaid carers and other social policies?

EIGHT

The paid adult social care workforce

Overview

Although much of the policy and research attention in recent years has been on social workers and childcare, there has been an increasing focus on the adult social care workforce, which is set to increase significantly in coming decades as demand rises. This chapter looks at the number and range of workers employed in social care and at workforce recruitment and retention challenges. It discusses the low status and low financial remuneration associated with many care jobs and questions how the apparent lack of value of and investment in this workforce can be reconciled with the policy rhetoric about the need for it to be well trained and skilled. The workforce implications arising from key policy developments, including personalisation, are also examined and the policy response to workforce issues is outlined.

Policy discussions and strategies about reform of adult social care in the UK have emphasised the importance of the social care workforce to the delivery of care in residential and domiciliary settings and to the quality of care outcomes (DH, 2011b; DHSSPS, 2011a and 2011c; Scottish Government, 2011; Welsh Assembly Government, 2011). This has been accompanied by calls for major reorganisation of and investment in workforce training and development. The term 'social care workforce' is used to describe those workers providing personal care and support. This includes the social work profession. This chapter begins by looking at developments relating to professional social workers but the main focus of the chapter is the wider group of workers who provide care and support.

Workforce issues in social work

With regard to social workers, policy has focused on training, registration and continuing post-qualifying qualifications. Social workers can be employed by a range of organisations but in Great Britain they work primarily for local authorities and in Northern Ireland for health and social care trusts. Social work is a regulated profession and all social workers in the UK are required to register. Workforce issues in social work need to be considered in the context of broader issues relating to more fundamental debates about the role of social work and standards in delivery, and a feature of developments in the UK has been the extent to which these have been a response to scandal or tragedy. As part of the New Labour modernisation drive, two workforce development bodies were created – the Children's Workforce Development Council and Skills for Care, which was charged with developments regarding adult social care. New workforce regulatory bodies and inspection bodies were also established. These are discussed in Chapter Ten. Each of the four countries of the UK has carried out reviews of the roles and tasks of social work.

In England, the GSCC (2008) review of the role and tasks of social work stressed the core value of social work although it gave relatively little attention to the role of social work in future social care provision (Lymbury and Postle, 2010). In the event, this review was overtaken by the setting up of a social work taskforce in 2008 by the Department of Health, which had responsibility for adult social care, and the Department for Children, Schools and Families (now the Department for Education). The catalyst for this was primarily concerns about the delivery of children's social work services after the Baby P case, but there were also issues regarding adult social care, including eligibility for services and funding, long-term care and personalisation. The final report (DH, 2009b) made 15 recommendations, including:

- strengthening the criteria governing the calibre of entrants;
- recommendations on curriculum and education reform and the delivery of social work education;
- the introduction of a formal probationary year;
- the creation of a more effective national framework for professional development;
- the development of a licence to practise.

The Social Work Reform Board was set up in 2010 to take forward the recommendations of the taskforce. One of its tasks has been to develop professional standards for social work – the Professional Capabilities Framework, which is to be a backdrop to initial social work training and continuing professional development. This is expected to be implemented in social work training in England from 2013. The probationary year – or Assessed and Supported Year in Employment – was introduced in England from September 2012. While employers are not legally obliged to offer this, a survey of local authorities suggests that three quarters are planning to do so (McGregor, 2012). Based on a recommendation in the Munro (2011) review of child protection, the Westminster government announced the creation of a post of chief social worker for England. This will cover both adult and child social work, with the post including responsibility for overseeing improvements in social work practice.

In Scotland, the backdrop to a review of social work was critical reports about the practice of social workers in two high-profile cases (Clark and Smith, 2011). The review was to include a fundamental review of the role of social work and recommendations for improving the standing and the standard of social work and social workers. The outcome – *Changing lives* (Scottish Executive, 2006) – pointed to the need for better governance, improved leadership and performance and a move towards personalisation.

A review by the Welsh Assembly Government (2007) prioritised work on defining the role of social workers and taking forward some of the recommendations of a 2005 review of social work (Social Services Improvement Agency, 2005), the development of a national action plan for the social care workforce and issues relating to workforce regulation – raising the question of whether regulation should be extended to all social care workers. *Sustainable social services for Wales: A framework for action* (Welsh Assembly Government, 2011) noted the progress made regarding the recruitment and retention of social workers and to social work education. It advocated further changes to the conception and delivery of social work, arguing, for example, that the concept of 'care management' is outmoded and not sufficiently user focused but rejecting 'personalisation' and 'consumer choice' in favour of the principle of 'citizen control'.

In Northern Ireland, the Northern Ireland Social Care Council was commissioned by the Department of Health, Social Services and Public Safety to conduct a review of the roles and responsibilities unique to social work. The council described this as 'a once-in-a-lifetime opportunity to identify the unique role, value and contribution of social work' (Northern Ireland Social Care Council, 2012). The outcome, a consultative document on a 10-year strategy for social work (DHSSPS, 2010), prioritised the development of a culture of continuous improvement and greater public understanding of social work. This was criticised for lacking focus on key issues – including the personalisation agenda, user involvement and tackling the impact of the governance and commissioning agendas (Heenan and Birrell, 2011). The final strategy published in April 2012 (DHSSPS, 2012a) set out 10 strategic priorities to build 'a strong foundation for social work', including an objective to strengthen the capacity of the workforce. Newly qualified social workers in Northern Ireland already have an assessed year in employment so the focus was largely on professional development. The strategy does contain an interesting suggestion about the introduction of caseload weighting for adult social services, however, while the document discusses the need for the workforce to be valued and for capacity to be strengthened to meet demand, there is little detail on how these objectives are to be achieved.

The analyses in the review documents have much in common – each pointing to the undervaluing of social work and the poor public image of social work and social workers, and the need to improve recruitment and retention and review education provision. While the English and Scottish reviews emphasise personalisation this is not a feature of the Northern Ireland review, and the most recent Welsh document rejects the focus on personalisation and commissioning in favour of a more collaborative 'citizen-focused' approach.

Social care workforce

Social care workers can be defined as 'people that are (typically) not professionally qualified but will hold vocational qualifications and undertake a wide range of care and support tasks. This includes individuals who provide care in people's own homes and other settings, such as care homes' (Centre for Workforce Intelligence, 2011). Since the rolling out of the modernisation agenda and the focus on personalisation, a number of new social care roles have been created. These include support workers working with users, where their role is to help the person achieve greater independence, and advocacy type roles. However, the term 'support worker' is only vaguely defined and is often used more generally, for example, when describing the work carried out by home care workers, those working in high-support-need housing and personal assistants directly employed by users. Manthorpe and Martineau, (2008) identified three characteristics that they felt could be applied to support workers:

- fostering independence among people being supported;
- generally without professional accreditation;
- tend to engage in both social care and healthcare tasks.

While estimates for the number of workers vary, overall, at least two million people work in adult social care in the UK and it is a major sector in the UK economy. Skills for Care (2011) estimates that the number of jobs in the adult social care sector will need to be about 2.8 million in 2025 in order to meet projected demand for social care support, with some predictions having suggested that the workforce will increase as much as ninefold in the coming decades (Eborall and Griffiths, 2008).

Social care workers are employed across a range of areas and by hugely diverse organisations but there are common characteristics. The social care workforce is generally a low-paid, predominantly female workforce, in an area where there is a strong legacy of under-investment. It is also a workforce that has become increasingly reliant on migrant workers. Since the 1990s, adult social care workers across the UK have been less likely to be employed by the statutory sector and the majority are now employed by the independent sector. The proportion of workers in the voluntary and private sector varies between the countries of the UK, with workers in Northern Ireland being much more likely to be employed by the voluntary sector than by private, for-profit organisations (UK Sector Skills Assessment, 2010). The use of direct payments and independent budgets has significantly increased the number of social care personal assistants. Skills for Care (2010) estimated that in 2009/10, about 150,000 adults and older people were using direct payments. These workers have been described as being in a position between formal, paid workers and unpaid carers (Land and Himmelweit, 2010).

Information on the adult social care workforce in England in 2009 is outlined in Box 31.

Box 31: The adult social care workforce in England (2009)

An estimated 21,900 organisations in England provided or organised social care for adults and older people and employed social care workers. These ranged from very large national organisations to very small community-based organisations.

- 40,600 separate establishments employed social care staff.
- There were an estimated 1.75 million paid jobs in adult social care.
- About 82% of all jobs in adult social care were being carried out by women.
- Fourteen per cent of adult social care workers were of a non-European Economic Area (EEA) nationality.
- Over two thirds of adult social care jobs were in the independent sector, while 46% were in the private sector and 15% were in the public sector.
- Forty-four per cent (774,000) of jobs were in domiciliary care and 35% were in residential care.
- The average age of a care worker in adult care was 47 years.
- Two fifths of the social care workforce held no formal qualifications.
- 263,000 jobs were with recipients of direct payments.

Source: Centre for Workforce Intelligence (2011)

Chapter Seven discussed the poor financial circumstances of many unpaid carers and the low level of state financial support. The low status and low reward attached to caring work is also very apparent in the paid adult social care workforce where there is a strong association with poor working conditions, especially among workers who are not professionally qualified. Rubery and Urwin (2011), in their case of study of human resource policies and practices among a range of agencies employing care workers, found that workers had limited employment protection across a range of variables including:

- lack of job security;
- variability in hours of employment and lack of guaranteed hours;
- lack of formal representation;
- lack of clarity about job and role boundaries;
- limited opportunities for career development.

Their findings suggested that private sector employers 'failed to provide even minimum employment protection' (Rubery and Urwin, 2011, p 134). These conclusions appear to be at odds with the rhetoric about developing excellence in the workforce and building sustainability (see, for example, DH, 2011b; Welsh Assembly Government, 2011). They are also concerning in light of the responsibilities, expertise, range of skills and qualities required by social care workers (Fleming and Taylor, 2007; Land and Himmelweit, 2010), who look after some of the most vulnerable people in society. Why then do such conditions prevail? One reason is the historical development of social care and indeed its continued existence as a residual service, underfunded relative to demand and need. That care work remains predominantly women's work is also a factor contributing to the undervaluing of it. The thinking is that it 'does not need to be rewarded by good employment conditions' but that job satisfaction and the ideal of putting the person being cared for first is enough reward (Rubery and Unwin, 2011, p 124).

Many caring jobs attract minimal remuneration with pay levels little more than or even below the statutory minimum wage. National Minimum Data Set for Social Care (NMDS-CS) data for August 2012 show a median pay rate for a care worker of £6.69 per hour (NMDS-CS, 2012). The Low Pay Commission has expressed concern about the number of social care workers being paid below the National Minimum Wage. It links this to 'evidence indicating that the level of fees paid by public sector bodies when purchasing care services from the independent social care sector did not reflect minimum wage costs' (Low Pay Commission, 2011, para 2.74). This point was also reflected in the impact assessment for the 2012 White Paper *Caring for our future* (DH, 2012j, p 10), which identified that 'Providers are concerned that commissioners are focusing too much on price rather than individual outcomes and value for money'.

Within the social care sector there is a strong reliance on migrant workers and the recruitment of migrant workers has been a key strategy adopted to address workforce shortages. Over 14% of care workers and over 16% of senior care workers in England are identified as 'not British' in NMDS-SC 2011 data. Migrant workers are more likely to work in the private sector where rates of pay are lowest. They are also more likely to be working in establishments where clients require higher levels of care – for example, in care homes where older people have dementia or mental health problems (Hussein, 2011). Working pattern information collected by NMDS-SC shows that non-British social care workers are more likely to have a zero hours contract and to work flexitime (NMDS-SC, 2011) and a study of migrants employed in the long-term care sector revealed that many were working in exploitative conditions (Shutes, 2012).

The relationship between the carer and the person they care for is one of the most important factors in determining user satisfaction so retaining staff is important for maintaining quality. Inadequate pay and poor working conditions, including limited support and opportunity for progression, are significant factors in difficulties regarding recruitment and retention of social care workers with vacancy levels for England approximately 25% higher than the level for all industrial, commercial and public sector employment. Problems with recruitment and retention of some social care workers have also been identified in Scotland, Wales and Northern Ireland. Although care workers are often expected to carry out demanding and sensitive tasks, they may be ill-prepared for these because of a lack of formal training and/or mentoring and supervision (discussed later in the chapter). Turnover rates are high, particularly in the private sector with less than 50% of care workers in England having been in their current position for more than three years (Skills for Care, 2010). Future workforce recruitment considerations include a possible reduction in the number of migrant workers in the sector. Hussein (2011) suggests that a worsening shortfall in social care could be one of the implications of the immigration policy cap on migrants from non-EEA countries.

The deficiencies with regard to poor training and working conditions and the difficulties caused by funding not keeping pace with demand for services have implications for the quality of care. A number of studies have shown that stress and low morale, resulting from the way that care staff are treated, can have a direct impact on service quality (Hatton et al, 2001; Thomas and Rose, 2009). The limited length of time that workers are allocated with each user is frequently cited as a negative factor by those receiving services and their unpaid carers. A UKHCA (2012) report on the commissioning practice of local authorities and health and social care trusts found that 82% are reducing both the number of visits to users and the number of hours of care they will pay for. Therefore the time spent with clients decreases as care workers are forced to make shorter visits. The average visit length is reported to have been reduced by 10 minutes to 38 minutes but many home care visits are commissioned in 15-minute slots. It has also become increasingly common for workers to be given very specific tasks to complete during their visit, limiting their ability to respond sensitively to the specific needs or wishes of users (Land and Himmelweit, 2010). Beresford et al (2011, p 123) suggest that relationships between workers and users have been 'restructured as transactions … timed and evaluated on the basis of readily quantifiable outcome measures', resulting in less contact and time with users.

The high staff turnover means that recipients of home care frequently find themselves with different care workers coming into their homes. An inquiry into older people and human rights in home care published by the Equality and Human Rights Commission (EHRC, 2011) drew on the experiences of people receiving care, their families and commissioners and providers. The findings illustrate the disruption and upset caused by workers having a lack of time to deliver care, a lack of flexibility in the system in terms of when carers could/ would visit, poor staff awareness and skills and high staff turnover. Extracts from the report are presented in Box 32.

Box 32: Extracts from the Equality and Human Rights Commission report on home care (1)

"The carers … get Mum ready for bed at 4.30pm. Mum would prefer this later but the only slot given was after 9.30pm and this was too late for her, and they sometimes did not come. So I agreed to 4.30pm. This does not always work; last week one carer arrived at 2.45pm to get her ready for bed. Apart from loss of dignity, she needs her stockings on longer."

Daughter of woman in her 90s, North of England (EHRC, 2011, p 34)

> "My mother was ... entirely dependent on visiting carers for all her needs. Ladies came on buses to provide the 30 minutes four times a day. Sometimes the journey could take them nearly 2 hours with a final half mile uphill to walk from the bus stop. They were exhausted and not paid for travel time. If they were unable to get to a shift it often went without cover."
>
> **Daughter of older woman previously receiving home care currently in residential care, South of England** (EHRC, 2011, p 73)

A survey by the Patient Client Council (2012) in Northern Ireland of older people's experiences of domiciliary care highlighted similar concerns. While the majority of people rated the quality of their care as very good or good, a significant minority felt that the care they received did not meet their needs, with some people paying for additional private provision. Reference was made to carers being too rushed: 'they have too many people to see. They can't wash you properly. They don't have time to shower me so I only get washed with a cloth in the bedroom. It's not good enough' (Patient Client Council, 2012, p 28). Another participant's comments reflected familiar complaints about home care services, in particular the limitations caused by time constraints and a system that is not sufficiently flexible and personalised:

> 15 minutes in the morning is not enough time to shower, dress and get breakfast. I'm old now and it takes me time to do stuff. A lot of the time the girls don't come. If the weather is bad I don't see anybody and they don't phone to say they are not coming. The morning visit is too late and the night visit is too early. I don't want to go to bed at 8pm, the soaps aren't even over. I don't like it that all the carers change so much. I had to leave a key so they can get in to me in the morning and I'm not happy that I don't know who is coming through the door – a stranger. The young summer staff didn't even know what bedroom I was in. Can these girls not be put on a rota so I know who I'm getting and when? Also, are the staff trained to do this work, because sometimes you wouldn't think so. (Patient Client Council, 2012, p 29)

Of course, studies also provide insight into what makes a positive difference, for example, as shown in Box 33.

> **Box 33: Extracts from the Equality and Human Rights Commission report on home care (2)**
>
> The following quotes show the importance of contact that goes beyond carrying out practical tasks and how care work is valued:
>
> "We have a good laugh which is what I need, they do the job, but we joke and laugh at the same time. It is important because when you are like us, you don't go out, you don't ... see anybody. They are friends.
>
> **Woman, 70, lives with partner, self funded** (EHRC, 2011, p 24)
>
> "The Council home care service is ultra-reliable, even in bad weather, and they are always cheerful ... I have tremendous respect for the work they do."
>
> **Husband of older woman, North of England** (EHRC, 2011, p 23)

The vast majority of social care staff (as acknowledged by the House of Commons Health Select Committee, 2012a) work hard in often difficult circumstances. Unfortunately, despite the political and policy emphasis on workforce development, significant challenges remain. Many care workers have strong emotional attachment to those they care for and attach a value to their work that goes beyond monetary recompense. An inability to do their job to an acceptable standard can carry a personal emotional cost. A 2007 survey of care workers revealed that 63% of care workers thought that the public did not understand much about the work they do and less than half (39%) thought that their work was valued by the public (Skills for Care, 2007).

Social care workers are increasingly working with clients who are older and who have more complex needs. They may also be responsible for tasks that would, in the past, have been seen as the domain of health professionals – such as giving medication, maintaining records and providing intimate personal care. Yet, most adult social care workers do not have to be registered, many lack any formal training and there is evidence that a significant proportion of workers do not receive even the minimum levels of induction and supervision. Standards established in the Care Standards Act 2000 and the National Minimum Standards and Regulations for Domiciliary Care include provisions relating to the training of social care workers. Yet, in 2009, 25% of private sector providers and 20% of voluntary sector and local authority providers did not meet the minimum standards required by regulations (CSCI, 2009). A new Qualifications and Credit Framework (Skills for Care, 2011), replacing National Vocational Qualifications, was launched across the UK in 2011. This allows for small chunks of training to be accredited, adding up to a qualification over time. Alongside this, a new Skills for Care Continuing Professional Development Framework will be introduced. In England, as a response to future management needs, the National Skills Academy for Social Care launched a national social care trainee programme for graduates in 2010. This may go some way towards helping to address the status of social care work. The changing nature of social care work, including the need for effective inter-professional work, familiarity and expertise in the use of assisted living technology and stronger regulation of quality, presents particular challenges for workforce development. At all levels of social care work the requirement will be for effective inter-agency working (Cameron et al, 2012). Criticism of the compartmentalisation of care in the home led the Care Council for Wales (2010, p 67) to refer to 'service and professional silos' and there is little doubt that the training needs of the workforce in terms of integrated services and multidisciplinary working will be a key issue for the future.

Personalisation and the adult social care workforce

Personalisation presents challenges in terms of the transformational change required of local government services and professionals and other providers and social care workers. This has direct implications for leaders and managers who have to create the conditions within which personalisation can operate – including bringing about cultural change in organisations and practices (Hudson and Henwood, 2009). Professionals have at times been portrayed as presenting barriers to change or as reluctant participants in a process that challenges their expertise and status. Social workers have been criticised for being part of a traditional system that has disempowered users and part of a bureaucracy that has rationed care through resource-led needs assessment. Yet, social work has a pivotal role in the implementation of personalised services and many of the values associated with personalisation are strongly related to the purpose of social work. There is still uncertainty about how the role of social workers may change as a result of personalisation and there are mixed views about whether changes will be positive or negative for the profession. Some view the changes as an opportunity for social workers to return to traditional social work focused on empowering users (Henwood and Hudson, 2007; Duffy, 2010), but there is also concern that the changes will result in a de-professionalisation of social work with deskilling, job losses and a more casualised workforce (Ferguson, 2007; Cunningham and Nixon, 2011; Lymbury, 2012) as job roles are changed, more provision is outsourced and other workers take on social work responsibilities.

Policy indications have been towards social workers taking on a brokerage and advocacy role (DH, 2008e) but some commentators and users have questioned whether social workers are sufficiently autonomous to do this given they are mainly employees of local government (Dowson and Greig, 2009; Leece and Leece, 2011). There are some examples of positive outcomes from the creation of new jobs such as independent brokers or advocates – see Beresford et al's (2011, p 126) discussion of the role of disability development workers who offer person-centred support to users. However, these workers do earn considerably less than qualified social workers, will have less job security and may in the future be viewed by local authorities as a way of cutting more qualified social work posts.

The central government target in England of everyone needing social care receiving a personal budget by spring 2013 will result in an increasing number of user employers and personal assistants. Personalisation has implications for all social care staff, including a large number of workers not normally defined as professionals such as care workers, ancillary staff and personal assistants. Attention has focused on the personal assistants directly employed by users in relation to their pay, working conditions, training, registration and regulation (Leece, 2008; Land and Himmelweit, 2010). These issues are also discussed in Chapter Ten. They present an additional set of workforce challenges that could be summarised for workers as:

- issues relating to lack of job security or guarantee of work;
- whether the level of direct payment or individual budget will be sufficient to meet the needs of the care receiver – if it is not, the personal assistant may do more than they are paid for;
- personal assistants and their employers being unaware of their rights and obligations (Leece, 2008).

UNISON (2011) has expressed concern that the increasing use of personal assistants in what it considers to be an unregulated and unmanaged way will result in the downgrading and downsizing of adult social care roles. The view that conditions of employment for workers are at risk was identified in a study looking at the barriers to self-directed support in Scotland (Manthorpe et al, 2011) in which it was thought that the 'casualisation' of care was contrary to rhetoric about the need to increase skills and standards. While many personal assistants have been employed directly by users, it is predicted that as personalisation is rolled out, more care will be purchased from provider organisations (Baxter et al, 2010). But there is not, as yet, a national regulative or registration framework for employers of personal assistants. There are no comprehensive data on the number of directly employed personal assistants. Directly employed personal assistants are not required to be trained or to have a Criminal Records Bureau check. In 2011, the Department of Health published a Framework for Personal Assistants (DH, 2011c). This is described as a toolkit to make the practical side of employment easier to understand, including job descriptions and interviewing; it also provides information on the Common Induction Standards developed by Skills for Care. While welcomed, it has not been enough to allay concerns, particularly given the lack of resources for staff development and training and the resource pressures on social care provision more generally.

The personalisation agenda will also impact on work in multidisciplinary teams and on a range of health professionals, including nurses, mental health teams, occupational therapists and physiotherapists. The Department of Health (DH, 2008f) has acknowledged that more sophisticated workforce planning is required as is more preparation and support for working across professional groups and sectors. Staff have reported feeling inadequately prepared, particularly with regard to safeguarding and financial issues, including the potential misuse of budgets (Ipsos MORI, 2011). International experience of personal budget schemes has identified the training of frontline staff as imperative for the implementation of aspects of personalisation. Professionals need to be well informed and have the confidence and knowledge to support people (SCIE, 2010a; Manthorpe et al, 2011). A new relationship will need to be established between users, professionals and a range of other staff, including care staff employed by agencies, personal assistants employed directly by users and new staff such as service brokers. Some authors have spoken of this new relationship in terms of 'relocating expertise' and accepting service users as experts in their own lives and as having a strong user voice (Poll, 2007). 'Co-production' is a term used to describe collaborative relationships between staff and users – for example, in the development of a person-centred care plan (Bartlett, 2009). It has been expressed as a more positive relationship between staff and users of services, which acknowledges the contribution of users, carers and informal support networks as well as staff (Needham, 2011). There is little evidence that genuine co-production is a common experience and it is likely that the ethos of co-production has yet to become firmly established in professional and organisational cultures.

The government's workforce strategy – *Capable, confident, skilled* (Skills for Care, 2011) – sets out how the workforce would need to change and, as shown in Box 34, the knowledge and skills that care workers require to be able to deliver the outcomes linked to the social care agenda. As can be seen from Box 34, more personalised and person-centred services require a highly skilled and trained workforce.

Box 34: Knowledge and skills required by care workers as identified in the 2011 workforce strategy

- Supporting self-assessment and person-centred planning, with an emphasis on self-directed care, health promotion, and growing and sustaining circles of support.
- Supporting risk taking, and helping to manage and minimise harm that may prevent people from directing their own lives.
- Outcomes-based and outcomes-driven practice.
- Protecting, where people who use services are deemed not to have the capacity themselves.
- Providing information, advice, advocacy, brokerage and guidance.
- Providing personalised social care services, in people's own homes, and in residential and other settings, that respect people's dignity, choice and self-direction.
- Providing care and support with flexibility and understanding in ways that reflect the circumstances, religion, cultural background and lifestyle of the person using services.
- Enabling employment, education, training and other valued activities.

- Supporting people who use services who are or who wish to become employers to acquire the organisational capabilities to manage their own care and support, including providing reliable information and advice about employment law and practice.
- Recognising the value of the expertise and contributions of people who use services, and involving them from the outset in designing local care provision, influencing commissioning and planning their own care.
- Creating capacity and confidence among people who use services to lead, manage and work in social care and other organisations, such as new and existing user-led organisations.
- Engaging people who use services in developing strong local communities, enabling them to have a family and community life.
- Facilitating people's participation in governance, commissioning, training and quality assurance of social care services.

Source: Skills for Care (2011, p 14)

Workforce issues in social care reform

A key question is to what extent these workforce development needs have been prioritised. The *Caring for our future* White Paper (DH, 2012a) set out a number of measures. A code of conduct for adult social care workers is to be drafted by sector skills councils for social care and health (by September 2012). Sector skills councils will also recommend minimum training standards for adult social care workers and healthcare support workers (by September 2012). By April 2013, the Department of Health is to publish clear and accessible information on staff training as part of the provider quality profile and there is to be a Workforce Development Fund to target personal assistants and employers with regard to training and support. Also announced is the doubling of the number of apprenticeships in social care over five years (DH, 2012a, p 51). Although these measures represent some acknowledgement of the need to address workforce issues, the government has been criticised for paying 'scant attention' to 92% of the social care workforce most involved in delivering the measures outlined in the 2012 White Paper and in the draft Care and Support Bill (DH, 2012a, 2012b) (Johnson, 2012).

Conclusions

There are significant future challenges and demands regarding the adult social care workforce:

- A growing number of people will need care and support at a time when social care services face significant reductions. The King's Fund (2011) puts the funding gap in England at £1.4 billion by 2014.
- The recruitment, retention and quality of the paid social care workforce are critical to future provision. Skills for Care (2011b) has stated that the adult social care workforce in England is set for a massive expansion in the next 15 years, with the number of jobs expected to nearly double.
- In order to sustain the workforce, considerable investment in training and continuing professional development will be required but will not be sufficient while care work is so undervalued and underpaid.
- Future developments regarding personalisation raise a set of new issues for social workers, care workers, those employing them and regulators.

Sources

The National Minimum Data Set for Social Care (NMDS-SC) provides statistical data on the paid social care workforce. Rubery and Unwin (2011) look at the employment conditions of paid workers across a range of agencies. A number of studies consider the impact of personalisation policy on social workers and other social care staff, including Leece and Leece (2011), Land and Himmelweit (2010) and Cunningham and Nixon (2011).

Questions

- What are the key challenges in relation to the recruitment and retention of the social care workforce? How adequate are current initiatives aimed at addressing these challenges?

- What are the main characteristics of the social care workforce?

- To what extent are the employment conditions of social care workers at odds or in keeping with rhetoric about developing excellence in the social care workforce?

- What knowledge and skills are required by the social care workforce to meet current and future policy outcomes for social care?

NINE

Public and user involvement

Overview

This chapter describes the development of a significant role for service users that has been established in the adult social care system. The scope and nature of user involvement and public participation are explained, covering the formulation of policy, planning and administration of service delivery, regulation and inspection, education and training, research and evaluation and assessment. The commitment of the UK government and devolved administrations and delegated and local government as set out in legislation, strategies and guidelines is set out. Also covered are structures for participation and involvement, user-led organisation and the role of advocacy.

Historically, four main trends have influenced the development of public and user involvement in the delivery of adult social care. First, the promotion of public participation in service delivery including adult social care became a major activity throughout local government in Great Britain. Second, public and user involvement also became an important issue within the NHS, leading to several initiatives and specific structures. With the increase in collaboration and partnership working between health and social care and between the NHS and local authorities, attention turned to common approaches and integrated structures to promote public involvement. Third, from the early 1990s, social work moved to the increased involvement of 'clients' in social work decisions (Beresford and Croft, 2004). Fourth, there were major developments in forms of user engagement geared specifically to adult social care.

The terminology used has raised issues. In health the terms 'public' and 'patient' are rather interchangeable as almost everyone has an engagement with health although 'patient' may have connotations of hospital treatment. The older term 'client' is still used in some instances in social care, for example, the Patient and Client Council set up in 2008 in Northern Ireland, but is not widely used. 'User involvement' and 'service user' are the most common terms and this may include potential users. However, the term 'service users' has been subject to some criticism, often on grounds that it restricts people's identities and may imply a passive recipient or someone who has things done to them. Heffernan (2006) suggests that the term can be interpreted to imply dependency in health and social care on services and service providers. Thus, it may be claimed that there are still undertones of an unequal relationship with providers, and the users' role in the concept of a service or the value of user experience is not recognised (Social Work Education Participation, 2011). However, increasingly, 'service user' has been defined as an active and positive term (SCIE, 2007b). 'Involvement' and 'participation' are the most commonly used phrases but 'engagement' and 'empowerment' may be used at times.

The public participation context

Local government has always seen itself as in an especially close position to local people and local communities and there is quite a long history of participatory initiatives, particularly in the past in tenant participation. New Labour gave a boost to increasing and improving public participation in local government (the Local Government Act 1999 included a statutory requirement on consultation). New participatory arrangements were seen as a means of improving public services, promoting social inclusion and facilitating the democratic renewal of local service delivery (Lowndes et al, 2001; Barnes et al, 2010). Subsequently, government policy making has endorsed the expansion of public participation as opposed to a consumerist model. In 2006, a government White Paper stated that local democracy could be reinforced by direct participation of citizens (DCLG, 2006). The Lyons (2007) report on the future of local government in England stated that improving public engagement was at the heart of a reformed place-shaping role and gave an example of involving older people in developing and tailoring the 'meals on wheels' service. From 2009, local authorities were under a statutory duty to inform, consult and involve local people in the running of local services. This period was marked by a major increase in the number and scope of initiatives to increase participation in local government and local accountability and engage with the public. A wide variety of methods can be identified: consultations, public meetings, forums, focus groups, citizen juries, issue forums, visioning exercises, satisfaction surveys and interactive websites (Wilson and Game, 2006). In Scotland there was a similar government demand that local authorities strengthen citizen participation in decisions taken about service delivery (McAteer and Orr, 2006). Wales has had a widely developed government position that all public services should be citizen centred. This policy of enhancing public participation and involvement has been seen by Newman (2009) as directed at sharpening the accountability downwards to citizens and users, eliciting pressure to drive up standards and with some focus on area-based initiatives. Assessments of this participative activity in local government identified some difficulty or lack of clarity in stating how these activities influenced mainstream decision making (Sullivan et al, 2004). Public participation can be a sensitive issue for councillors as it has been seen as undermining their elected position and a form of threat to their traditional representative role on behalf of the public. Furthermore, the views of participative processes may clash with the decisions of formal council processes and thus place councillors in a defensive relationship with public participants (Copus, 2004).

Influence of public involvement in health

The period 1995 to 2005 saw a major emphasis on strengthening patient and public involvement in health. The internal market reforms, consumerism and user-orientated standards led to a number of responses to increase the involvement of the public in decisions about health services, with the Conservative government producing a patient partnership strategy (Baggott, 2005) and community health councils being set up in local areas. The New Labour government, as part of rebuilding the NHS with a more responsive and participatory approach, published *Patient and public involvement in the new NHS* (DH, 1999a), which urged that patient and public involvement should be embedded in NHS structures. *The NHS Plan* (DH, 2000) stated that for the first time patients will have a real say in the NHS, through surveys and forums and the expression of patient views. This was translated into statutory terms in the Health and Social Care Act 2001, which created a duty on health bodies to consider and involve patients and the public in the planning, development and operation of services. The development of patient and public involvement in health became strongly focused on organisational innovations. In 2003, patient forums were established in each trust in England, subsequently revised as patient and public involvement forums to represent the community, including the public, patients and carers. This structure was complemented by another new organisational tier, Patient Advice and Liaison Services (PALS), to mainly provide advice but also act as a catalyst for improving services. The new system was criticised for its complexity and lack of clarity between patient and public involvement forums and PALS (Baggott, 2005, p 543). Milewa (2004) saw the new architecture of patient and public involvement as creating a degree of normative ambiguity about whether enhanced access to decision making would lead to greater empowerment.

Another criticism of these structures was to be taken up by government – that they did not acknowledge the growing importance of partnership and collaboration between health and social care. In 2006, the Department of Health published the White Paper *Our health, our care, our say: A new direction for community services* (DH, 2006a), which set a new direction by including community health with social care and gave a commitment to a stronger voice for individuals and communities in influencing the shape and delivery of local services, described as 'giving people choice and control over the services they use' (DH, 2006a, p 157). Another government paper quickly followed – *A stronger local voice* (DH, 2006b) – with the stated aim of creating health and social care services that are user centred, responsive, flexible, open to challenge, accountable to local communities and constantly improving. This strategy was also presented as a commitment to revitalise community empowerment and particularly emphasised more explicit duties on providers and commissioners of services to involve and consult. The inclusion of social care did not receive a detailed explanation in these papers and to some extent appeared as a natural development to the growing integration and collaboration between health and social care and the NHS and local government.

A stronger local voice proposed new structural arrangements built on the work of patient forums and the engagement activities of social care organisations. New Local Involvement Networks (LINks) would replace the patient and public involvement forums and would provide a way for local people and communities to engage with both health and social care organisations. The development of participation in social services had been left to individual local authority initiatives or to the new National Service Frameworks, for example for mental health and for older people.

LINks were established by the Local Government and Public Involvement in Health PCT in 2007 within each area served by a local authority for social services in England, meaning that there were some 150 bodies covering adult health and social care. The aim was to give local communities a way to influence local health and social care services. A LINk was made up of individuals and community groups and is best considered a network, empowered to determine their own form of governance without a mandatory structure. The formation of some was based on patient and public involvement, but expanded into social care. Their main tasks were to:

- ask the views of people on local services;
- request information;
- communicate directly with those planning, commissioning and providing services;
- make reports and recommendations;
- receive responses.

LINks also had powers to carry out visits when necessary to view health and social care premises. These 'enter and view' arrangements also applied to health and social care services provided by the independent sector. Those bodies commissioning or providing health and social care were expected to contact the LINk in their area and LINks provided information and intelligence for PCTs, NHS trusts, foundation trusts and social care providers. LINks could also develop an active relationship with the regulators of health and social care and the CQC, which could draw on LINks' views on how NHS bodies and councils were performing. They planned to have a strong relationship with all decision makers in health and social care, could collect and assess evidence to influence commissioning, monitor services rigorously and reach out to local people. If dissatisfied with responses to any recommendations or reports, LINks were able to refer matters to the Health Overview and Scrutiny Committee of the local council.

Patient and public involvement continued to develop in some respects distinctive from social care, with the Darzi report *High quality care for all* (DH, 2008b) having a vision of effective change empowered by the views and preferences of users and patients, the public and NHS staff involved in securing improvements. The Department of Health guidance on engaging with patients – *Real involvement:*

Working with people to improve services (DH, 2008e) – and the NHS constitution, published in January 2009, firmly embedded the principle of involving people in the design and development of health and social care services. A number of initiatives and structures based in health thus extended to social care in the way LINks did, with the intention of better reflecting a joined-up approach to care provided to individuals.

Another vision document in 2008 stated patient and public engagement was an approach that puts the people who use services at the heart of care (DH, 2009c). At the same time as those developments, local councils were adopting more radical approaches to user involvement in social care. The Coalition government was committed to a principle of devolving power from central to local government. Its published *Vision for adult social care* (DH, 2010a, p 4) declared: 'We want to see a real shift of power from the state to people and communities'. The White Paper on reform of the NHS (DH, 2011a) continued the commitment to shared decision making covering health and social care. The analytical strategy published for consultation purposes referred to evidence that increased involvement can improve outcomes, and the consultation paper (DH, 2011a) acknowledged that too many decisions were made without enough public involvement. The proposals for implementation put much emphasis on enhancing 'local democratic legitimacy'. The White Paper *Caring for our future: Reforming care and support* (DH, 2012a) gave priority to the principle that people should be in control of their own care and support, and ensuring that services respond to what they want, although detailed strategies specifying user involvement were confined to personal budgets and the HealthWatch arrangements (see below).

Rationale for user involvement in social care

User involvement has developed as a specific form of public participation that involves individual users in decisions that affect them. The emergence of user involvement as a key element of social care modernisation stemmed from self-help and advocacy organisations that had sought to speak for users themselves (Bochel and Bochel, 2004), rather than depend on professionals, managers, politicians or appointed board members. Service users and user organisations developed approaches to user involvement and an empowerment approach (Beresford, 2010). The user movement was also promoted by the social inclusion and equality agendas, leading to the appeal of user-centred services rather than provider-centred services. At the level of individual user participation, social care can be seen as having led the way in engaging with service users (Glendinning, 2009). Since the early 1990s, major strategies and legislation have included the involvement of service users and there have been continuing developments in practice, described as to an extent without real precedent (Beresford and Croft, 2004). The approach was underlined in *Putting people first* on transforming adult social care, which stated the government's aim to make adult social care the first public service reform programme to be co-produced, co-developed and co-evaluated and recognised that change will only be achieved by the participation of users and carers at every stage (DH, 2008f).

As well as the growth of the user movement, other factors identified as promoting user involvement were the shift from passive to active modes of professional practice and theory (Brown and Young, 2008). Policies empowering users also had the effect of threatening the power of existing social services organisations (Rummery, 2007). User involvement developed significantly in a broad framework, encompassing the planning, processing, delivery and evaluation of adult social care.

Box 35 outlines the rationale and justification for user involvement as identified by SCIE (2010b).

Box 35: Rationale and justification for user involvement

- It is a mechanism for improving the standard and quality of adult social care by making providers more aware and responsive to the needs and expressed preferences of users and receiving their feedback. This can reduce the risk of unsuitable provision and lead to increased user satisfaction.
- User perspectives bring a wide range of ideas on needs and delivery, personal experiences and the authentic expression of lived experience. Such an approach helps to mould provision and practice in new directions and promote new ideas.
- User involvement empowers people who had previously been excluded or had been passive clients or recipients of services. Thus, user participation can remove dependency and be a form of active citizenship, which can end exclusionary structures and practices and alter power relationships in the delivery of social care (Carr, 2007). Such empowerment also realises local accountability.
- User involvement is justified on the grounds of its contribution to social capital through widespread participation, voluntary contributions and community-based activity.
- It improves efficiency (reducing costs and securing better value for money) by more closely addressing people's needs.
- It increases the knowledge base for delivery of information and advice on social care among providers, users and carers; improving capacity for choice.
- It is a means to improve training, education, regulation and research.
- It shapes provision to suit the needs of service users rather than people fitting the service provision.

Devolved administrations' approach to user involvement

The Welsh devolved administration has espoused a model of delivery for all its services, including social care, of collaboration and citizen engagement as an alternative to competition and markets (Martin and Webb, 2009). The Welsh Government has emphasised the individual as an active citizen rather than a passive consumer. The paper *Sustainable social services for Wales: A framework for action* (Welsh Government, 2011, p 9) listed as the first principle 'a strong voice and real control'. It suggested that social services can feel proud of their track record of being citizen centred. Service providers were expected to put in place stronger arrangements to involve those who use services directly and a much higher range of services were to be run by citizens themselves (Welsh Government, 2011, p 15). The Social Services Bill placed a relatively low-key emphasis on the provision of information, advice and assistance to promote a stronger voice and real control (Welsh Government, 2012b, p 16). Jones (2012) conducted research on how the citizen voice model could be made more effective for older people and how they could become more vociferous in complaining and identifying areas for improvement. In a groundbreaking approach, the Welsh minister announced in 2012 a new 'citizen panel' to give users and carers involved in social services a voice in important strategic decisions taken at an all-Wales level (Welsh Government, 2012b).

A major contribution in Scotland to user involvement has been through self-directed support. A national strategy document (Scottish Government, 2010d) sought to give service users more control, choice and flexibility in directing their own care. The subsequent Bill seeks to view users and carers as equal citizens with rights rather than people who receive services. A principle of the Bill is involvement – that a person must have as much involvement as the person wishes in relation to assessment of the person's needs and the provision of support (Scottish Government, 2012d, p 19). The plan in Scotland for statutory health and social care partnerships proposes a membership to include service users' representation. In Scotland there has also been support for strengthening advocacy and extensive involvement of mental health service users.

User involvement in Northern Ireland has not been promoted as a major value. The *Transforming your care* review (DHSSPS, 2011a) and follow-up implementation plans (DHSSPS, 2011b, 2012b) make only occasional general references to user involvement. The major mechanism for user participation is through a Patient and Client Council, which is organised for the whole country as a centralised quango with an appointed board. Its functions are limited largely to a consultative role, giving information and advising on complaints. It has been argued that there has been a dominance of managerialist values in health and social care (Greer, 2004) and a top-down approach in Northern Ireland. It also has few user-led organisations. Trusts and other health and social care boards are required to have a personal and public involvement strategy based on mainstream principles but questions exist about their implementation.

Concepts of user involvement and participation

User involvement may cover different concepts of participation. An important aspect of user involvement is its contribution to the development and delivery of services at policy formulation and implementation levels. The concept has been used in a low-key way in the sense of 'user friendly' and 'user centred', where involvement is minimal and interpretation of the phrases and all decisions are taken by management (Moullin, 2002). A more useful typology of participation is outlined by Bochel et al (2008), based on the identification of three modes of governance by Kooiman (2005), which makes a distinction between hierarchical governance, co-governance and self-governance. User involvement can operate in social care in those three settings.

First, user involvement in hierarchical governance is demonstrated mainly in consultation processes with users and these largely correspond to the practices adopted in local government and health generally, including focus groups, surveys, satisfaction questionnaires, feedback processes, and user and public panels. In this mode, the actual method of consultation and impact of the data and views analysed will be finally determined by the existing management and decision-making structure. A committee/forum convened by a local authority in which hierarchical power relations continue to be exerted will probably be in practice strongly hierarchical (Simmons et al, 2011). The legislation creating new delivery structures in Northern Ireland contains a statutory requirement to consult and involve people, and guidance was published on strengthening personal and public involvement (DHSSPS, 2007), but in practice schemes have moved little beyond consultation.

Second, user involvement as co-production means cooperation between providers and users and may relate to joint involvement in planning, commissioning, designing, managing, delivering and evaluating a service (Bovaird, 2007). The co-production approach sees service users as equal partners involved centrally with service professionals, managers and policy makers in planning and delivering services. A key difference between participation and co-production has been identified as a move from service users and carers being consulted, to being brought into work when it is already under way, to being co-creators (Turner, 2012), that is, co-producing is producing together.

Thus, service users are working with practitioners, professionals and managers to produce an agreed outcome. Co-production requires some cultural shift among professionals and managers from their traditional role. A distinction can be made between an individualist context for co-production and a collectivist or programme-wide context. Co-production in delivery implies a redefinition of a service as the user moves from passive recipient to occupy a role in joint design and delivery. Needham (2008) refers to the different manifestations in service of co-production and that in some areas, for example, mental health, co-productive relationships may have therapeutic benefits. Aspects of personalisation, direct payments or supported housing also fall into the category of co-production. Government strategies and narratives have not expanded greatly on the implementation of co-production. Needham and Carr (2009) have identified co-production as operating on three different levels:

- at the least transformative level, simply some productive input from users;
- at the intermediate level, creating better channels for people to shape services;
- at the most transformative level, a relocation of power and control through new mechanisms of planning, delivery, management and governance.

Co-production in adult social care has been seen as implying participation by users and carers at every stage and services co-produced, co-developed and co-evaluated (Needham and Carr, 2009). Co-production can involve individuals and user-led bodies, with voluntary and community groups, the private sector and statutory bodies. User organisations may be the base or hub for the other sectors. The Department of Health (2010d), in a report on practical approaches to co-production, saw a change needed to the design, planning, commissioning and delivery of services where a greater proportion of decision-making processes were led by the people who use services. The Scottish Government endorsed co-production in 2007 in its health and social care strategy. The *Better health, better care* action plan (Scottish Government, 2009) set out what it described as a new mutual ethos, which saw Scottish people and staff as partners in the delivery of care. This was seen as requiring new ways of thinking and shifts in control, status and participation in health and social care. This mutual involvement can even be defined as a move beyond the concept of the 'user' as it indicates a preference for an emphasis on users as co-producers.

Co-production of social care can take place at different levels of service provision, encompassing different degrees of interaction from one to one, to teams and organisations. The concept does not necessarily imply that co-production involves an equal relationship or no differentiation of roles. Thus, the design of a service may reflect co-production or a solely professional design, while the delivery may reflect user co-delivery or user sole delivery (Bovaird, 2007, p 849), implying that co-production may imply multiple relationships. SCIE has set up a co-production network to develop policies and practices on co-production. To realise the full potential of this model, users have to be empowered to act as partners, staff need training in the benefits of co-production and new decision-making structures and commissioning practices need to be established. Financial support is necessary to embed co-production as a long-term strategy (Needham, 2009) and current financial pressures may limit co-production initiatives. The Department of Health has published best practice guidance covering who should be involved, engaging carers in co-production and budgetary participation (DH, 2010d).

The third context in which user involvement can operate is in self-management or self-governance within a framework of statutory provision of care. Conceptually, self-management by users can operate at the level of the individual or household or a collectivist entity or organisation. In this model, decision-making power is delegated to the user, who directs and controls the pattern and nature of services and may also have personal control over the use of funding, as with individual payments. The alternative form of self-governance is through groups of users coming together to deliver and self-manage a service. There is a tradition of self-management in social housing tenant management but Bochel et al (2008) suggest that this more radical form of user participation is difficult to achieve and is still often subject to hierarchical governance. Examples of this model may exist in such activities as community resource centres, advice centres and other services provided by user organisations. A defining criterion may be the element of delegation of power and responsibility for the services from the state to users and this is different from voluntary sector activity.

Organisation of users

The exact format and configuration of user involvement can vary, mainly between participation by individual users and participation by group representatives. The form of representation is largely determined by structures and access principles set up by governments or providers rather than determined by users and carers. At the level of participation by individuals, a distinction can be drawn between:

- involvement by an individual amateur, who may respond to an open request or invitation and take part in panels, discussion groups or consultations;
- involvement of expert individuals who have been trained, are members of a user group or network and are normally paid;
- involvement by an appointed individual on the board of a public body, advisory body or partnership body – this position may arise from a personal application or a nomination by a group.

Involvement can also be based totally on a group basis, normally referred to as user-led organisations (ULOs), and groups participating in user involvement activities can also have different characteristics. The essential feature of a ULO is that it is run and controlled by service users, promotes involvement, is independent and provides support. It may be a dedicated local user organisation or a network of user organisations operating at a regional or national level, a self-help group that also engages in user involvement or a large voluntary organisation that has user involvement as one of its activities. The format for group involvement can also differ between:

- a group supplying people to act as user representatives;
- a group or network having the right to nominate a member(s) of a user committee, focus group or panel;
- a group that is itself a member of a user committee or forum and decides how it is represented.

User group involvement in commissioning and designing services

ULOs have been described as the authentic voice of service users (DH, 2010d, p 16). They base their activities on direct experience and are often seen as the most legitimate and credible voice from the perspective of other agencies. Local authorities in Great Britain can develop and strengthen ULOs through commissioning processes, especially in areas of participation, advocacy, self-help or personalisation. Box 36 lists the typical activities of a ULO.

Box 36: Typical activities of a user-led organisation
- Information and advice.
- Advocacy.
- Support with direct payments.
- Assistance with assessment.
- Support in employing personal assistants.
- Equality training.
- Campaigning.
- Involvement with provider bodies.
- Support to statutory agencies in fulfilling their equality duties.

ULO activity may be limited in some areas. Some existing ULOs are small, have few resources, are not given recognition or do not have the capacity to tender.

The idea has been promoted that users should be involved at all stages of commissioning, to make sure that services meet their needs and preferences. This does not exist in all councils but in Scotland it was suggested that the user contribution could be directed at user involvement in commissioning through the processes set out in Box 37.

Box 37: Potential user involvement in commissioning
- Identifying needs and what the services should achieve.
- Identifying what services should be in place.
- Considering how the right range of services should be available.
- Working with providers to develop services.
- Developing procurement strategies and plans.
- Undertaking procurement exercises.
- Monitoring and reviewing services

Source: Audit Scotland (2012, p 33)

The Centre for Policy on Ageing (Clarke, 2011) has given illustrations of different practices enabling older people to practise self-directed support. 'Expert Elders' Sheffield was a network of older people involved in service reviews, evaluations and quality assurance in the POPPs. Cambridgeshire Older People's Reference Group was set up to strengthen the voice of older people across the county. There has also been strong user support for low-intensity handyman schemes, care and repair agencies in Wales, place-based support and advice services. Examples of users having a real say in commissioning are limited, but projects in Dorset and Salford produced service change and improvements but within narrow limits (Wistow, 2011).

User participation in research and evaluation

There is a long history of user involvement in research and evaluation as a matter of course and with most such work the researchers would wish to include the views and perspectives of users on the quality of services and delivery. There has been a trend to involve users in all aspects of research in social care. Warren (2009, p 15) identifies a distribution of power between those conducting research and those being researched. This is the idea that users should not just be treated as subjects but should be involved in all stages, in preliminary discussions, in designing the proposal, in commissioning if applicable, in sitting on research steering committees and in the dissemination of results. The rationale for such participation has been expressed as valuing user knowledge and expertise, collaboration and increasing the relevance of research (Brown and Young, 2008, p 92). Some user groups have also been carrying out research in partnership with academics. INVOLVE is a Department of Health-sponsored organisation in England to promote public involvement in health and social care research. This approach has faced a difficulty with the demands of ethical approval for social care research, which largely give control over research access to users or subjects to managers and formal committees.

User involvement in education and training

In the last decade the involvement of users has become central to professional education and training in social work at all levels and in other qualifications in social care. Education providers of social work have shown a strong commitment to collaboration between social work academic staff and users. From 2003 it became Department of Health policy in England to require the inclusion and participation of users in the design, delivery and evaluation of programmes and in the selection of social work students; while in 2003 the GSCC allocated special funding to higher education providers to support user involvement (GSCC, 2006). It is a requirement of the standards in social work education, the framework for the new social work degree, that users are involved in all aspects of the degree. In

2003 the requirement to involve service users was changed to include carers. The value of the knowledge of users and carers is seen as different from but equal to professional and academic knowledge. Studies have shown a wide range of user involvement whether individually or in groups. In the classroom, involvement has meant teaching, participation in discussions and the individual personal story or 'testimony' case study approach, giving the user's experience, perspectives and views and the realities of experiencing social work intervention and throwing practical light on anti-oppressive practice. Some involvement may be on a one-to-one basis or even involve visits (Stevens and Tanner, 2006). It has become practice to involve user groups in curriculum design, programme monitoring and review, quality assessment (Ferguson and Ager, 2005) and also programme management. More radical for higher education has been user involvement in student recruitment and assessment, including practice assessment.

The involvement of service users in social work education and training is set out in Box 38.

Box 38: Focus of service user involvement in teaching
- Design of degree, all areas of curriculum.
- Contribution of written material, videos, audio.
- Student selection.
- Teaching and learning through participation in seminars, conversation,
- role play.
- Preparation for practice learning.
- Operation of placements.
- Student visits.
- Assessment of students.
- Quality assurance.
- Course management.

Source: Based on Sadd (2011, p 11)

By 2009, the GSCC had reported that user involvement was now a central and invaluable part of social work training (GSCC, 2010). The Social Work Reform Board in developing new proposals for social work education and training set a basic underpinning principle that service users and carers should be consistently and substantially involved in the design and delivery of courses (Department for Education, 2011). The newly established College of Social Work as the professional social work body, and intended as a powerful voice for the profession, has as part of its mission building relationships with user- and carer-led organisations and involving service users and carers in everything it does (The College of Social Work, 2011). The GSCC ceased to exist in July 2012. With an expected lessening of requirements to participate there may be a loss of resources to support involvement. The replacement organisation, the Health and Care Professions Council, will be under pressure to recognise the value of user involvement. This change will provide an opportunity to review capacity, support and dissemination of good practice in involvement, but a move to more employment-based training may diminish user involvement.

User involvement has to be underpinned with practical training and support, in such matters as presentations and communication in teaching settings. Duffy (2006) cites the small group/seminar as most favoured by users. Instruction in social work values, anti-discrimination practices and equality duties has formed part of the training. Building the capacity and the selection of users has raised issues. Should users be affiliated to ULOs and can they be selected to represent the diversity of user categories? It may be difficult to attract marginalised representatives or find users willing to participate (Simmons and Birchall, 2005). It is customary to pay users as with part-time or occasional teachers. There has been a process of development of an experienced cadre of users and the term 'experts by experience' has been used although this means in part a professionalisation of users and even a career opportunity. It has also been noted that user involvement can benefit those participating in other ways in building skills, self-confidence and esteem and encouraging their own reflection (Simmons and Birchall, 2005, p 277). User involvement does require time and resources but the evidence is that all educational institutions have adapted to user involvement in teaching and selection (GSCC, 2008) and have been innovative in overcoming barriers. Wallcraft et al (2012, p 6) identify two different approaches to creating an infrastructure for involvement: higher education institutions either develop their own internal user and carer forum or they contract with an external organisation.

The benefits are usually described in terms of the influence on student attitudes and understanding, challenging and reducing stereotyping, creating empathy with users and users' knowledge improving practice. User involvement can strongly influence the quality of care and may also contribute to it being based on theorising as, for example, with their contribution to the social model of disability (Beresford, 2000). The key benefits of user involvement in education and training are listed in Box 39.

Box 39: Benefits of service user involvement in education

- Improving the performance of social work.
- Understanding of how it is to be in receipt of services.
- Understanding the power of social workers and power imbalances.
- Giving diverse perspectives from personal experiences.
- Helping prepare studies for practice.
- Promoting respect from connecting with users.
- Assisting awareness of seniors.
- Linking theory and practice and bringing theory to life.

- Highlighting gaps in services.
- Changing the image of users away from passive recipients.
- Giving voice and recognition to carers.
- Keeping academic staff up to date.

Source: Adapted from Sadd (2011)

A study of the impact of participation in social work education following the introduction of the new degree curriculum in 2003 found that the requirement to involve service users and carers made a real difference to the quality of social work education (GSCC, 2006). There tend to be high levels of student satisfaction with user and carer involvement.

This report also highlighted factors facilitating beneficial outcomes, such as participation and regular reviews as well as identifying some barriers over payments and practice experience. Service user and carer participation was identified (Sadd, 2011) as most developed in selection and recruitment, involvement in teaching and learning and assessment and preparation for practice, but less well developed in the design of courses, placement and quality assurance. Studies have demonstrated that the mandatory involvement of users and carers is a very powerful policy development (SCIE, 2009b). These reports have identified examples of good practice in some areas but patchy performance in others. A major study (Wallcraft et al, 2012) found some difference by programme. In qualifying social work degrees the strongest areas of involvement were recruitment, selection and teaching and the weakest was assessment. In post-qualifying programmes the strongest were teaching course design, quality assurance and development.

As user and carer participation is a relatively new development it requires stable and adequate resourcing. The original GSCC funding has not been adequate and has had to be supplemented by higher education institutions from their own resources. This important role for user involvement does have some unusual features in that it has been introduced in a more systematic way in social care education and training than in other comparable professions. Some criticisms have emerged relating to a degree of incongruence with the underdeveloped user participation in actual service delivery and to the practical rather than theoretical focus of user involvement. Molyneux and Irvine (2004) found no single successful format and some users being over-consulted. Taylor and LeRiche (2006) could not identify any research that substantially claimed that user involvement in education improved the quality of practice. While acknowledging that social care user and carer involvement required a shift in the local culture of social work education, Anghel and Ramon (2009), in an active research evaluation, stressed the value of service users' and carers' involvement. Wallcraft et al (2012, p 5) assessed the evidence as showing involvement bringing positive changes in the perceptions of learning of service users and carers, as well as staff, and the acquisition of knowledge and skills. However, they found no evidence of this learning being transferred to practice, or changes in organisational policy to directly benefit service users. A review of 29 studies on user and carer involvement also found little empirical evidence that it improved outcomes for students or affected social work practice (Robinson and Webber, 2012). There is still a need to produce a research base for the outcomes of user and carer involvement in social work education.

User involvement in regulation and inspection

Regulation and inspection bodies have given a major role to users and the principles of user involvement. This means an acceptance that users' views and experience must play an important part in the regulation and inspection process for adult social care conducted by the relevant agencies. The introduction of devolution has had a major impact on the structures of governance, with different inspection and regulation bodies for each of the four countries of the UK, as shown in Box 40.

Box 40: UK inspection and social care regulatory bodies

UK inspection bodies
Care Quality Commission (England)
Scottish Commission for the Regulation of Care
Care and Social Services Inspectorate Wales
Regulation and Quality Improvement Authority (Northern Ireland)

UK social care regulatory bodies
Health and Care Professions Council (England)
Scottish Social Services Council
Care Council for Wales
Northern Ireland Social Care Council

The inspection bodies have all taken the view that the input of users and the public should be central to the regulators' work in assessing service quality and improving services for everyone. It is important that people who use services contribute to the information that regulators gather and use and engage directly with regulators. By inviting participants, regulators are entering a relationship with users and need to outline their expectations and what users can expect. The CQC as the newest body has given prominence to getting people involved. It has published *Voices into action* (CQC, 2007), a statement of involvement that sets out how the commission will involve people in its work and was subject to a consultation. *Voices into action* endorsed a number of principles:

- Involvement must be real, ensure a diverse range of people are involved and no group should be overlooked.
- Involvement should be flexible and provide feedback on involvement provided.
- There should be clear guidelines and standards to inform people's involvement activities.
- Barriers to participation should be removed.
- There should be outreach to a wide range of people.
- Evidence of outcomes should be produced.

The CQC has set up panels to give advice from across the sector, promotes involvement by email and also runs focus groups. The CQC has set up a number of bodies:

- a Mental Health Improvement Board with a membership of users, carers and representatives of mental health organisations to advise on priority areas and improve outcomes;
- a People with Learning Disabilities Advisory Panel to share ideas and experiences about services;
- a LINks advisory group to build a special relationship with local involvement networks
- an innovative Speak Out Network of some 80 groups that are often not heard, to enable them to have a strong voice.

The Scottish Commission for the Regulation of Care has adopted a key ethos of putting people at the heart of regulation. Among the ways of getting involved has been an Involving People Group, which had the aim of developing new user-friendly ways to improve care. Members could take part by post or email. The Care and Social Services Inspectorate Wales covers inspection and evaluation of local authority social services and care settings and agencies.

There has been some significant progress in fully involving people who use services in inspections. This means not only inspectors talking to service users but in the case of the CQC having experts by experience taking part in inspections. Experts by experience are trained and supported and also go on council adult services inspections, meet staff and contribute to overall findings. The CQC has also a service user reference panel to provide a service user perspective on activity around the Mental Health Act. The panel is made up of people who are currently or have recently been detained. The Scottish Commission for the Regulation of Care has a system of lay assessors, which is seen as a crucial mechanism for supporting the involvements of users. They have a background of being a service user or carer and are seen as very suited to communicating with users and their own experience adds value to inspections. Training and support through coordinators are provided.

While there have been some claims that there is no evidence to indicate that the involvement of service users has improved the quality of inspections, in discussing the issue, Scourfield (2010, p 1904) has suggested the use of the term 'experts by experience' as leading to conceptual confusion and the use of the term is contestable in the context of service inspections.

Four care councils in the UK are responsible for workforce regulation and registration and also for regulating education and training. Research in 2003 found some service users on boards of councils but not an organisation-wide user focus and a lack of coordination (Hasler, 2003). The GSCC (2005) produced a set of eight principles, which also covered the Commission for Social Care Inspection that preceded the CQC and workforce skills bodies. These principles were minimum standards for involving service users and carers:

- clearly identifying benefits of involving service users or carers;
- working with those who use services to agree the way they are involved;
- letting service users and carers choose the way they become involved;
- developing methods to provide feedback on the outcome of involvement;
- overcoming barriers to involvement;
- including the widest possible range of people;
- paying or compensating service users;
- using the experience of users and carers to influence changes.

The Care Council for Wales developed a service user and carer participation strategy in 2007, setting out principles, standards and priorities (Care Council for Wales, 2007). This framework involved shaping the standards for social care workers, the codes of practice and the skills of social care workers in national occupational standards and also the standards for user participation in planning and delivering social work training programmes.

The Northern Ireland Social Care Council has a participation group to promote user and carer reference groups and to provide a user perspective, but the participation group's role is limited.

The establishment of adult safeguarding boards has also raised the issue of user and carer involvement options. Safeguarding boards in England have not as a matter of routine had users and carers represented on their boards (Barnes et al, 2010). Some boards do have one or two 'lay membership' posts but these individuals may or may not be users. The establishment of sub-groups of boards has created more opportunities for user involvement. Wallcraft and Sweeney (2011) also describe a number of specific innovations through service user reference groups or safeguarding adults forums to link with the safeguarding board. Service users can also play a major role in the training of staff and providing user experience of having been through a safeguarding procedure.

HealthWatch England

Following the White Paper *Equity and excellence* (DH, 2010f) and the consultation processes, the Coalition government's Health and Social Care Bill made provisions for the establishment of HealthWatch to champion service users and carers. The government saw this as part of 'no decision about me without me' and that citizens, not service providers or systems, should have choice and control over how their care and support are provided (DH, 2011c). This new system will from 2013, as with LINks, cover health and social care. HealthWatch will exist in two distinct forms – local HealthWatch organisations and national HealthWatch England. It is also closely aligned with local authorities, so it was an evolution from LINks. Local authorities will be able to commission activities from local HealthWatch organisations. Local HealthWatch organisations will be expected to be highly visible in the local community, draw on diverse groups and provide a strong, independent, local consumer voice. They will monitor local services and recommend improvements to providers and commissioners and will have the power of entry to visit any core services. They will ensure that the views and feedback from patients and carers influence local commissioners and providers across health and social care and will provide information and advice to support people in making choices. They can report concerns to national HealthWatch about the quality of services independent of local government.

HealthWatch England will provide advice and support to local HealthWatch organisations. HealthWatch England will also advise the NHS Commissioning Board, Monitor and the Secretary of State, including advice on the provision of care services. An innovative and controversial aspect is that local HealthWatch will be a statutory part of the much-criticised NHS regulator, the CQC, but a separate arm, to retain independence. HealthWatch England will have powers to propose CQC investigations of poorly performing health and social care services. While the HealthWatch provisions have been put forward as giving people more say in how services are delivered, it may suggest more a consumer or consultative voice rather than a commitment to greater user involvement. The Department of Health claims that HealthWatch will give people real influence over decisions made about local services (DH, 2011d). Box 41 shows how HealthWatch is intended to be a local consumer voice.

Box 41: Local HealthWatch – promoting local consumer voice

Local HealthWatch
'Local consumer voice for health and social care'
Influencing – help shape the planning of health and social care services
Signposting – help people access and make choices about care
Advisory – advocacy for individuals making complaints

Key differences between local HealthWatch and LINks

From	To
Influence local services	Participate in decision making via local authority health and wellbeing board

Focus on community voice	Help and support for individuals
Local voice	Local and national voice through HealthWatch England *Source:* DH (2011d, pp 16-18)

Impact and assessment

Assessments of user participation have continued to find some problems and difficulties in the implementation of principles and strategies. There is still some evidence that user involvement strategies have not been totally effective or realised their objectives and there are still criticisms of tokenism and users being left powerless, with user involvement grafted on to existing decision-making structures (Warren, 2009, p 56). Lewis (2009) suggested that in mental health the aims of user involvement are not fully realised in practice and the use of compulsory powers does not help. Research by Duffy (2008) in Northern Ireland states that the extent to which meaningful involvement has been achieved is questionable. Users themselves have been able to articulate barriers to better participation: costs, time, transport, childcare, communication, environment and flexible arrangements with professional partners (Tyler, 2006). Questions can be raised about the representativeness of user involvement, limits to their capacity and a continuing disengagement of some service users and populations with heightened levels of need that are hard to reach.

A number of seldom-heard groups have been identified who are often excluded from service user participation, for example, people from black and minority ethnic communities and people with addictions. Some staff in health and social care may believe that people with certain conditions, communications impairments or dementia are not able to contribute. Developing mechanisms through which frail older people can influence planning and provision and have their voices heard can require a strong commitment (Barnes and Walker, 1996). In a study of seldom-heard users, Hernandez et al (2010) identified practices that would facilitate participation, including flexible and confidence-building approaches and meeting groups' practical needs before involvement in research and development projects.

It is also the case that users have a variety of perspectives and motives with regard to why they wish to get involved (Robson et al, 2008). These may include personal enthusiasm, interest or identification with a service or group, or be a consequence of an individual experience or complaint. Some research has indicated that users exercise choice about voice and are willing to use different mechanisms as best appropriate to the circumstances, whether statutory processes, group-based activities or individual initiatives (Simmons, 2011). There may also be attitudinal barriers, for example, users may not wish to be critical as they may think it will affect their own treatment by a provider; or they largely think that their view will be ignored anyway; or they may be encroaching on the role of local elected representatives. Robson et al (2008, p 11) identified tensions and uncertainties between traditional provider approaches and expectations and user approaches. Table 10 presents an adapted version.

Table 10: Tensions in user involvement

Traditional providers	Users
Clear purpose of service	Varieties of choice
Clear expectation of people using service	Flexibility and adaptation of response
Output-based expectations/targets	Responsive to user views and priorities
Focus-led/directed consultation	Open consultation
High expectation of involved users	Realistic about user capacity
Role of professional expertise	Contribute expertise by experience
Management role	Sharing of decision making
Constrained/defined role for users	Participate in all aspects of a service
Limited to certain activities	Flexible
Controlled by a management strategy	Bottom-up determination
Accountability as line management	Accountability to the public

In securing necessary cultural change in the attitude of providers and professionals, Simmons (2011, p 552) notes that while many users are willing to share their views with providers in the interests of the service, there are mixed views about the extent to which providers are interested in making opportunities for this. In adult social care there may still be a dominance of a traditional managerial ethos and traditional committee structures. There can also be problems with the required interaction with elected councillors. It is still judged complex to assess the outcome of user participation in terms of the impact on service improvement. A study (Carr, 2004) on the main differences that user participation added to social care services found the evidence patchy and problems with organising representatives. It is difficult to isolate user involvement as a causal factor and more longitudinal studies may be necessary or more specialist analysis such as network analysis (Webb, 2008). There are also more sceptical views about the whole exercise as still embedded in neoliberal agendas and individualist approaches (Carr, 2007; Carey, 2009), while Beresford (2010, p 245) sees even co-production strategies as at risk of incorporation into developments antithetical to users' interests and of being submerged into managerialist/consumerist projects or subject to manipulation. The emergence of groupings of professional users to participate in policy making and implementation has also been criticised (Cowden and Singh, 2007). At the practical level the capacity of users to engage has been affected by expenditure cuts, particularly impacting on innovative schemes and new areas of involvement.

There is some uncertainty about the future pathway or user involvement, as it possibly faces degrees of marginalisation because of reduced financing, scepticism and lower policy priority.

Conclusions

- A wide range of initiatives and areas of activity for user involvement can be identified covering forms of formal representation and mechanisms for user involvement.
- The principles, forms, subject and outcomes of user involvement may differ between service areas, that is, between mental health, older people, physical disability and learning disability.
- The form, shape and outcome of user involvement may also vary between administrative levels in:
  - local government;
  - partnerships with health trusts and boards;
  - national bodies in four countries;
  - specialist ad-hoc forums.
- Following devolution, an increasing importance has been given to user involvement, with some policy and strategy differences emerging based on underlying principles and ideology. The Scottish and Welsh administrations have developed commitments to more radical forms of user involvement and England has developed policies with a strong localist dimension. Only in Northern Ireland has the restructuring of health and social care not led to priority being given to strong, localised systems of public involvement.
- Co-production has emerged as a popular principle encompassing user participation and as a contribution to greater efficiency.

Sources

The rationale for user involvement in social care is well covered by Beresford (2002 and 2010) and Beresford and Croft (2004). Bochel et al (2008) provide a useful typology of participation. Needham (2008) looks at the concept of co-production; Needham and Carr (2009) and Bovaird (2007) explore issues relating to the realisation of co-production. Hernandez et al (2010) discuss the involvement of 'seldom heard users'. The involvement of users in social work education is covered by Sadd (2011) and Wallcraft et al (2012).

Questions

- What are the main factors underpinning government interest in the concept of public participation?

- What initiatives have been introduced to promote and develop user involvement in adult social care and do these differ substantially between the countries of the UK?

- What are the characteristics of the co-production model of user involvement and to what extent does this represent a more radical and innovative way of achieving better outcomes for users?

- What has research identified as the key challenges to effective user involvement in adult social care policy and provision?

TEN

Regulatory frameworks, inspection and safeguarding

Overview

On 31 May 2011 the BBC *Panorama* programme broadcast secret filming showing a pattern of serious abuses at Winterbourne View residential hospital, a private facility for people with learning disabilities and autism. Although the case had been reported to the CQC in December 2010, the commission had taken no action. A few months later, revelations of poor standards and neglect in home care were revealed in an inquiry by the Equality and Human Rights Commission (2011) and in residential care in a report published by the Northern Ireland Human Rights Commission (NIHRC, 2012). This chapter looks at the regulation and inspection of adult social care provision and considers policy and provision for the safeguarding of vulnerable adults. It also considers the policy response to some long-term problems and examines new challenges relating to safeguarding emerging from different ways of providing care.

Panorama reporter Joe Casey spent five weeks filming undercover in Winterbourne View private care hospital after getting a job as a support worker. The extract from his report in Box 42 illustrates the abuse and neglect he witnessed.

Box 42: Extract from the *Panorama* report on Winterbourne View private care hospital

'My experience at Winterbourne View will stay with me for a very long time.

The hitting, slapping, bullying, dousing with water, cruel and often pointless use of physical restraint on people – many with a child-like understanding of the world – all happened in front of my eyes. On a near-daily basis, I watched as some of the very people entrusted with the care of society's most vulnerable targeted patients – often, it seemed, for their own amusement. The targets had no way of defending themselves or speaking out. Anyone who questioned the abuse met a wall of silence....

During my first days in the hospital I was struck by the sense of boredom that permeated the days. With little to do, the patients were either watching television in the lounge or sleeping in their rooms. The smattering of activities were rarely inspired. At one point, staff resorted to reading to patients from a general knowledge textbook.

While some support workers seemed to genuinely enjoy their work, others seemed just as bored and frustrated as the patients.'

Source: Panorama report on Winterbourne View (2011), www.bbc.co.uk/panorama/hi/front_page/newsid_9501000/9501531.stm

The Northern Ireland Human Rights Commission (NIHRC), in the report of its inquiry into nursing home care (NIHRC, 2012), provides examples of individual experiences and views, including contributions from staff, often expressing frustration at not having enough time to speak with residents. The views of one worker are reproduced in Box 43.

Box 43: Extract from the NIHRC inquiry report into nursing home care

'You go off a wee bit frustrated sometimes because you think you haven't given your best. I haven't spent long enough talking to somebody and then I thought, "there is a lady there I haven't spoken to all day hardly because I hadn't time". I think that is terrible but it happens and there you are. We don't even have time to talk to the residents or anything. You would love to sit down and have a yarn with them and find out about their past and what they did, what they worked as – and I couldn't even tell you....You don't have time to have a conversation with them to find out.'

Source: NIHRC (2012, p 32)

These reports and revelations about standards of care raised fundamental issues and provoked a significant media and public response. One of the questions often asked was how, despite the existence of regulatory frameworks, quality standards and inspecting bodies, these appalling cases of abuse and neglect could occur and go unaddressed. Box 44 presents some of the newspaper headlines relating to adult care provision in 2011 and 2012.

Box 44: Newspaper headlines in 2011 and 2012 relating to adult care provision

* 'Care home quango faces claims it put patients at risk after failing to spot serious abuse' (*Daily Mail*, 16 November 2011)
* 'Patients robbed and abused by their carers' (*Daily Express*, 23 November 2011)
* 'Cruelty of the carers: damning report into home help for the elderly finds neglect so appalling some wanted to die' (*Daily Mail*, 23 November 2011)
* 'Winterbourne View staff charged with neglect and ill-treatment' (*The Guardian*, 28 November 2011)
* 'Homecare for elderly "disgraceful"' (*The Guardian*, 16 March 2012)

Media coverage in the wake of the above revelations would suggest that people were profoundly shocked and disturbed. Many of those watching the *Panorama* programme or reading about the inquiries would have had a relative or friend being looked after at home or in a residential setting; some may have been contemplating going into care. Others may themselves have been victims of abuse. The disclosures raised questions about how society cares for and protects or fails to protect vulnerable people, about the vetting and training of staff, the adequacy of safeguarding measures and the rigour of the inspection regime.

Framework for regulation

While the regulation of health professionals is devolved to the Northern Ireland Assembly (and to some extent the Scottish Government), there is a UK-wide regulatory machine. In social care, however, regulation of the workforce is devolved and there are separate regulatory systems and bodies in the four countries of the UK. While social work is a regulated profession and all social workers in the UK have to be registered, the majority of the social care workforce is unregulated. Currently, social care workers in the UK are regulated by four separate councils, which came into operation in 2001. The GSCC in England, the Northern Ireland Social Care Council, the Scottish Social Care Council and the Care Council for Wales had similar responsibilities for a registration scheme, training standards, the accreditation of social work qualifying and post-qualifying qualifications and codes of practice. Following a review of arm's length bodies (DH, 2010c), the Coalition government announced the abolition of the GSCC and the transfer of its regulatory functions to the Health Professions Council – renamed the Health and Care Professions Council (HCPC) (DH, 2012g). The councils in Scotland, Wales and Northern Ireland will continue. The HCPC will assume responsibilities for regulating social work education but post-qualifying courses will not be accredited by the HCPC. A new professional body – The College of Social Work – will be responsible for producing clear career frameworks and guidance for continuing professional development. Set up in January 2012, it emerged from the Social Work Taskforce, which had recommended the establishment of an independent college of social work to champion the profession (DH, 2009b). It has a primary focus on professional standards, including the professional capabilities framework, and its remit includes social work policy development. It is initially being run by an appointed board but this will be replaced by an elected board in 2013.

Workforce registration

Registration requirements for social care workers, although not for social workers, vary across the UK. Each jurisdiction requires social workers to be registered with the relevant council. Requirements across the UK regarding workforce registration are set out in Table 11.

Table 11: Workforce registration requirements

Scotland	Since 2009, managers of adult day services (and managers of residential and childcare services) have had to register. By 2015, a wide range of social care workers will be compelled to register.
Wales	Residential childcare workers and managers have to register with the Care Council for Wales and this has also been the case for managers in adult care services from 2012.
Northern Ireland	The compulsory registration of social care workers with the Northern Ireland Social Care Council is taking place on a staged basis. Social care managers of residential, day care and domiciliary care were to be registered by September 2011 and social care workers in adult residential or nursing homes settings by December 2012. When they register, social care workers will also be required to undertake specific training.
England	No compulsory registration for social care workers exists, although it does exist for social workers.

A Law Commission review of regulation of health and social care professionals concluded that the current system was complex, fragmented and expensive and in a consultative document (Law Commission, 2012) it recommended revising existing legislation that governs regulators, with new measures that would include regulators having the power to fine those found unfit to practice. This consultative document is a joint paper by the Law Commission, the Scottish Law Commission and the Northern Ireland Law Commission, although the remit of the review with regard to the social work profession is restricted to England.

Regulation and inspection bodies

Systems for inspection and quality improvements have gone through a number of changes in each of the countries of the UK since devolution but while there are some differences in structure, the policy direction has been broadly similar. Across the UK the scrutiny of public services has been influenced by a number of reviews, including the Hampton Review (2005) in England and the Crerar Review of regulation, audit and inspection in Scotland (Scottish Government, 2007), which advocated a more risk-based and proportionate response to regulation and inspection.

In England, the CQC is the regulator for health and social care and is also responsible for people detained under the Mental Health Act. It was created in 2009 as a result of a merger of three organisations – the Healthcare Commission, the Commission for Social Care Inspection and the Mental Health Commission. It was also the third social care regulatory body in eight years – the National Care Standards Commission set up in 2002 was replaced in 2004 by the Commission for Social Care and Inspection. Since April 2010, all health and adult social care providers (including providers of domiciliary care) have had to be registered and licensed with the Commission, which regulates against 28 standards, 16 of which are 'essential standards' of quality and safety (see Box 45). Each of the standards has an associated outcome (CQC, 2010). Under the previous system, care homes were registered and given quality ratings against a set of national minimum standards. The decision to move away from this attracted criticism that it would make the system less transparent for the public. Providers need to show that they are meeting the essential standards through a process of compliance monitoring carried out by the commission. The case study in Box 46 outlines the process of inspection and the outcome. The commission has a range of enforcement powers and has power of prosecution.

Box 45: Essential standards focused on by the CQC

1. *Respecting and involving people who use services:* People should be treated with respect, involved in discussions about their care and treatment and able to influence how the service is run.

2. *Consent to care and treatment:* Before people are given any examination, care, treatment or support, they should be asked if they agree to it.

3. *Care and welfare of people who use services:* People should get safe and appropriate care that meets their needs and supports their rights.

4. *Meeting nutritional needs:* Food and drink should meet people's individual dietary needs.

5. *Cooperating with other providers:* People should get safe and coordinated care when they move between different services.

6. *Safeguarding vulnerable people who use services:* People should be protected from abuse and staff should respect their human rights.

7. *Cleanliness and infection control:* People should be cared for in a clean environment and protected from the risk of infection.

8. *Management of medicines:* People should be given the medicines they need when they need them, and in a safe way.

9. *Safety and suitability of premises:* People should be cared for in safe and accessible surroundings that support their health and welfare.

10. *Safety, availability and suitability of equipment:* People should be safe from harm from unsafe or unsuitable equipment.

11. *Requirements relating to workers:* People should be cared for by staff who are properly qualified and able to do their job.

12. *Staffing:* There should be enough members of staff to keep people safe and meet their health and welfare needs.

13. *Supporting workers:* Staff should be properly trained and supervised, and have the chance to develop and improve their skills.

14. *Assessing and monitoring the quality of service provision:* The service should have quality checking systems to manage risks and assure the health, welfare and safety of people who receive care.

15. *Complaints:* People should have their complaints listened to and acted on properly.
16. *Records:* People's personal records, including medical records, should be accurate and kept safe and confidential.

Source: CQC, 2010

Box 46: CQC case study

'In August 2011, our inspectors visited a care home in the South West, which cares for 40 older people, some of whom need nursing as well as personal care. We found concerns with eight of the 16 government standards and in four of these cases our concerns were serious enough for us to issue warning notices.

In February this year, our inspectors returned to the care home to check what kind of action the care home management had taken in response to our warnings and concerns. We spoke to the people in the home, to their relatives visiting them and to staff at the home, not only the nursing and care staff but to laundry, kitchen staff and the cook.

Last summer our inspectors found that people in the home were not being treated with dignity and respect and there were failings over their care and welfare. Serious concerns included communal use of laundered continence underwear, lack of privacy in toileting, the use of a hoist in the living room to relieve pressure, no choice of activity offered to people in the home and failure to knock before entering bedrooms.

One resident complained of the lack of activity and respect for her individual needs: "There is nothing to do here," she said, "I was asked if I'd like to make a pom-pom."

Our inspectors issued a warning notice to the home relating to this outcome, demanding an action plan to make improvements. A similar warning notice related to the poor level of food and drink provided and a third demanded repairs to the inadequate bathing facilities at the home where some of the rooms had no running hot water. The final warning notice we issued mandated improvements in record-keeping.

Further concerns related to insufficient staff to meet people's needs, to the management of medicines and the monitoring on a continual basis of the quality of service provided.

When our inspectors returned four months later, we found that fair progress was being made in overcoming the home's failings. A new acting manager was in post and additional staff had been recruited.

Our inspectors spoke again with people in the home to understand their experience of being treated with dignity and recorded their views in the report such as "Staff knock and wait more than they used to". The laundry and the kitchen staff now follow new rules of hygiene and meet nutritional needs and keep meticulous records on the personal care and nutritional needs of the people in the home.

New hoist equipment and hot water to rooms is now in place although our inspectors noted that there are still inadequate bathing facilities. There is still room for improvement too in how the care home will audit the quality of the service it provides to people on a continuous basis although the acting manager was able to share with us her plans for doing so.

We have informed the home that they are still required to respond to us with an action plan to make sure they are fully compliant. Our inspectors will return to the home this spring to report on the home's further progress with meeting all government standards.

Source: www.cqc.org.uk/public/news/case-study-warning-notices-over-failure-treat-people-respect

Recent health and social care policy developments have included a number of new initiatives in the area of quality standards and monitoring. The Health and Social Care Act 2012 extended the remit of the National Institute for Health and Clinical Excellence (NICE) to include developing quality standards for social care in England (from 1 April 2013, NICE will be renamed the National Institute for Health and Care Excellence). NICE provides national guidance and standards in relation to healthcare promotion and provision, with a strong emphasis on this guidance being built on evidence and knowledge. The first two care quality standards – on dementia care and the health and wellbeing of looked-after children – were published by NICE for consultation in August 2012 (NICE, 2012). The Department of Health has indicated that one focus for NICE in the immediate future will be the production of a social care quality standard on home care (DH, 2012a). NICE and the CQC are expected to work together to ensure that standards are complementary. Measures to increase transparency and access to information about poor-quality services are outlined in the 2012 White Paper on adult social care (DH, 2012a), including the publication by the Ombudsman of the names of local authorities or providers against which complaints have been upheld and the requirement on every home care provider to have a provider quality profile on the NHS and social care information website (www.nhs.uk/carersdirect/guide/practicalsupport/pages/carehomes.aspx), which should include details on how the care provider meets the CQC's essential standards (DH, 2012a).

In Northern Ireland, it is also a single body – the RQIA – set up in 2005, which governs health and social care. Child protection and children's residential homes are also part of its remit. In 2009, it took over regulation of mental health services from the Mental Health Commission. A set of minimum standards for adult social care has been developed for a range of services, including nursing homes, residential care and day care settings and these are based on a number of principles, including dignity, independence, equality, diversity and choice (DHSSPS, 2011d).

At the local level, there are adult safeguarding partnerships in each trust. A new RQIA inspection process was introduced in 2009 with a focus on outcomes for users, targeting inspection at areas where the greatest improvement was needed and making more information publicly available. A Northern Ireland Audit Office report (2010, para 3.3) was critical of aspects of the RQIA's work, stating that it could do more to collate requirements and recommendations across a range of inspections and use this information to determine training needs. It also expressed concern that the complaints monitoring failed to capture the *record* of complaints in independent sector homes, which could help to identify an accumulation of minor issues that could adversely affect quality of life and/or be indicative of abuse.

Post devolution, the regulation of health and social care services in Scotland was split. Social care services in Scotland were the responsibility of two bodies – the Care Commission and the Social Work Inspection Agency. A review into the regulation of public services in Scotland – the Crerar Review (Scottish Government, 2007) – recommended a simplification of scrutiny bodies. The Public Services Reform (Scotland) Act 2010 legislated for the replacement of the two with a single body – the Social Care and Social Work Improvement Scotland (its everyday name became the Care Inspectorate in September 2011), which became operational in April 2011. The Care Inspectorate is an independent scrutiny and improvement body for adult care and children's services. All Care Inspectorate-authorised inspectors have to be registered and are required to gain a qualification in regulation. A separate body – Healthcare Improvement Scotland – is responsible for the scrutiny of healthcare services. The Care Inspectorate regulates 18 out of the 23 National Care Standards (with the remainder the responsibility of Health Improvement Scotland). These were first developed in 2002 and revised in 2004 and accompanied by a set of benchmarks that adopted a person–centred approach to assessment (Stein et al, 2010). The standards are based on six main principles:

- dignity;
- privacy;
- choice;
- safety;
- realising potential;
- equality and diversity.

Since April 2008, inspections have been based on a set of quality statements using a Quality Assessment Framework, which was argued to be easier for assessors, providers and the public (Care Commission, 2007). An inquiry into the regulation of care for older people (Scottish Parliament, 2011a) recommended a review of the standards to take into account developments such as the number of older people with dementia and the need to embed equality and human rights into the delivery of services. It also recommended that consideration be given to the establishment of a single point of entry for complaints about integrated services given the policy moves towards more integration of health and social care.

The catalyst for a Health and Sport Committee inquiry was a series of high-profile events in the care sector, including a police investigation into the death of a resident at an Edinburgh nursing home in May 2011, and the issues raised by the closure of the care home provision by the Southern Cross Group in July 2011, which affected more than 90 care homes in Scotland. The remit of the inquiry included a review of the regulatory regime, and subsequent to it changes to the regulatory system in Scotland were announced in the Scottish Parliament in September 2011. Specifically, the inquiry asked for a revised statutory inspection regime for all care homes and personal care and support services to be inspected at least once every year rather than once every two years (Scottish Parliament, 2011a) – the Public Services Reform (Scotland) Act 2010 had removed the statutory minimum frequency for inspections. This recommendation was accepted and new statutory minimum frequency rules were introduced in early 2012, meaning that every care home and care at home service would receive at least one unannounced inspection each year (Scottish Government, 2012b).

As in Scotland, two regulatory bodies had initially been established in Wales after devolution – a Social Services Inspectorate for Wales and a Care Standards Inspectorate for Wales. In 2007, the Welsh Assembly Government announced the amalgamation of the two bodies and the Care and Social Services Inspectorate for Wales was created, which regulates and inspects all social care provision (plus early years), deals with complaints and enforcement and is responsible for quality improvement. Unlike the other UK inspection bodies it is part of a department within the Welsh Assembly Government, although it is stated that safeguards are in place to protect its independence. There has been an emphasis on joint working with the healthcare inspection bodies and the Wales Audit Office. An example of this is the joint review by Healthcare Inspectorate Wales and the Care and Social Services Inspectorate on the impact of the National Service Framework for Older People (Commission for Social Care Inspectorate Wales and Healthcare Inspectorate Wales, 2012).

Before devolution, the poor standards of some adult care services and the inadequacy of provision together with the expansion of the independent sector were indicating that existing regulatory frameworks and practices were not sufficient (Stein et al, 2010). Since devolution, each of the countries of the UK has developed its own regulatory and inspection structures. The structures adopted post devolution have a number of common features: the creation of care standards; the stipulation of the frequency and numbers of inspections; the key role of inspectors and the inspection visits; although as highlighted by Stein et al (2010) the Scottish system is unique in terms of its development of measurements of risk and quality.

The effectiveness of the regulatory and inspection systems was brought into sharp focus as a result of the care scandals outlined at the start of this chapter. The CQC in particular has been the subject of a series of critical reports, which led the chief executive to resign. Criticisms have focused on its failure to manage risks (DH, 2012h), poor leadership and governance, inconsistencies in the judgements of individual inspectors and failure to provide the public with sufficient information on the quality of care (House of Commons Public Accounts Committee, 2012). The revelations of abuse at Winterbourne View led to major reviews being conducted. The Department of Health commissioned a review of Winterbourne, which included a wider investigation into how the health and care system supports vulnerable people with learning disabilities and autism. It is the latter which is the focus of the interim report (DH, 2012h). The initial findings identified referred to a 'model of care [which] goes against government policy and has no place in the 21st century' (para 3.1). It also reported evidence of poor quality of care, poor care planning, lack of meaningful activities to do in the day and too much reliance on restraining people (p 7). The review identified 14 national actions with a focus on promoting home care and setting and achieving higher standards, including the development of quality standards on learning disabilities by NICE. A serious case review on Winterbourne View commissioned by South Gloucestershire's Adult Safeguarding Board (Flynn and Citarella, 2012) detailed numerous cases of physical restraint and serious assault. This highlighted major deficiencies on the part of the owners and managers of the facility and a number of organisations, which had resulted in the violence and abuse that had been exposed by the BBC *Panorama* programme. Staff were mostly unregulated support workers despite the hospital's focus on rehabilitation. The review concluded: 'Although "person-centred" care, participation and empowerment characterise national policy priorities, these were alien to the experiences of Winterbourne View Hospital patients and their families' (p 143). Some of the main findings are summarised below:

- There was a lack of leadership among commissioners who had continued to place people in the facility even though the providers were not meeting their contractual obligations.
- The response to the whistleblowing notification had been ineffective.
- While a number of safeguarding referrals were known to the local authority adult safeguarding board, this had not been treated as a significant *body* of evidence so the board had only a limited version of events at Winterbourne View.
- On paper the policy, procedures, practices and clinical governance were impressive but there were serious failings in practice.

The ramifications of events at Winterbourne View extend well beyond the hospital. The subsequent inquiries identified systems failure on a large scale and revealed attitudes and practices far removed from policy priorities and guidelines. Organisations, including the CQC, have made changes to procedures as a result of the inquiries – including classifying residential services for people with learning disabilities and challenging behaviours as 'higher risk', thereby being subject to more inspections, and setting up a specialist team to deal with whistleblowers and ensure that every contact is followed up. But more generally the inquiries have highlighted the need for more transformative change in terms of where care is provided, the qualifications and suitability of staff and the regulation and complaints system.

Complaints

Of the four regulatory and inspection bodies, only the Care Inspectorate in Scotland investigates individual complaints. The bodies in Wales, England and Northern Ireland encourage people with concerns to make them aware of them so that they can use the feedback to inform inspections. By law, every care home and social care service must have a procedure for dealing with complaints. If resolution cannot be reached at that level there is recourse to an Ombudsman in each of the four countries – in England this is the Local Government Ombudsman (LGO). In April 2009, a single, joint, complaints procedure for health and social care was introduced based on the Local Authority Social Services and National Health Services Complaints (England) Regulations 2009. Prior to this there had been two separate complaints procedures for health and social care. Research commissioned by the Local Government Ombudsman for England (Office for Public Management, 2011) into complaints in privately funded and arranged social care and how these were handled in the adult social care sector found much consistency in the issues giving rise to complaints. These included:

- poor standards and quality of care;
- poor communications with users/relatives;
- food, nutrition and mealtimes;
- fees and contracts;
- the conduct of local authorities with regard to assessment for direct payments;
- how complaints were handled.

A key finding was that some people had great difficulty even lodging a complaint in the first place, thus preventing it from entering the system.

Many users have needs that cross health and social care boundaries and, as highlighted in Chapter Six on integration, there is increasing emphasis on more effective joint working by health and social care services and the need to achieve a more seamless service. The extract in Box 47 summarises the findings from a joint review by the Local Government Ombudsman and the Health Ombudsman in England. The Ombudsmen emphasised that power to investigate complaints jointly is particularly important when health and local government join together to provide a service.

Box 47: Joint review by the Local Government Ombudsman and the Health Ombudsman

'A joint investigation by the Health Service Ombudsman and the Local Government Ombudsman revealed how a vulnerable adult in Merseyside, referred to as Mr B, was let down by the joint service provided by the NHS trust and council responsible for his care. In the report, the two Ombudsmen describe how the joint Community Mental Health service of the 5 Boroughs Partnership NHS Trust and St Helens Metropolitan Borough Council failed to monitor Mr B and respond to signs that he was at risk, resulting in the serious deterioration of his living conditions and the neglect of his personal health. Mr B had schizophrenia and had lived in his own home for more than ten years with a support package, jointly managed by the Trust and the Council through a Community Mental Health Team (CMHT). This included regular visits from a support worker and a community psychiatric nurse from the CMHT together with practical help from Council cleaners. Mr B's health and living conditions deteriorated and he was unable to care for himself. He developed a serious physical illness. His cousin, Ms A, alerted the Trust and the Council when she became concerned about his personal health and hygiene and the state of his flat. Unhappy with their response, she then complained to the Health Service Ombudsman and the Local Government Ombudsman. Ms A described how Mr B had come to their aunt's home, was extremely dirty and unkempt, had lost a great deal of weight and was feeling unwell. Ms A went to Mr B's flat and was horrified by what she saw. By Ms A's account, there were cockroaches and flies, food that was over a year out of date, uneaten takeaway food, stains on every surface, and faeces and urine stains on the carpets and furniture. She said she spent several days cleaning the flat.

When Mr B returned home, his physical health quickly deteriorated and he was admitted to hospital as an emergency. He was found to be severely malnourished, dehydrated, lethargic and confused.

The Ombudsmen found that the joint CMHT had failed Mr B. Their report highlights how Mr B's care plan was not properly implemented. Evidence given during the investigation revealed how there was poor communication and gaps in records as well as a failure to review Mr B's care, to assess in depth his mental state, capacity or risk, and to act on concerns raised about his welfare. The Council's cleaners raised concerns but little action by appropriate professionals followed.'

Source: Extract from the joint investigation by the Local Government Ombudsman and the Health Ombudsman, 4 July 2011, www.lgo.org.uk/news/2011/jul/ombudsmen-investigation-reveals-failings-care-vulnerable-adult/

There has been increasing discussion in debates about quality of social care provision of the need to adopt a stronger human rights perspective in all countries of the UK and there is some evidence that this is influencing policy. The Welsh Assembly Government in its 2007 strategy for social services (Welsh Assembly Government, 2007) talked of a rights–based approach linked to United Nations principles and conventions. In Scotland, the Health and Sport Committee (2011) report into the regulation of care for older people recommended that a review of the National Care Standards should have a human rights focus underpinned by principles of dignity, privacy, choice, safety, realising potential and equality and diversity. The Equality and Human Rights Commission and the CQC in England have produced equality and human rights guidance for compliance inspectors and registration assessors (EHRC and CQC, 2011). The CQC has argued that human rights should be at the centre of everything it does and that the emphasis should be on people's rights and entitlements, as opposed to their needs and requirements. In Northern Ireland, the RQIA (2012) states that human rights is at the heart of its policy and planning, citing fairness, respect, equality, dignity and autonomy as being at the core of its work. Ultimately, the extent to which this policy rhetoric impacts on practice will be down to acceptance of the principles, appreciation and understanding of a human rights-based framework for social care. This in turn is dependent on the training and professional development opportunities provided to social care staff.

Protection, risk and safeguarding

Protection was one of the seven principles underpinning the *Vision for adult social care* (DH, 2010a), which included the statement: '[a] modern social care system needs to balance freedom and choice with risk and protection' (para 6.4). However, achieving the balance is challenging. Promoting choice and control may require professionals adopting a very different approach to risk assessment.

The *No Secrets* policy (DH and Home Office, 2000) was the first national policy statement on protecting vulnerable adults across the UK and its general principles were implemented in policies in the devolved countries. *No secrets* defined abuse as 'a violation of an individual's human and civil rights by any other person or persons' and a vulnerable adult as '[a] person aged 18 or over who is or may be in need of community care services by reason of mental health or other disability, age or illness, and who is or may be unable to take care of him or herself or unable to protect him or herself from harm or exploitation' (DH and Home Office, 2000, para 2.3).

Although providing a set of national guidelines, *No secrets* advocated a local response. In Great Britain, local authorities were to play a lead role in developing local policies, setting up local safeguarding boards and developing a multidisciplinary approach to protecting vulnerable adults. Powell and Steele (2011) describe *No secrets* as drawing from experience of safeguarding children, but lacking the statutory basis of child protection legislation and the duty on organisations to share information. A Commission for Social Care Inspection (2008) review found variable practice across councils in relation to measures to prevent abuse and argued for an emphasis on safeguarding as a way of improving preventative measures.

These limitations were acknowledged in a consultation on a review of *No secrets* (DH, 2009d). The consultation showed that the *No secrets* policy had significantly raised the profile of adult safeguarding but respondents also talked of the difficulties of trying to get some organisations to participate in safeguarding boards and limited developments regarding effective multi-agency working. The review process also revealed the diversity of policy and practice because of the localised approach and identified strong support for the term 'vulnerable adult' to be replaced with a term that would more readily reflect the objectives of the personalisation agenda. There were also calls for the legislation on vulnerable adults to be revised in line with more stringent revised legislation in Scotland where the Adult Support and Protection (Scotland) Act 2007 provided councils with a statutory duty to make inquiries and carry out investigations. Although used sparingly since its introduction, this Act gave social workers the right to enter any premises as part of an investigation and the right to apply for a legal order to remove an older or disabled adult from premises where it is suspected they are at risk of harm or to request an order to remove an alleged perpetrator.

Northern Ireland had actually led the way in terms of vetting and barring arrangements when in 1993, as a result of an inquiry into a major scandal relating to the abuse of a vulnerable adult, a pre-employment consultancy service was set up by the-then Department for Health and Social Services. The arrangements were put onto a statutory footing in 2003. Further legislative changes on safeguarding impacted across the UK. Following the Birchard inquiry (Home Office, 2004), set up after the Soham murders of Jessica Chapman and Holly Wells, which, among other things looked at the way employers recruit people to work with children and vulnerable adults, the Safeguarding Vulnerable Groups Act 2006 was introduced. This led to the setting up of the Independent Safeguarding Authority (ISA) (covering England, Wales and Northern Ireland) and established the Vetting and Barring Scheme whereby the ISA was responsible for barring those considered to pose a risk to vulnerable adults (and children) and maintaining a list of those barred from engaging in regular activity with children and vulnerable groups. The list was shared across the UK.

Controversy about aspects of the vetting and barring scheme and in particular the definition of regulated activity, which was argued by some to be too expansive, prompted the Coalition government to conduct a review of the scheme on the grounds that it was a disproportionate response to the risk posed by a small minority of people. Changes resulting from the review have been incorporated in the Protection of Freedoms Act introduced by the Home Office in 2012 and have been rolled out in England, Wales and Northern Ireland. The barring function of the scheme will be maintained but registration and monitoring requirements will be abolished and the scope of activities defined as 'regulated' will be scaled back (DH, 2012i). In England the functions of the Criminal Records Bureau (which carries out criminal record checks) and the ISA will be merged and replaced by a new quango – called the Disclosure and Barring Service.

In Scotland, a new scheme, the Protecting Vulnerable Groups Scheme, came into existence in 2011 as a result of legislation introduced by the Scottish Government in 2007. It is managed by Disclosure Scotland and is a checking system for individuals who work with children and/or protected adults. Under the legislation it is an offence for an organisation to employ a person who is barred from working with children and/or protected adults and for an individual to put themselves forward for regulated work while barred.

The system and policy for preventing and detecting abuse and safeguarding vulnerable adults is complex, with a number of different agencies having some responsibility. With the exception of Scotland, policy has also lacked a strong statutory basis. In all parts of the UK, concern about the adequacy of policy has also been increased by incidences of abuse and statistical evidence that the systems are not effective enough. The issue of safeguarding was taken up by the Law Commission (2011) in its report on social care. The commission agreed that the term 'adult at risk' should replace 'vulnerable adult' (recommendation 40). It defined 'adult at risk' as those who appear to:

- have health or social care needs, including carers (irrespective of whether or not those needs are being met by services);
- be at risk of harm;
- be unable to safeguard themselves as a result of their health or social care needs (2011, p 114).

It also recommended that local authorities should have a legal duty to investigate suspected instances of adult abuse when an adult is at 'risk of harm', that they take the lead role in multi-agency safeguarding procedures and that adult safeguarding boards should include representatives from NHS trusts and the police.

The White Paper on adult social care (DH, 2012a, p 43) took on board many of the commission's recommendations and includes provision for greater powers to local authorities including a lead role on multi-agency safeguarding adults boards, which are to be given a new statutory footing. These will have a core membership from local authorities, the police and the NHS to strengthen joint working but decisions can be made locally about which other agencies should be involved. These boards will be empowered to make safeguarding enquiries, and will also have a responsibility to carry out safeguarding adults reviews. The draft Care and Support Bill (DH, 2012b) proposes a duty on local authorities to make enquiries where there is a safeguarding concern. This had been recommended by the Law Commission (2011) in its review of adult social care law. The Department of Health issued a consultation on a new safeguarding power (DH, 2012i) on whether this should be supported by a new 'power of entry' for local authorities in relation to a person they believe may be at risk of abuse and neglect and on the safeguards that would need to be in place if such a power were to be introduced. Although, as noted earlier, powers to remove vulnerable adults from premises have existed in Scotland for a number of years, this is a controversial area. Proponents of such powers being used as a last resort argue that they are required to protect some of the most vulnerable while opponents are concerned about the threat the powers represent to the human rights of individuals.

Personalisation and safeguarding

The consultation report on *No secrets* (DH, 2009d) showed that there was concern about the balance between safeguarding and achieving the outcomes associated with personalisation. Of particular concern was the potential for financial abuse. The contesting views on direct payments and personal budgets are evidence of fundamental differences in how people perceive this issue. While some strongly argue that personal budgets promote choice and give people more control, thereby reducing risk, others argue that the potential for abuse and exploitation puts users and carers at increased risk. The Commission for Social Care Inspection (2008), discussing concerns raised by some local authority staff that people using direct payments could be at risk of abuse from the workers they employ or from family managing payments on their behalf, suggested that risk could be alleviated by good information on safeguarding, obtaining Criminal Records Bureau and career history checks and references for personal assistants, training for users/ carers on employment issues and routine council checks on progress through care plan reviews. There has continued to be criticism about personal assistants not having to have a Criminal Records Bureau and previous employment check and of the lack of clarity about where responsibility for safeguarding against financial abuse rests (Gilbert and Powell, 2011). Studies have also pointed to the dearth in knowledge about how risk is understood by users, providers, care workers, carers and families (Glendinning et al, 2008; Wiseman, 2011). This includes the difficulty for workers in balancing their duty towards the protection and wellbeing of service users and supporting user choice. For many workers the anxiety around promoting and enabling choices that may involve risk is that they fear the consequences (Glendinning et al, 2008; Carr, 2011), a perspective exacerbated by the lack of clarity about' safeguarding in this context. A review of research on risk and adult social care published between 2007 and 2012 (Mitchell et al, 2012, p 33) concluded that '[o]verall, there appears to be widespread uncertainty and a lack of evidence in how professionals can best support different groups of service users in positive risk taking'.

While personalisation has undoubtedly resulted in very significant benefits and improved quality of life for many users, there remain questions about the impact in the longer term and in relation to specific groups of users. Risk has been discussed in terms of the potential adverse impact linked to inadequate resourcing and concern that the personalisation agenda will result in reduced or less appropriate provision for some individuals as local authorities experience increased financial restrictions, or if other services are closed down or reduced as personalisation is rolled out, leaving users and carers with less choice (Ferguson, 2007; Land and Himmelweit, 2010; Rummery, 2011). Some of these relate to risks to the individual from inadequate provision if direct payments are insufficient to meet needs or individuals find it difficult to purchase appropriate services with the allocated budget – an important point given the current and future financial pressures on social services. A useful analysis of risk and personalisation can be found in Glasby's (2011) overview paper on risk, regulation and personalisation for the Joseph Rowntree Foundation. In this he writes of his own response to personalisation and risk and safety being influenced by six key principles (see Box 48).

Box 48: Glasby's principles regarding personal risk and safety

1. Risk is important – but people using services often perceive this in a disempowering way as something that is imposed on them by the system.
2. We make people safe not by segregating them, but by building their confidence and by more fully connecting them to their communities.
3. We reduce risks if we identify them in advance and plan what to do in an emergency.
4. We might protect people better if we could focus our safeguards on those people who really need it.
5. Personalisation and safeguarding are (or at least should be) two sides of the same coin.
6. We set people up to fail if they don't have enough support.

Source: Glasby (2011)

Glasby (2011, p 16) concludes that '[t]he history of adult social care is littered with things that looked promising at pilot stage but that we killed stone dead in the implementation. The challenge in the current context will be to find ways of working with some very real issues about risk and regulation without allowing this to happen again'.

Conclusions

- Responsibility for standards and quality improvement has been placed with regulatory bodies in each of the countries of the UK and this chapter has described the ways in which policy and guidance have developed.
- The continuing problems in relation to quality of provision and care and risk and abuse are evidence that regulatory and inspection systems are not adequate as they are operating.
- Research and inquiries have identified fundamental issues regarding the care, respect and dignity of users, with the move from institutional to more personalised home care seen as an important factor in improving care and support for users.

- However, concerns have been raised about the potentially increased risk associated with personalisation for some users and how personalisation needs to be balanced with safeguarding.

There is also the difficulty of achieving quality improvement and safeguarding in the context of very restricted resources, especially with increased outsourcing by local authorities and multiple provider organisations – many of them very small. Resource pressures are also increasingly apparent in residential care. Asenova et al (2011) point to the tension between the optimisation of quality factors and the economic efficiency of running a care facility on the one hand, and of minimising negative risks to service users on the other.

Sources

The regulatory and inspection bodies in the countries of the UK produce information and data on regulation and inspections in each jurisdiction. Recent policy papers and government reports are cited in the chapter. Useful sources on emerging issues regarding personalisation, safeguarding and risk include Gilbert and Powell (2011), Wiseman (2011) and Glasby's (2011) review of risk, regulation and personalisation for the Joseph Rowntree Foundation.

Questions

- What are the main ways in which adult social care is regulated and inspected in the UK?

- How adequate has the policy response been to the persistent problems relating to standards and quality of care?

- To what extent do future developments regarding the personalisation of care give rise to greater safeguarding concerns?

ELEVEN

Conclusions

Since adult social care was established as a distinctive area, the development of policy and provision has often been described as embracing a transformation. The transformational aspects are mainly identified in reforms to the way services are delivered, underpinning values and principles and innovative strategies. The term 'transformation' can be questioned as applying to all aspects of developments in adult social care, as in practice a number of developments represent a continuation from existing or previous policies. This book has identified a number of categories or areas of transformational change in adult social care.

Transformation into a separate care sector

The establishment of adult social care as distinct from children's services in England from 2006 has been particularly significant. It has raised the profile of adult social care, led to its recognition as an important area of policy and provision and raised its importance within government policy, programmes and structures. The organisational separation of adult social care from children's social care applies only in England. In Scotland and Wales local authorities retain unified social care or social work departments and in Northern Ireland children's and adults' services are part of the integrated health and social care structure. However, the change in England and the consequent attention paid to new policy formulations have had a major influence on developments in Scotland and Wales, if less so in Northern Ireland.

Transformation through policy shifts vis-à-vis health

There has been a commitment to a shift in policy from the use of the acute health sector to community care. In practice this means the increasing use of adult social care in the community, with the aim of reducing demand and pressure on the acute health sector. This also implies a shift in resources to adult social care, which has happened, to some extent, across the UK. However, to be transformational the shift in resources would have to be significant. Substantive transformation would also need to be supported by more focus on and resourcing of preventative work, rather than the concentration of resources on those with high-level needs as has been the case. The shift to community-based care has also placed attention on home as the hub and people supported to live independently at home. A consequence of keeping people out of hospital is social care taking over more functions from the NHS, with the need to work out how to remodel services. This means more focus on rapid response services, reablement and initiatives in intermediate care. This shift in policy has emerged as part of government policy throughout the four administrations of the UK but has been perhaps most openly elucidated in Scotland and Northern Ireland.

Transformation and vision principles

Three policies have dominated the transformation agendas in terms of what may be called 'vision principles' although to an extent these themes have been features of pre-2006 modernisation agendas. However, a great deal of attention has been paid to the development of these principles in recent years and they are seen as fundamental to transformational outcomes. The three core themes are personalisation, integration and user involvement.

Personalisation

The personalisation agenda has moved to dominate values and principles for the delivery of adult social care. This direction of travel is marked out by a focus on person-centred services, self-directed care, direct payments and individual budgets. Personalisation aims to put people at the centre of the process of identifying their needs, giving them choices about how they are supported, of shaping services to more closely meet people's definition of their care needs. Personalisation is thus a vehicle for increasing people's control over services, increasing their independence and facilitating more innovative approaches to care and as a mechanism for achieving greater efficiencies. The expansion of direct payments is a key element in advancing the personalisation agenda. The aim in England is for all social care users to have personal budgets (Williams, C., 2012). There has been a marked increase in the number of personal budgets – a 40% increase in 2011/12 compared to the previous year – but the bulk of this increase is in relation to local authority-managed budgets, with numbers of users receiving direct payments just remaining stable. This is significant given the research evidence, which suggests that users with direct payments have better outcomes than those with managed personal budgets. With home care a key component of the vision for personalisation needs to be accepted by the independent sectors. Think Local, Act Personal in England is a partnership of over 30 national social care organisations committed to personalisation in social care and for people to have better lives through more choice and control over the support they use (Think Local, Act Personal, 2012). Their work shows that many value the opportunity to make decisions about the care they need and think there are benefits from delivering care that is core customised to the expressed needs of users. However, concerns have emerged about problems with the implementation of personalisation and about the impact of public expenditure cuts and imposed efficiency savings. Constraints can result from the formal requirements put on users, for example, regarding the use of personal budgets, and requirements may also stifle potential innovation in service delivery. Some users may prefer service to be provided to them on a collective basis rather than on an individual basis. Personalisation stands out as the key theme to drive forward higher-quality and more responsive services for the individual. The main justification for increasing personalisation is not to save money, with most analysts agreeing that this would not be the case if high-quality care is the desired outcome.

Integration

The promotion of more integrated working between health and social care has been the other dominant principle alongside personalisation in transformation narratives. In Scotland it is the topic of a major legislative initiative. In England and Wales it is a key agenda item in strategies, consultations and practitioner and academic debates on transformation and the future of health and social care. The House of Commons Health Committee has given its full support to the promotion of integration as a key element of future development. In Northern Ireland a distinctive feature has been the existence of fully integrated structures for health and social care since the 1970s. The operation of integration has perhaps more than any other topic related to adult social care been the major focus of research and evaluation, in work carried out by government departments, audit commissions, parliamentary committees, research institutes and academics. Examined in this book have been the strategies and structures used to promote integration and produce more collaborative working between health and social care. It has been possible to identify the role of joint commissioning, pooled budgets, integrated delivery teams, integrated management and leadership, and unified assessment and formal partnerships as having a key role in developments in Great Britain. It has also been possible to identify continuing barriers in terms of professional differences, accountability mechanisms and failings in partnership working. Some special initiatives involving integrated structures also provide significant evidence including care trusts and the fully integrated structure in Northern Ireland. There are differences in assessments of the achievements of integration and evaluations of performance. Some evidence has been produced of benefits in terms of reduced use of acute hospitals and care hours and more appropriate and timely services for people with complex needs. An area of some concern for the future relates to the impact of the restructuring of PCTs in England and the need for new partnership arrangements between new clinical commissioning groups and local authorities.

The development of joint health and wellbeing strategies at the local level through the local health and wellbeing boards is being seen by government as a way to agree commissioning decisions across the NHS/local authority interface. Integration remains a key theme of transformation as a method of achieving better joined-up care and also as a way of making better use of resources.

User involvement

User involvement has become a significant principle in narratives on the transformation of adult social care. The role of users in service design, delivery and evaluation has been of particular significance in some areas of adult social care. The principle is widely accepted and promoted in England, Scotland and Wales although sometimes expressed in terms of greater voice, greater control or the related principle of co-production. User involvement is also closely linked to carer involvement, more general public participation and the more specific approach of advocacy. User involvement is most developed in certain services – mental health and learning disability – and in the operational activities of policy formulation and consultation, policy and service assessment and evaluation, education and training and research. User involvement has also become more important in the commissioning of services and in the development and delivery of new services where user-led organisations have developed some of the most innovative provision. Also significant has been the widespread emergence of user-involvement organisations with their role in lobbying, formal consultations, policy implementation, partnership arrangements and the appraisal of provision. User-led organisations serve to put user involvement on a strong institutional basis. There has been a growing recognition of the valued role played by user groups and the contribution they can make to basic future developments on user expectations and aspirations, user experience, co-produced services and user-focused outcomes. In terms of user control, the principle has of course links to the personalisation agenda.

Together the three principles of personalisation, integration and user involvement have major theoretical implications in raising issues about the relationship between the individual and the state, and the provider and the user, in the system of adult social care.

Transformation through legislation

The recognition that adult social care has not had a clear statutory basis and acceptance that this requires legislation have been quite significant. Previously there has been a disparate range of legislation, mostly permissive with a lack of clear entitlement to services and overall confusing complexity. The Law Commission (2011) review recommended a radical reform of legislation to clarify a full range of legal rights in adult social care. The Care and Support Bill for England will encompass most of the Law Commission's recommendations. The review also covered Wales, and the Welsh Government has acted to bring in a new Social Services Bill, which will include most of these recommendations. In Scotland several pieces of legislation have been enacted or proposed, which will serve to put some key aspects of adult social care on a new legislative footing, including advocacy, carers' support, self-directed support and the integration of health and social care. The existence of devolution has encouraged the devolved administrations to embark on legislative initiatives, although legislation in Northern Ireland has been confined to structural reorganisation of health and social care. The enactment of social services legislation in England and Wales has the advantage of a single new statute, which should pave the way for a more coherent and comprehensive statutory foundation. A legal framework imposes duties and also sets out entitlement to services. Setting out legal rights for carers is a particularly significant development.

Transformation through devolution

Adult social care is a completely devolved matter and Wales has now joined Scotland and Northern Ireland in being empowered to pass primary legislation. For Scotland and Wales in particular, social care is a major component of devolved social policy. It is seen as a service with close connections to the principles of social justice and equality, and strong and traditional value commitments for most Scottish and Welsh politicians. Devolution has resulted in a degree of policy divergence between Scotland, Wales and Northern Ireland and also between the devolved administrations and England in some areas of adult social care. This is demonstrated in some major policy divergence, called flagship policies (Birrell, 2009) such as the free nursing and personal care policy in Scotland, and the Older People's Commissioner for Wales, now copied by Northern Ireland. The possible outcome of divergence may be demonstrated in future by four different systems of funding support for residential care in the UK. So far devolution can be seen as producing not just divergence in provision but somewhat different models of adult social care in respect of aspects of provision, priorities and underpinning values and principles.

Transformation through structural reform

Structural and organisational reform has been a feature in recent policy developments. In fact, health and social care restructuring has dominated health and social care agendas in England with the new Health and Social Care Act and fundamental restructuring of primary healthcare. The restructuring has major implications for the relationship between local authority adult social care departments and the new clinical commissioning groups. The local authorities will also be operating with a new configuration of new health and wellbeing boards in developing integrated services. Possible difficulties may arise with the variation across England in terms of the number of clinical commissioning groups to each local authority area. The new structures may encourage a closer engagement of GPs with adult social care than is often the case at present. Structural reform has also been seen as important in Scotland, with proposals for a system of health and social care partnerships across the country. In Northern Ireland, structural reform was also undertaken in 2006/07 to produce a reconfiguration of quangos for health and social care and, while further structural reform is alluded to in the *Transforming your care* (DHSSPS, 2011a) policy document, there is no specific detail on what this might involve. In Wales, local authority social care departments have also had to adapt to a restructuring and reduction in the number of health boards.

Transformation through new financial arrangements

Much of the transformation debate has been dominated by the costs of residential care and possible options for a new funding system, and in particular the recommendations of the Dilnot Commission (2011) on the funding of long-term care in England and the reaction to these. There is widespread acceptance that a new funding model is required involving both public and private contributions. The Dilnot approach of a cap of £35,000 on a lifetime contribution towards social care costs remains on the table but not yet endorsed by government. The further development of private and voluntary sector involvement continues with its overall significant change impact. Almost all adult social care in England, as much as 90%, is now in the private sector. It is still the case that one in four staff in the voluntary sector work in social care. In a sense the older mixed economy of welfare has been transformed significantly in that it can be said that statutory bodies provide few services directly but what happens is that services are contracted out to the private sector, the voluntary sector, or people receive a budget to arrange their own care. The current financial situation has been dominated by financial pressures on local authority budgets, with requirements for efficiency savings. This is having impacts on rationing and cutting care and entitlements, and increasing charges. A survey of adult services senior managers found that services for older people are the biggest strain on council resources, followed by dementia services and the funding of learning disability services (Williams, C., 2012). These are the fastest-growing part of the adult social care budget. There are fears that the present budgetary pressures will impact on strategies for the shift from acute care to focus on preventative action, with priority having to go to those with substantial or critical needs, and there being less money for specialist voluntary services. The outcomes may make commissioning more complex and overall there may be some pressure to try innovative approaches, for example, to transfer services into social enterprises, establish sustainable formal partnerships with the independent sector or experiment with local authority in-house trading companies.

Transformation through new services

A number of largely new services have emerged or been developed, some as part of wider policy agendas. Reablement services may be the clearest example with their focus on short intensive support to enable people to live independently and with their emphasis on integrated support. Another example may be rapid response services based on ideas of rapid assessment on an integrated basis and aiming at preventing unnecessary hospital admissions. Some services are well established but some new or different dimension has developed, for example, Extra Care out of the wider housing-based support programmes, specialising in maintaining healthy older people in independent living. Direct payments is an older policy but the move to give it priority is new and the evidence points to users who hold direct payments having better outcomes than those with managed personal budgets. Some other developments from existing policies are intermediate care at home and frail older people mental health teams. The use of telecare continues as holding out prospects of new services with technology to enable people to stay at home and give them confidence to live independently.

Transformational mainstream support

A number of more traditional forms of social care provision have continued to be at the centre of most government strategies and can be seen as making a contribution to developing policy and provision and to a process of transformation. These are: carer support, workforce developments, outcome frameworks, daycare provision, housing-led support and safeguarding.

Carer support has a vital role and there have been a number of initiatives aimed at enhancing support for adult and young carers and to facilitate carer involvement. Carer support has been a priority in the devolved administrations and addressed in a number of subject-specific strategy documents. Developments in relation to the large social care workforce are under discussion but in this area developments are more ad-hoc, with a lack of a coherent and comprehensive strategy. A range of new employment opportunities have arisen as a result of the new social care agendas and have included development workers, direct payment officers, directly employed personal assistants and social care officers. Some recognition of the need to increase the size of the social care workforce and to address quality and professionalisation issues could be seen in the decision by the Department of Health in England to double the number of social care apprenticeships within five years from 2012 (DH, 2012a, p 52). Also noted has been the need to develop better leadership competency and to look at the need for more managerial positions in social care. There has been some discussion of the impact of the new social care agendas on social work, with reviews of social work taking place in all the countries of the UK. Most of these have included some discussion of the need to improve the status and public perception of social work and some approach the issue of the specific roles and responsibilities of social workers. This is perhaps an increasingly pertinent issue given the shift to self-directed support and the emergence of new groups of advocacy and support workers. The emphasis on collaboration and multidisciplinary working can also be seen in discussions about workforce development, with some suggestion that closer integration in training and education is needed to promote team working (Ham et al, 2012, p 29). Overall, new ways of working in social care have major implications for workforce policies.

The use of outcomes frameworks to achieve improvements in social care and assess changes in provision has been a feature of social care policy for some time but there has been an increasing focus on the development of more comprehensive frameworks in England with a key role for users and carers. Safeguarding has moved to become a major topic of concern in all comprehensive strategies. A range of policies and measures have been introduced, which are fairly standardised across the UK, and similar frameworks have been introduced across local authorities. Yet, there remain many questions and concerns about the adequacy of regulatory frameworks and institutions and inspection processes and complaints procedures.

There is increasing acceptance by government that issues of quality and safety cannot be separated from workforce issues but, as noted above, there is as yet no comprehensive strategic development in this area.

Transformation implies very major changes, reforms and innovations. There has been a very strong policy rhetoric around the transformation of adult social care – but has there actually been a real transformation in policy and practice, or is such a transformation under way? It is useful to distinguish between two different scenarios or models of transformation or significant change. Major changes or developments in existing services may be driven by external forces and pressures. Other major changes can be seen more in terms of principles, values and forms of delivery and practice and may be driven by internal debate and analysis of social care issues. The major external factors have been first, demographic change increasing the demand for services and increasing the size of the adult social care sector. Second has been the impact, in recent years and in the future, of financial pressures, with reductions in resources and requirements for efficiencies leading to fewer entitlements, the imposition of higher charges and the need for innovative commissioning. One major future decision is the funding of long-term care. Third are structural changes, which, while not having adult social care as a key component, have had a significant impact. In England, structural change has seen adult social care emerge as a separate and distinct service and policy area. Fourth have been changes introduced mainly in relation to the NHS, but which have had an impact on adult social care. This includes changes in England concerning the replacement of PCTs by clinical commissioning groups and, also, policy changes throughout the UK encouraging a shift in emphasis from acute healthcare to care in the community. Fifth has been the impact of devolution as the new devolved administrations in Scotland, Wales and Northern Ireland have used their devolved responsibilities for adult social care to develop some divergent policies and provision, from each other and from England.

In the second scenario it is possible to identify a range of new principles, service innovations and forms of delivery that have had what can be called a transformational impact or near-transformational impact. This covers the principles of personalisation, integration, user involvement and co-production and prevention, all of which have had an impact in terms of the development of new ways of delivering services. Other principles and practices have contributed to significant change but have evolved more gradually over time and may not merit the transformational description. This could include carers' support, advocacy, independent living, safeguarding, workforce development and outcome frameworks. Service innovations, formulated within adult social care practice, can also be seen as contributing to transformation in a cumulative fashion. Examples are reablement, rapid response and Extra Care.

The future pathway for adult social care will bring conflicting demands and pressures for governments, commissioners, providers, managers and practitioners in terms of aims and priorities. Goals of achieving improved outcomes and promoting wellbeing will be set against the push for more cost efficiencies and reduced expenditure. Central to the 'transformation agenda' are ideas about personalisation and self-directed support, which offer new opportunities but also carry risks. While having the potential to promote individual rights, autonomy and choice, there are political constraints on personal funding and resources. Ultimately, it may be that as adjustments are made within the boundaries of modernising agendas, resources and expressed need, real transformational change is limited.

Bibliography

Abbott, D. and Marriott, A. (2012) 'Money, finance and the personalisation agenda for people with learning disabilities in the UK: some emerging issues', *British Journal of Learning Disabilities*, doi: 10.1111/j.1468

Adams, R. (1996) *The personal social services*, London: Longman.

ADASS (Association of Directors of Adult Social Services) (2011) *Personal budget survey: March 2011*, London: ADASS.

ADASS (2012) *ADASS personal budget survey*, London: ADASS.

Ahmad, W. and Atkins, K. (eds) (1996) *'Race' and community care*, Buckingham: The Open University.

Anghel, R. and Ramon, S. (2009) 'Service users and carers' involvement in social work education: lessons from an English case study', *European Journal of Social Work*, vol 12, no 2, pp 185-99.

Arksey, H. (2002a) 'Combining informal care and work: supporting carers in the workplace', *Health and Social Care in the Community*, vol 10, no 3, pp 151-61.

Arksey, H. (2002b) 'Rationed care: assessing the support needs of informal carers in English social service authorities', *Journal of Social Policy*, vol 31, no 1, pp 81-101.

Arksey, H. and Glendinning, C. (2007) 'Choice in the context of informal care giving', *Health and Social Care in the Community*, vol 15, no 2, pp 165-75.

Asenova, D., Stein, W. and Marshall A. (2011) 'An innovative approach to risk and quality assessment in the regulation of care services in Scotland', *Journal of Risk Research*, vol 14, no 7, pp 859-79.

Audit Commission (1986) *Making a reality of community care*, London: Her Majesty's Stationery Office.

Audit Commission (1992) *Community care: Managing the cascade of change*, London: Her Majesty's Stationery Office.

Audit Commission (2007) *Progress made in improving housing-related Supporting People services*. Available at: www.audit-commission.gov.uk

Audit Commission (2009) *Means to an end: Joint financing across health and social care*, London: Her Majesty's Stationery Office.

Audit Commission (2011) *Joining up health and social care*, London: Audit Commission.

Audit Scotland (2011) *Review of community health partnerships*, Edinburgh: Audit Scotland, www.audit-scotland.gov.uk

Audit Scotland (2012) *Commissioning social care*, Edinburgh: Audit Scotland, www.audit-scotland.gov.uk

Baggott, R. (2004) *Health and health care in Britain*, Basingstoke: Macmillan.

Baggott, R. (2005) 'A funny thing happened on the way to the forum? Reforming patient and public involvement in the NHS in England', *Public Administration*, vol 83, no 3, pp 533-51.

Baldock, J. (1994) 'The personal social services: the politics of care', in V. George and S. Miller (eds) *Social policy towards 2000*, London: Routledge.

Baldwin, S. and Parker, G. (1989) 'The Griffiths Report on community care', in M. Brenton and C. Ungerson (eds) *Social policy review 1988–89*, London: Longman.

Balloch, S. and McLean, J. (2000) 'Human resources in social care', in B. Hudson (ed) *The changing role of social care*, London: Jessica Kingsley Publishers.

Barnes, M. and Walker, A. (1996) 'Consumerism versus empowerment: a principled approach to the involvement of older service users', *Policy & Politics*, vol 24, no 4, pp 375-93.

Barnes, M., Gell, C. and Thomas, P. (2010) 'Participation and social justice', in I. Greener, C. Holden and M. Kilkey (eds) *Social policy review 22: Analysis and debate in social policy, 2010*, Bristol: The Policy Press.

Bartlett, J. (2009) *At your service: Navigating the future market in health and social care*, London: Demos.

Bauld, L., Chesterman, J., Davies, B., Judge, K. and Mangalore, R. (2000) *Caring for older people: An assessment of community care in the 1990s*, Aldershot: Ashgate.

Baxter, K., Wilberforce, M. and Glendinning, C. (2010) 'Personal budgets and the workforce implications for social care providers: expectations and early experiences', *Social Policy and Society*, vol 10, no 1, pp 55-65.

BBC (British Broadcasting Company) (2010) 'Hidden young carers in the UK', 16 November, www.bbc.co.uk/news/education-11757907

Beresford, P. (2000) 'Service users' knowledges and social work theory: conflict or collaboration?', *British Journal of Social Work*, vol 30, no 3, pp 489-503.

Beresford, P. (2002) 'Participation and social policy: transformation, liberation or regulation?', in R. Sykes, C. Bochel and N. Ellison (eds) *Social policy review 14*, Bristol: The Policy Press.

Beresford, P. (2010) 'Service users and social policy: challenging dominant discourses', in I. Greener, C. Holden and M. Kilkey (eds) *Social policy review 22: Analysis and debate in social policy, 2010*, Bristol: The Policy Press.

Beresford, P. and Andrews, E. (2012) *Caring for our future: What service users say*, York: Joseph Rowntree Foundation.

Beresford, P. and Croft, S. (2004) 'Service users and practitioners reunited: the key components of social work reform', *British Journal of Social Work*, vol 34, no 1, pp 53-68.

Beresford, P., Fleming, J., Glynn, M., Bewley, C., Croft, S., Branfield, F. and Postle, K. (2011) *Supporting people: Towards a person-centred approach*, Bristol and York: The Policy Press and Joseph Rowntree Foundation.

Berthoud, R. (2010) *The take-up of Carer's Allowance: A feasibility study*, London: Department for Work and Pensions.

Berry, K. (2008) Social Work Services in Scotland, Scottish Parliament Information Spice Briefing Paper 08/52, Edinburgh: Scottish Parliament.

Birrell, D. (2009) *The impact of devolution on social policy*, Bristol: The Policy Press.

Birrell, D. and Heenan, D. (2012) 'Implementing the Transforming your Care agenda in Northern Ireland within integrated structures', *Journal of Integrated Care*, vol 20, no 6, pp 359-66.

Blewett, J., Lewis, J. and Tunstill, J. (2007) *The changing roles and tasks of social work*, London: General Social Care Council.

Bochel, C. and Bochel, H. (2004) *The UK social policy process*, Basingstoke: Palgrave Macmillan.

Bochel, C., Bochel, H., Somerville, P. and Worley, C. (2008) 'Marginalised or enabled voices? User participation in policy and practice', *Social Policy and Society*, vol 7, no 2, pp 201-10.

Bovaird, T. (2007) 'Beyond engagement and participation: user and community coproduction of public services', *Public Administration Review*, vol 67, no 5, pp 846-60.

Brown, K. and Young, N. (2008) 'Building capacity for service user and carer involvement in social work education', *Social Work Education: The International Journal*, vol 27, no 1, pp 84-96.

Bruce, A. and Forbes, T. (2005) 'Delivering community care in Scotland: can local partnerships bridge the gap?', *Scottish Affairs*, no 52, pp 89-109.

Bryan, M. (2011) *Access to flexible working and informal care*, Colchester: Institute for Social and Economic Research, University of Essex.

Burgess, L. (2012) *Integration of health and social care: International comparisons*, Scottish Parliament Information Centre Briefing, Edinburgh: Scottish Parliament.

Burstow, P. (2012) 'No "structural merger" of health and social care, MPs told', www.localis.org.uk/article/955

Bynoe, I. Oliver, M. and Barnes, C. (1991) *Equal rights for disabled people: The case for a new law*, London: Institute of Public Policy Research.

Callaghan, L., Netten, A., Brooks, N. and Fox, D. (2011) *Personalisation of services scoping study*, London: National Institute for Health Research.

Cameron, A., Lart, R., Bostock, L. and Coomber, C. (2012) *Factors that promote and hinder joint and integrated working between health and social care services*, Research Briefing 4, London: Social Care Institute for Excellence.

Campbell, J. and Oliver, M. (1996) *Disability politics: Understanding our past, changing our future*, Basingstoke: Macmillan.

Care Commission (2007) *Scotland quality assessment framework*, Edinburgh: Care Commission.

Care Council for Wales (2007) *Service User and Carer Participation Strategy*, Cardiff: Care Council for Wales.

Care Council for Wales (2010) *Care at home: challenges, possibilities and implications for the workforce in Wales*, Final Report, Cardiff: Care Council for Wales.

Carers UK (2011) *Caring at a distance: Bridging the gap*, London: Carers UK.

Carers UK (2012) *Cost of caring*, London: Carers UK.

Carers UK and Employers for Childcare (2011) *Caring at a distance: Bridging the gap*, London: Carers UK

Carers UK and Ipsos MORI (2009) *The cost of caring*, London: Carers UK.

Carers UK and University of Leeds (2011) *Valuing carers 2011: Calculating the value of carers' support*, London: Carers UK.

Carey, M. (2009) 'Happy shopper? The problems with service user and carer participation', *British Journal of Social Work*, vol 39, no 1, pp 179–88.

Carmichael, F., Charles, S. and Hulme, C. (2010) 'Who will care? Employment participation and willingness to supply informal care', *Journal of Health Economics*, vol 29, no 1, pp 182–90.

Carr, S. (2004) *Has service user participation made a difference to social care services?*, London: Social Care Institute for Excellence.

Carr, S. (2007) 'Participation, power, conflict and change: theorising dynamics of service user participation in the social care system of England and Wales', *Critical Social Policy*, vol 27, no 2, pp 266–76.

Carr, S. (2011) 'Enabling risk and securing safety: self directed support and personal budgets', *Journal of Adult Protection*, vol 13, no 3, pp 122–36.

Carr, S. and Robbins, D. (2009) *The implementation of individual budget schemes in adult social care*, London: Social Care Institute for Excellence.

Cass, B. and Yeandle, S. (2009) 'Policies for carers in Australia and the UK: social policy ideas, practices and their cross-national transmission: social movements, parliamentary inquiries and local innovations', Paper prepared for RC19 2009 Montreal, www.cccg.umontreal.ca/rc19/PDF/Cass-B_Rc192009.pdf

Cavaye, J. (2006) 'Care of older people in Scotland', in G. Mooney, T. Sweeney and A. Law (eds) *Social care, health and welfare in contemporary Scotland*, Paisley: Kynoch and Blaney.

Centre for Workforce Intelligence (2011) *The adult social care workforce in England – Key facts*, Centre for Workforce Intelligence: London.

Cestari, C., Munroe, M., Evans, G., Smith, A. and Huxley, P. (2006) 'Fair access to care servives: implementation in the mental health context of the UK', *Health and Social Care in the Community*, vol 14, no 6, pp 474–81.

Challis, D., Stewart, K., Donnelly, M., Weiner, K. and Hughes, J. (2006) 'Does integration make a difference?', *Journal of Interprofessional Care*, vol 20, pp 335–48.

Clark, C. and Smith, M. (2011) 'Changing lives: what is really changing for Scottish social work?', *European Journal of Social Work*, www.tandfonline.com/doi/abs/10.1080/13691457.2010.543892

Clarke, A. (2011) *How can local authorities with less money support better outcomes for older people?*, York: JRF.

Clarke, J. and Glendinning, C. (2002) 'Partnership and the remaking of welfare governance', in C. Glendinning, M. Powell and K. Rummery (eds) *Partnerships, New Labour and the governance of welfare*, Bristol: The Policy Press.

Clements, L. and Bang, J. (2012) *Young carers and the Draft Care and Support Bill*, Oxford: Oxfordshire Carers' Forum.

College of Social Work (2011) *Mission, vision and values*, London: College of Social Work, www.collegeofsocialwork.org/standard-2-rhm

College of Social Work (2012) *Vision and governance*, London: College of Social Work, www.collegeofsocialwork.org/about-us/vision-and-governance

Connor, M. and Kissen, G. (2010) 'Tackling whole-systems change: The Trafford Framework for Integrated Services' *Journal of Integrated Care*, vol 18, no 3, pp 4–14.

Cook, T. (2007) *The history of the carers' movement*, London: Carers UK.

Copus, C. (2004) *Party politics and local government*, Manchester: Manchester University Press.

Cornwell, J. (2012) *The care of frail older people with complex needs: Time for a revolution?*, London: The King's Fund.

Cowden, S. and Singh, G. (2007) 'The "user": friend, foe or fetish? A critical exploration of user involvement in health and social care', *Critical Social Policy*, vol 27, no 1, pp 5-23.

CQC (Care Quality Commission) (2007) *Voices into action: The Care Quality Commission's statement of involvement*, London: CQC.

CQC (2010) *The essential standards of quality and safety*, www.cqc.org.uk/organisations-we-regulate/registering-first-time/essential-standards

CQC (2011) *The state of health care and adult social care in England*, HC 1487, London: The Stationery Office.

CSCI (Commission for Social Care Inspection) (2004) *Leaving hospital: The price of delays*, London: CSCI.

CSCI (2008) *Safeguarding adults: A study of the effectiveness of arrangements to safeguard adults from abuse*, London: CSCI.

CSCI (2009) *The state of social care in England 2007–2008*, London: CSCI.

CSSIW (Care and Social Services Inspectorate Wales) and HIW (Healthcare Inspectorate Wales) (2012) *Growing old my way: Review of the impact of the National Service Framework (NSF) for Older People in Wales*, Merthyr Tydfil and Caerphilly: CSSIW and HIW.

Cunningham, I. and Nixon, D. (2011) *The personalisation agenda: Implications for work and employment*, Stirling: Voluntary Sector Social Services Workforce Unit.

Davidson, J., Baxter, K., Glendinning, C., Jones, K., Forder, J., Caiels, J., Welch, E., Windle, K., Dolan, P. and King, D. (2012) *Personal health budgets: Experiences and outcomes for budget holders at nine months*, London: Department of Health.

DCLG (Department for Communities and Local Government) (2006) *Small and prosperous communities*, Local Government White Paper, London: Her Majesty's Stationery Office.

DCLG (2007) *Independence and opportunity: Our strategy for supporting people*, London: DCLG.

Department for Education (2011) *Service user and carer participation in social work education*, London: Department of Education, www.education.gov.uk/swrb/serviceusers-carers

Devine, P. and Lloyd, K. (2011) *Young carers too*, ARK Research Update, no 76, www.ark.ac.uk/publications/updates/update76.pdf

DH (Department of Health) (1989) *Caring for people: Community care in the next decade and beyond*, Cm 849, London: Her Majesty's Stationery Office.

DH (1998a) *Modernising social services: Promoting independence, improving protection, raising standards*, Cm 4169, London: DH.

DH (1998b) *Partnership in action*, London: DH.

DH (1999a) *Patient and public involvement in the new NHS*, London: DH.

DH (1999b) *Caring about carers: A national strategy for carers*, London: DH.

DH (2000) *The NHS Plan*, Cm 4818, London: DH.

DH (2001a) *Valuing people: A new strategy for learning disability for the 21st century*, London: DH.

DH (2001b) *A National Service Framework for Older People*, London: DH.

DH (2002) *Care trusts background briefing*, London: DH.

DH (2005) *Independence, well-being and choice: Our vision for the future of social care for adults in England* (Green Paper), Cm 6499, London: DH.

DH (2006a) *Our health, our care, our say: A new direction for community services* (White Paper), Cm 6737, London: DH.

DH (2006b) *A stronger local voice: A framework for creating a stronger local voice in the development of health and social care services*, Cm 6759, London: DH.

DH (2007) *Putting people first: A shared vision and commitment to the transformation of adult social care*, London: DH.

DH (2008a) *Transforming social care*, Local Authority Circular LAC (DH) (2008), London: DH.

DH (2008b) *High quality care for all: NHS next stage review: Final report*, London: DH.

DH (2008c) *The evidence base for integrated care*, London: DH.

DII (2008d) *Carers at the heart of 21st-century families and communities*, London: DH.

DH (2008e) *Real involvement: Working with people to improve services*, London: DH.

DH (2008f) *Putting people first: Working to make it happen: Adult social care workforce strategy – interim statement*, London: DH.

DH (2009a) *Shaping the future of care together*, London: DH

DH (2009b) *Building a safe confident future: Social Work Taskforce*, London: DH.

DH (2009c) *Putting patients at the heart of care*, London: DH.

DH (2009d) *Safeguarding adults: Report on the consultation on the review of No Secrets*, London: DH.

DH (2010a) *A vision for adult social care: Capable communities and active citizens*, London: DH.

DH (2010b) *Building the national care service*, London: DH.

DH (2010c) *Liberating the NHS: Report of the arms-length bodies review*, London: DH.

DH (2010d) *Practical approaches to co-production*, London: DH and Transforming Adult Social Care Co-production Group.

DH (2010e) *Recognised, valued and supported* (refreshed carers' strategy), London: DH.

DH (2010f) *Equity and excellence: Liberating the NHS* (White Paper), London: DH.

DH (2010g) *Everything you need to know about personal budgets*, London: DH, www.personalhealthbudgets.dh.gov.uk/about/faqs/

DH (2011a) *Caring for our future: Shared ambitions for care and support*, London: DH, www.caringforourfuture.dh.gov.uk

DH (2011b) *Enabling excellence: Autonomy and accountability for healthcare workers, social workers and social care workers*, London: DH.

DH (2011c) *Working for personalised care: A framework for supporting personal assistants working in adult social care*, London: DH.

DH (2011d) *Liberating the NHS: Legislative framework and next steps*, Cm 7993, London: DH.

DH (2012a) *Caring for our future: Reforming care and support* (White Paper), Cm 8378, Norwich: The Stationery Office.

DH (2012b) *Draft Care and Support Bill*, London: The Stationery Office.

DH (2012c) *Caring for our future: Progress report on funding reform*, London: DH, www.dh/gov/uk/health/2012/07/scfunding

DH (2012d) 'Care and support White Paper published', www.dh.gov.uk/health/2012/07/careandsupportwhitepaper/

DH (2012e) *Transparency in outcomes: A framework for quality in adult social care*, London: DH, www.dh.gov.uk/publications

DH (2012f) *Personal health budgets and NHS continuing health care*, London: DH.

DH (2012g) *Regulated activity (adults)*, London: DH.

DH (2012h) *Department of Health review: Winterbourne View Hospital: Interim report*, London: DH.

DH (2012i) *Consultation on a new adult safeguarding power*, London: DH.

DH (2012j) *Quality care providers and the workforce: Accompanying IA for the White Paper 'Caring for our future: reforming care and support'*, London: DH.

DH and Home Office (2000) *No secrets: Guidance on developing and implementing multi-agency policies and procedures to protect vulnerable adults from abuse*, London: DH.

DHSS (Department of Health and Social Security) (1981) *Growing older*, Cm 8173, London: Her Majesty's Stationery Office.

DHSSNI (Department of Health and Social Services Northern Ireland) (1990) *People first: Community care in Northern Ireland in the 1990s*, Belfast: Her Majesty's Stationery Office.

DHSSPS (2004) *A healthier future: A twenty-year vision for health and wellbeing in Northern Ireland*, Belfast: DHSSPS.

DHSSPS (2005) *Who cares? The future of adult care and support in Northern Ireland*, Belfast: DHSSPS.

DHSSPS (2006) *Caring for carers*, Belfast: DHSSPS.

DHSSPS (2007) *Guidance on strengthening personal and public involvement in health and social care*, Belfast: DHSSPS, www.dhsspsni.gov.uk

DHSSPS (2010) *A 10 year strategy for social work in Northern Ireland 2010–2020*, Belfast: DHSSPS.

DHSSPS (2011a) *Transforming your care: A review of health and social care in Northern Ireland*, Belfast: DHSSPS.

DHSSPS (2011b) *Transforming your care: Implementation plan*, Belfast: DHSSPS.

DHSSPS (2011c) *Review of the social services workforce: Final report*, Belfast: DHSSPS.

DHSSPS (2011d) *Residential care homes minimum standards*, Belfast: DHSSPS.

DHSSPS (2012a) *Improving and safeguarding social wellbeing: A strategy for social work in Northern Ireland 2012–2022*, Belfast: DHSSPS.

DHSSPS (2012b) *Transforming your care: Draft strategic implementation plan* Belfast: DHSSPS.

DHSSPS (2012c) *Who cares? The future of adult social care and support in Northern Ireland (consultation)*, Belfast: DHSSPS.

Dickens, J. (2011) 'Social work in England at a watershed – as always: from the Seebohm Report to the Social Work Taskforce', *British Journal of Social Work*, vol 41, no 1, pp 22-39.

Dickenson, H. (2006) 'The evaluation of health and social care partnerships: an analysis of approaches and synthesis for the future', *Health and Social Care in the Community*, vol 14, no 5, pp 375-83.

Dickenson, H. and Peck, D. (2008) 'Is leadership and management in inter-agency settings really that different? Perspectives from the literature', *International Journal of Integrated Care*, vol 8 (supplement).

Dilnot Commission (2011) *Fairer care funding: Report of the Commission on Funding of Care and Support*, London: Department of Health.

Dominelli, L. (2002) *Anti-oppressive social work theory and practice*, Basingstoke: Palgrave Macmillan.

Donnelly, T. (2008) 'Care in the community', in J. Osmond (ed) *The Welsh health battleground: Policy approaches to the third term*, Cardiff: Institute of Welsh Affairs.

Dowling, B., Powell, M. and Glendinning, C. (2004) 'Conceptualising successful partnerships', *Health and Social Care in the Community*, vol 12, no 4, pp 309-17.

Dowson, S. and Greig, R. (2009) 'The emergence of the independent support broker role', *Journal of Integrated Care*, vol 17, no 4, pp 22-30.

Drakeford, M. (2005) 'Wales and a third term of New Labour: devolution and the development of difference', *Critical Social Policy*, vol 25, 497-596.

Driver, S. and Martell, L. (2002) *Blair's Britain*, Cambridge: Polity Press.

DSD (Department for Social Development) and DHSSPS (Department of Health, Social Services and Public Safety) (2009) *Review of the support provision for carers*, Belfast: DSD and DHSSPS.

Duffy, J. (2006) *Participating and learning: Citizen involvement in social work education in the Northern Ireland context: A good practice guide*, London: Social Care Institute for Excellence.

Duffy, J. (2008) *Looking out from the middle: User involvement in health and social care in Northern Ireland*, Report 18, London: Social Care Institute for Excellence.

Duffy, S. (2010) 'The citizenship theory of social justice: exploring the meaning of personalisation for social workers', *Journal of Social Work Practice*, vol 24, no 3, pp 253-67.

Duffy, S. (2012) *Is personalisation dead?*, London: Centre for Welfare Reform.

Dumbleton, S. and McPhail, M. (2012) 'The coming of age of Scottish social services?', in G. Mooney and G. Scott (eds) *Social justice and social policy in Scotland*, Bristol: The Policy Press.

Duncan-Turnbull, H. (2010) 'It's your life, take control: evaluating self-directed support in Hertfordshire', *Journal of Care Services Management*, vol 4, no 3, pp 250-8.

DWP (Department for Work and Pensions) (2012) *The future of the Independent Living Fund*, London: DWP.

Eborall, C., and Griffiths, D. (2008) *The State of the Social Care Workforce 2008: The Third Skills Research and Intelligence Annual Report*, Leeds: Skills for Care.

Eccles, A. (2008) 'Since shared assessment: the limits to quick fix implementation, *Journal of Integrated Care*, vol 16, no 1, pp 22-30.

EHRC (Equality and Human Rights Commission) (2011) *Close to home: An inquiry into human rights and older people and home care*, London: EHRC.

EHRC and Care Quality Commission (2011) *Equality and human rights in the essential standards of quality and safety: An overview*, London: EHRC.

Ellison, N. and Pierson, C. (1998) 'Developments in British social policy', in N. Ellison and C. Pierson (eds) *Developments in British social policy*, Basingstoke: Macmillan.

Equality Commission for Northern Ireland (2012) *Strengthening protection for all ages: Legislative reform*, Belfast: Equality Commission for Northern Ireland.

Evandrou, M., Falkingham, J. and Glennerster, H. (1991) 'The personal social services: "everyone's poor relation but nobody's baby"', in J. Hills (ed) *The state of welfare*, Oxford: Clarendon Press.

Evans, D. and Forbes, R. (2009) 'Partnerships in health and social care: England and Scotland compared', *Public Policy and Administration*, vol 24, no 1, pp 67-83.

Ferguson, H. and Devine, P. (2011) *An ordinary life: Caring in Northern Ireland today*, ARK Research Update, no 75, www. www.ark.ac.uk/publications/updates/update75.pdf

Ferguson, I. (2007) 'Increasing user choice or privatizing risk? The antinomies of personalization', *British Journal Social Work*, vol 37, no 3, pp 387-403.

Ferguson, I. (2012) 'Personalisation, social justice and social work: a reply to Simon Duffy', *Journal of Social Work Practice: Psychotherapeutic Approaches in Health, Welfare and the Community*, vol 26, no 1, pp 55-73.

Ferguson, I. and Ager, G. (2005) *Integrated assessments: Involvement of users and carers*, Dundee: Social Institute for Excellence in Social Work Education, www.iriss.org.uk/docs

Field, J. and Peck, E (2003) 'Mergers and acquisitions in privatisation: what are the lessons for health and social services', *Social Policy & Administration*, vol 37, no 7, pp 742-55.

Finch, J. and Groves, D. (1980) 'Community care and the family: a case for equal opportunity', *Journal of Social Policy*, vol 9, no 4, pp 487-511.

Fleming, G. and Taylor, B.A. (2007) 'Battle on the home care front: perceptions of home care workers of factors influencing staff retention in Northern Ireland', *Health and Social Care in the Community*, vol 15, pp 67-77.

Flynn, M. and Citarella, V. (2012) *Winterbourne View Hospital: A serious case review*, Thornbury: South Gloucestershire Safeguarding Adults Board.

Forder, J., Jones, K., Glendinning, C., Caiels, J., Welch, E., Baxter, K., Davidson, J., Windle, K., Irvine, A., King, D. and Dolan, P. (2012) *Evaluation of the Personal Health Budget Pilot Programme*, Discussion Paper, 2840_2, PSSRU, University of Kent, Canterbury.

Fox, A. (2012) *Personalisation: Lessons from social care*, London: 2020 Public Services Hub.

Freeman, I. and Moore, H. (2008) 'Community health (and care) partnerships in Scotland', *Journal of Integrated Care*, vol 16, no 3, pp 38-47.

Freeman, T. and Peck, E. (2006) 'Evaluative partnership: A case study in integrated specialist mental health services', *Health and Social Care in the Community*, vol 14, no 5, pp 408-17.

Fry, G., Singleton, B., Yeandle, S. and Buckner, L. (2011) *Developing a clearer understanding of the Carer's Allowance claimant group*, London: Department for Work and Pensions.

Fulop, N., Mowlan, A. and Edwards, N. (2005) *Building integrated care: Lessons from the UK and elsewhere*, London: NHS Confederation.

Fyson, R., Tarleton, B. and Ward, L. (2007) *The impact of the Supporting People programme on adults with learning disabilities*, York: Joseph Rowntree Foundation.

Garboden, M. (2010) 'High Court rules against refusal to assess carers' needs in Northern Ireland autism case', *Community Care*, 21 September.

Gibb, M. (2001) 'Seebohm: an ambition ahead of its time', in I. Allen (ed) *Social care and health: A new deal*, London: Policy Studies Institute.

Gilbert, T. and Powell, J.L. (2011) 'Personalisation and sustainable care', *Journal of Care Services Management*, vol 5, no 2, pp 79-86.

Gladstone, D. (1995) 'Introducing the personal social services', in D. Gladstone (ed) *British social welfare*, London: Routledge.

Glasby, J. (2004) 'Discharging responsibilities? Delayed hospital discharges and the health and social care divide', *Journal of Social Policy*, vol 33, no 4, 593-604.

Glasby, J. (2005) 'The integration dilemma: how deep and how broad to go?', *Journal of Integrated Care*, vol 13, no 5, pp 27-30.

Glasby, J. (2007) *Understanding health and social care*, Bristol: The Policy Press.

Glasby, J. (2011) *Whose risk is it anyway? Risk and regulation in an era of personalization*, York: Joseph Rowntree Foundation.

Glasby, J. and Dickenson, H. (2008) *Partnership working in health and social care*, Bristol: The Policy Press.

Glasby, J. and Littlechild, R. (2006) 'An overview of the implementation and development of direct payments', in J. Leece and J. Bornat (eds) *Developments in direct payments*, Bristol: The Policy Press, pp 19-32.

Glasby, J. and Littlechild, R. (2004) *The health and social care divide: The experiences of older people*, Bristol: The Policy Press.

Glasby, J. and Littlechild, R. (2009) *Direct payments and personal budgets: Putting personalisation into practice*, Bristol: The Policy Press.

Glasby, J. and Peck, E. (2005) *Partnership working between health and social care: The impact of care trusts*, Birmingham: Health Study Management Centre.

Glasby, J., Dickenson, H. and Miller, R. (2011) *All in this together? Making best use of health and social care resources in an era of austerity*, Birmingham: Health Services Management Centre.

Gleave, R., Wong, I., Porteus, J. and Harding E. (2010) 'What is "more integration" between health and social care? Results of a survey of primary care trusts and directors of adult social care in England', *Journal of Integrated Care*, vol 18, no 5, pp 29-44.

Glendinning, C. (1992) *The costs of informal care: Looking inside the household*, London: Her Majesty's Stationery Office.

Glendinning, C. (2009) 'The consumer in social care', in R. Simmons, M. Powell and I. Greenor (eds) *The consumer in public services: Choices, values and differences*, Bristol: The Policy Press.

Glendinning, C., Jones, K., Baxter, K., Rabiee, P., Curtis, L., Wikle, A., Arksey, H. and Forder, J. (2010) *home care re-ablement services: Investigating the longer-term impacts*, York/Canterbury: SPRU/PSSRU.

Glendinning, C., Arksey, H., Jon, K., Moran, N., Netten, A. and Rabiee, P. (2009) *The individual budgets pilot projects: Impact and outcomes for carers*, York: Social Policy Research Unit.

Glendinning, C., Challis, D., Fernandez, J., Jacobs, S., Jones, K., Knapp, M., Manthorpe, J., Moran, N., Netten, A., Stevens, M. and Wilberforce, M. (2008) *Evaluation of the Individual Budgets Pilot Programme: Final report*, York: IBSEN.

Glendinning, C., Powell, M. and Rummery, K. (eds) (2002) *Partnerships, New Labour and the governance of welfare*, Bristol: The Policy Press.

Goldman, C. (2010) 'Joint financing across health and social care: money matters, but outcomes matter more', *Journal of Integrated Care*, vol 18, no 1, pp 3-10.

Goldman, C. and Carrier, J. (2010) 'Joint financing in the new NHS, thinking to the future', *Journal of Integrated Care*, vol 18, no 6, pp 27-34.

Gray, A.M. and Birrell, W.D. (2012) 'Devolution, social security and welfare reform', paper presented at the Social Policy Association Annual Conference, University of York, July.

Great Britain Ministry of Housing and Local Government (1968) *Report of the Committee on Local Authority and Allied Personal Social Services* (the Seebohm Report), Cmnd 3703, London: Her Majesty's Stationery Office.

Greer, S. (2004) *Territorial politics and health policy*, Manchester: Manchester University Press.

Griffiths, R. (1988) *Community care: Agenda for action: A report to the Secretary of State for Social Services* (Griffiths Report), London: Her Majesty's Stationery Office.

Grootegoed, E., Knijn, T. and da Roit, B. (2010) 'Relatives as paid care-givers: how family carers experience payments for care', *Ageing & Society*, vol 30, no 3, pp 467–89.

GSCC (General Social Care Council) (2005) *Working towards full participation*, London: GSCC.

GSCC (2006) *Working towards full participation: A report on how social work courses have begun to involve service users and carers in social work training*, London: GSCC.

GSCC (2008) *Raising standards in social work education in England*, London: GSCC.

GSCC (2010) *Raising standards in social work education in England*, London: GSCC.

Hafford–Letchfield, R. (2009) 'Leadership and management in integrated services', in J. McKimm and K. Philips (eds) *Leadership and management in integrated services*, Exeter: Learning Matters.

Ham, C. (2009) *Only connect: Policy options for integrating health and social care*, London: Nuffield Trust.

Ham, C. (2012) *A report to the Department of Health and the NHS Future Forum*, London: The King's Fund and Nuffield Trust.

Ham, C. and Oldham, J. (2009) 'Integrating health and social care in England: Lessons from early adopters and implications for policy', *Journal of Integrated Care*, vol 17, no 6, pp 3-9.

Ham, C., Dixon, A. and Brooke, B. (2012) *Transferring the delivery of health and social care*, London: The Kings Fund.

Hampton, P. (2005) *Reducing administrative burdens: Effective inspection and enforcement*, London: HM Treasury.

Harlock, J. (2009) *Personalisation: Rhetoric to reality*, London: National Council for Voluntary Organisations.

Hasler, F. (2003) *Users at the heart: User participation in the governance and operations of social care regulatory bodies*, SCIE Report 5, London: Social Care Institute for Excellence.

Hasler, F., Campbell, J. and Zarb, G. (1999) *Direct routes to independence: A guide to local authority implementation and management of direct payments*, London: Policy Studies Institute.

Hatton, C. and Waters, J. (2011) *The National Personal Budget Survey*, Wythall: In Control, www.in-control.org.uk/media/92851/national%20personal%20 budget%20survey%20report

Hatton, C., Emerson, E., Rivers, M., Mason, H., Swarbrick, R., Mason, L., Kiernan, C., Reeves, D. and Alborz, A. (2001) 'Factors associated with intending staff turnover and job search behaviour in services for people with intellectual disability', *Journal of Intellectual Disability Research*, vol 45, no 3, pp 258-70.

Hay, P. (2012) President's blog, www.adass.org.uk/index.php?option=com_con tent&view=article&id=790:march-201The

Health and Social Care Information Centre (2012) *Personal Social Services Expenditure and Unit Costs 2010–2011*, London: Health and Social Care Information Centre.

Health and Sport Committee (2011) *3rd report, 2011 (session 4): Report on inquiry into the regulation of care for older people*, Edinburgh: Scottish Parliament.

Heenan, D. and Birrell, W. D. (2006) 'The integration of health and social care: the lessons from Northern Ireland', *Social Policy and Administration*, vol 40, no 1, pp 47-66.

Heenan, D. and Birrell, W.D. (2009) 'Organizational integration in health and social care: some reflections on the Northern Ireland experience', *Journal of Integrated Care*, vol 17, no 5, pp 3-12.

Heenan, D. and Birrell, W.D. (2010) 'Devolution and social security: the anomaly of NI', *Journal of Poverty and Social Justice*, vol 18, no 3, pp 281-93.

Heenan, D. and Birrell, W.D. (2011) *Social work in Northern Ireland: Conflict and change*, Bristol: The Policy Press.

Heffernan, K. (2006) 'Does language make a difference in health and social care practice?', *International Social Work*, vol 49, no 6, pp 825-30.

Hendry, A. (2010) 'Lanarkshire's managed care network: an integrated improvement collaborative', *Journal of Integrated Care*, vol 18, no 3, pp 45-51.

Henwood, M. (1992) *Through a glass darkly: Community care and elderly people*, London: The King's Fund.

Henwood, M. (2006) 'Effective partnership working: a case study of hospital discharge', *Health and Social Care in the Community*, vol 14, no 5, pp 400-7.

Henwood, M. (2012) 'Commons Health Committee's report fails to make its case', *The Guardian*, 13 February.

Henwood, M. and Grove, B. (eds) (2006) *Here to stay? Self-directed support: Aspiration and implementation: A review for the Department of Health*, Towcester: Melanie Henwood Associates.

Henwood, M. and Hudson, B. (2007) 'Here to stay? Self-directed support: aspiration and implementation: a review for the Department of Health', www.changecards.org/evidence/files/2010/09/here_to_stay.pdf

Henz, U. (2006) 'Informal caregiving at working age: effects of job characteristics and family configuration', *Journal of Marriage and Family*, vol 68, no 2, pp 411-29.

Hernandez, L., Robson, P. and Sampson, A. (2010) 'Towards integrated participation: involving seldom heard users of social care services', *British Journal of Social Work*, vol 40, no 3, pp 714-36.

Herod, J. and Lymbery, M. (2002) 'The social work role in multi-disciplinary teams', *Practice*, vol 14, no 4, pp 17-27.

Hill, M. (2000) *Local authority social services*, Oxford: Blackwell.

Himmelweit, S. and Land, H. (2011) 'Reducing gender inequalities to create a sustainable care system', *Kurswechsel*, vol 4, pp 49-63.

HMSO (Her Majesty's Stationery Office) (1969) *The administrative structure of the health and personal social services in Northern Ireland*, Belfast: HMSO.

Home Office (2004) *The Birchard Inquiry report*, London: The Stationery Office.

House of Commons Communities and Local Government Committee (2009) *The Supporting Programme Committee*, London: House of Commons, www.publications.parliament.co.uk/pm/cm/200809/cmselect/emcomloc/649/64903

House of Commons Health Committee (2010) *Social care*, third report, HC22, London: House of Commons, www.publications.parliament.uk/pa/cm200910/cmselect/cmhealth/22/2202.htm

House of Commons Health Committee (2012a) *Social care*, fourteenth report, vol I, HC1583, London: House of Commons, www.publications.parliament.uk/pa/cm201012/cmselect/cmhealth/1583/158302.htm

House of Commons Health Committee (2012b) *Public expenditure*, HC1499, London: House of Commons, www.publications.parliament.uk/pa/cm201012/cmselect/cmhealth/1499/1499.pdf

House of Commons Library (2012) *The Supporting People Programme*, Research Paper 12/40, London: House of Commons.

House of Commons Public Accounts Committee (2012) *The Care Quality Commission: Regulating the quality and safety of health and adult social care*, seventy-eighth report of session 2010–12, London: House of Commons.

Hudson, B. (ed) (2000) *The changing role of social care*, London: Jessica Kingsley Publishers.

Hudson, B. (2006) 'Integrated team working: you can get it if you really want it: part I', *Journal of Integrated Care*, vol 14, no 1, pp 13-21.

Hudson, B. and Henwood, M. (2002) 'The NHS and social care: the final countdown', *Policy & Politics*, vol 30, no 2, pp 153-66.

Hudson, B. and Henwood, M. (2009) *Working for people: The workforce implications of putting people first – a report for the Department of Health*, Towchester: Melanie Henwood Associates.

Hussein, S. (2011) 'The contributions of migrants to the English care sector', *Social Care Workforce Periodical*, no 11, February, online.

Huxley, P., Evans, S., Munroe, M. and Cestaro, L. (2008) 'Integrating health and social care in community mental health teams in the UK: a study of assessments and eligibility criteria in England', *Health and Social Care in the Community*, vol 16, no 5, pp 476-87.

Improvement and Development Agency (2009) *Adult social care*, London: Centre for Public Scrutiny.

Independent Commission on Social Services in Wales (2010) *From vision to action: The report of the Independent Commission on Social Services in Wales*, Cardiff: Independent Commission on Social Services in Wales.

Ipsos MORI (2011) 'Written evidence from Ipsos MORI (SC48)', www.publications.parliament.uk/pa/cm201012/cmselect/cmhealth/1583/1583vw39.htm

Johnson, J., Rolph, S. and Smith, R. (2010) *Residential care transformed: Revisiting 'The Last Refuge'*, Basingstoke: Palgrave Macmillan.

Johnson, N. (1999) 'The personal social services and community care', in M. Powell (ed) *New Labour, new welfare state?*, Bristol: The Policy Press.

Joint Improvement Team (2011) *Work areas*, www.jitscotland.org.uk/supporting-partnership/work-areas/

Johnson, N. (2012) 'Reforms must not ignore the challenges facing the social care workforce', *Guardian Professional*, 5 September.

Jones, I. (2012) 'Effective public service delivery for older people: exploring the views of policy actors in Wales', *Contemporary Wales*, vol 25, pp 58-72.

Jones, N., Thomas, P. and Rudd, L. (2004) 'Collaborating for mental health: a process evaluation', *Public Administration*, vol 82, no 1, pp 109-21.

Kendall, J. (2000) 'The voluntary sector and social change for older people', in B. Hudson (ed) *The changing role of social care*, London: Jessica Kingsley Publishers.

Kooiman, J. (2005) *Governing as governance*, London: Sage Publications.

Kotsadam, A. (2010) 'Does informal eldercare impede women's employment? The case of European welfare states', *Feminist Economics*, vol 17, no 2, pp 121–44.

Land, H. and Himmelweit, S. (2010) *Who cares: Who pays? A report on personalisation in social care,* London: UNISON.

Langan, M. (1998) 'The personal social services', in N. Ellison and C. Pierson (eds) *Developments in British social policy*, Basingstoke: Macmillan.

Larkin, M. (2009) *Vulnerable groups in health and social care*, London: Sage Publications.

Law Commission (2011) *Adult social care*, HC941, London: The Stationery Office.

Law Commission (2012) *Regulation of health and social care professionals consultation*, London: Law Commission, Scottish Law Commission and Northern Ireland Law Commission.

Leadbeater, C. (2004) *Personalisation through participation: A new script for public services*, London: Demos.

Leece, J. (2006) 'It's not like being at work': a study to investigate stress and job satisfaction in employees of direct payments users', in J. Leece and J. Bornat (eds) *Developments in direct payments,* Bristol: The Policy Press.

Leece, J. (2008) 'Personalisation: who cares about personal assistants?', *Community Care*, 24 November.

Leece, J. and Bornat, J. (2006) *Developments in direct payments*, Bristol: The Policy Press.

Leece, J. and Leece, D. (2011) 'Personalisation: perceptions of the role of social work in a world of brokers and budgets', *British Journal of Social Work*, vol 41, no 2, pp 204–23.

Lewis, J. (2001) 'Social services departments and the health/social care boundary: players or pawns?', in I. Allen (ed) *Social care and health: A new deal?*, London: Policy Studies Institute.

Lewis, J. (2002) 'The boundary between health and social care for older people', in B. Bytheway, V. Bacigalupo, J. Bornat, J. Johnson and S. Spurr (eds) *Understanding care, welfare and community*, Abingdon: Routledge.

Lewis, J. and Glennerster, H. (1996) *Implementing the new community care*, Buckingham: Open University Press.

Lewis, L. (2009) 'Politics of recognition: what can a human rights perspective contribute to understanding users' experience of involvement in mental health services?', *Social Policy and Society*, vol 8, no 2, pp 257–74.

Local Government Association (2012) *Towards Excellence in Adult Social Care*, London: Local Government Association.

Local Government Association (2012) *Funding outlook for councils from 2012/11 to 2019/20*, London: Local Government Association.

Long, R. and Powell, T. (2012) Draft Care and Support Bill, www.parliament.uk/briefingpapers/SN0642.pdf

Low Pay Commission (2011) *National Minimum Wage report*, London: The Stationery Office.

Lowndes, V., Pratchett, L. and Stoker, G. (2001) 'Trends in public participation: local government perspectives', *Public Administration*, vol 9, no 1, pp 5–22.

Lucas, L. (2012) *Interim results: LGiU survey on outcome based commissioning in adult social care*, policy briefing, London: Local Government Information Unit.

Lymbery, M. (2006) 'United we stand? Partnership working in health and social care and the role of social work in services for older people', *British Journal of Social Work*, vol 36, no 7, pp 1119-34.

Lymbery, M. (2010) 'A new vision for adult social care? Continuities and change in the care of older people', *Critical Social Policy*, vol 30, no 1, pp 5-26.

Lymbery, M. (2012) 'Social work and personalisation', *British Journal of Social Work*, vol 42, pp 782-93.

Lymbery, M. and Postle, K. (2010) 'Social work in the context of adult social care in England and the resultant implications for social work education', *British Journal of Social Work*, vol 40, no 8, pp 2502-22.

Lyons, M. (2007) *Lyons Inquiry into local government: Final report*, www.lyonsinquiry.org.uk

McAteer, M. and Orr, K. (2006) 'Public participation in Scottish local government: strategic and corporate confusions, *Public Money and Management*, vol 26, no 2, pp 131-38.

McDonald, A. (2006) *Understanding community care*, Basingstoke: Macmillan.

McGregor, K. (2012) 'Government to invest in newly qualified social workers', *Community Care*, 26 July, www.communitycare.co.uk/Articles/26/07/2012/118403/government-to-invest-in-newly-qualified-social-workers.htm

McKimm, J. and Held, S. (2009) 'The emergence of leadership theory: from the twentieth to the twenty first century', in J. McKimm and K. Phillips (eds) *Leadership and management in integrated services*, Exeter: Learning Matters.

McTavish, D. and Mackie, R. (2003) 'The Joint Future Initiative in Scotland: the development and early implementation experience of an integrated care policy', *Public Policy & Administration*, vol 18, no 3, pp 39-56.

Malin, N., Wilmot, S. and Manthorpe, J. (2002) *Key concepts and debates in health and social policy*, Buckingham: The Open University.

Manthorpe, J. and Martineau, S. (2008) *Support workers: Their roles and tasks: A scoping review*, London: Social Care Workforce Research Unit, King's College London.

Manthorpe, L., Hindes, J., Martineau, S., Cornes, M., Ridley, J., Spandler, H., Rosengard, A., Hunter, S., Little, S. and Gray, B. (2011) *Self-directed support: A review of the barriers and facilitators*, Edinburgh: Scottish Government Social Research.

Martin, S. and Webb, A. (2009) '"Citizen-centred" public services: contestability without consumer-driven competition', *Public Money & Management*, vol 29, no 2, pp 123-30.

Maslin-Prothero, S. and Bennion, A. (2010) 'Integrated team working: A literature review', *International Journal of Integrated Care*, vol 10, April–June Supplement, pp 1-11.

Means, R. (2012) 'A brave new world of personalised care? Historical perspectives on social care and older people in England', *Social Policy & Administration*, vol 46, no 3, pp 302-20.

Means, R. and Smith, R. (1998) *From Poor Law to community care*, Bristol: The Policy Press.

Means, R., Morbey, H. and Smith, R. (2002) *From community care to market care?*, Bristol: The Policy Press.

Means, R., Richards, S. and Smith, R. (2008) *Community care*, Basingstoke: Palgrave Macmillan.

Melis, R. (2004) 'What is intermediate care?', *British Medical Journal*, vol 329, no 7462, pp 324-69, www.bmj.com/content/329/7462/360

Miers, M. (2010) 'Professional boundaries and inter-professional working', in K. Polland, J. Thomas and M. Miers (eds) *Understanding inter-professional working in health and social care*, Basingstoke: Palgrave Macmillan.

Milewa, R. (2004) 'Local participatory democracy in Britain's health service: innovation or fragmentation of a universal citizenship', *Social Policy & Administration*, vol 38, no 3, pp 240-52.

Miller, E. and Cameron, E. (2011) 'Challenges and benefits in implementing shared inter-agency assessment across the UK: a literature review, *Journal of Interprofessional Care*, vol 25, no 1, pp 39-45.

Mitchell, W., Baxter, K. and Glendinning, C (2012) *Updated review of research on risk and adult social care in England*, York: JRF.

Mithran, S. (2012) 'Councils to get Independent Living Fund cash after 2015 abolition', *Community Care*, 12 July, www.communitycare.co.uk/Articles/12/07/2012/118374/councils-to-get-independent-living-fund-cash-after-2015-abolition

Molyneux, J. and Irvine, J. (2004) 'Service user and carer involvement in social work training: a long and winding road', *Social Work Education*, vol 23, no 3, pp 293-308.

Mooney, G., Sweeney, T. and Law, A. (eds) (2006) *Social care: Health and welfare in contemporary Scotland*, Paisley: Kynoch and Blaney.

Moore, J., West, R., Keen, J., Godfrey, M. and Townsend, J. (2007) 'Networks and governance: the case of intermediate care', *Health and Social Care in the Community*, vol 15, no 2, pp 155-64.

Moran, N., Arksey, H., Glendinning, C., Jones, K., Netten, A. and Rabiee, P. (2011) 'Personalisation and carers: whose rights? Whose benefits?', *British Journal of Social Work*, doi: 10.1093/bjsw/bcr075

Morris, J. (2012) 'Defending the Independent Living Fund', www.jennymorrisnet. blogspot.co.uk/2012/01/defending-independent-living-fund

Moullin, M. (2002) *Delivering excellence in health and social care*, Buckingham: Open University Press.

Munro, E. (2011) *The Munro review of child protection: Final report: A child-centred system*, London: Department of Education.

National Audit Office (2009) *Supporting carers to care*, London: National Audit Office.

National Institute for Clinical Excellence (2011) *Service user experience in adult mental health: Guidance and quality standard consultation*, London: National Institute for Clinical Excellence, www.nice.org.uk/guidance

National Institute for Health and Clinical Excellence (2012) *Dementia – supporting people to live well with dementia: Consultation on draft quality standard*, London: National Institute for Health and Clinical Excellence.

Needham, C. (2008) 'Realising the potential of co-production: negotiating improvements in public services', *Social Policy and Society*, vol 7, no 2, pp 221-32.

Needham, C. (2009) *Co-production: An emerging evidence base for Adult Social Care transformation*, Research Briefing 31, London: Social Care Institute for Excellence.

Needham, C. (2010) *Commissioning for personalisation: From the fringes to the mainstream*, London: Public Management and Policy Association.

Needham, C. (2011) 'Personalisation: from story-line to practice', *Social Policy & Administration*, vol 45, no 1, pp 54-68.

Needham, C. and Carr, S. (2009) *Co-production: An emerging evidence base for adult social care transformation*, SCIE Research Briefing 31, London: Social Care Institute for Excellence.

Netton, A. (2005) 'Personal social services', in M. Powell, C. Bauld and J. Clarke (eds) *Social policy review 17*, Bristol: The Policy Press.

Newbronner, L., Chamberlain, R., Bosanquet, K., Bartlett, C., Cass, B. and Glendinning, C. (2011) *Keeping personal budgets personal: Learning from the experiences of older people, people with mental health problems and their carers*, London: Social Care Institute for Excellence

Newman, J. (2009) *Modernising governance*, London: Sage.

Newman, J., Glendinning, C. and Hughes, M. (2008) 'Beyond modernisation? Social care and the transformation of welfare governance', *Journal of Social Policy*, vol 37, no 4, pp 531-57.

NHS Commissioning Board (2012) *Commissioning support: Key facts*, London: NHS Commissioning Board.

NHS Confederation (2010) *Where next for health and social care integration?*, discussion paper, issue 8, London: NHS Confederation.

NHS Confederation (2011a) *Facing up to the challenge of personal health budgets: The view of frontline professionals*, London: NHS Confederation and National Mental Health Development Unit.

NHS Confederation (2011b) *The legacy of primary care trusts*, London: NHS Confederation.

NHS Confederation (2012a) *Operating principles for health and wellbeing boards*, London: NHS Confederation.

NHS Confederation (2012b) *Survey of NHS chief executives and chairs*, London: NHS Confederation, www.nhsconfed.org/documents

NHS Confederation (2012c) *A stitch in time – the future is integration*, London: NHS Confederation.

NHS Confederation and National Health Development Unit (2011) *Facing up to the challenge of personal health budgets: The view of frontline professionals*, London: NHS Confederation and National Mental Health Development Unit.

NHS Information Centre (2010) *Personal social services survey of adult carers in England – 2009-10*, London: NHS Information Centre.

NIHRC (Northern Ireland Human Rights Commission) (2012) *In defence of dignity:*
The human rights of older people in nursing homes, Belfast: NIHRC.

NILT (Northern Ireland Life and Times Survey) (2010) *Attitudes to caring*,
Belfast: ARK, www.ark.ac.uk/nilt/results/carers

NMDS-SC (National Minimum Data Set for Social Care) (2011) *Migrant workers*, briefing issue 14, London: Skills for Care.

NMDS-SC (2012) *National key statistics report*, London: Skills for Care.

Northern Ireland Audit Office (2010) *Arrangements for ensuring the quality of care in homes for older people*, Belfast: Northern Ireland Audit Office.

Northern Ireland Housing Executive (2009) Supporting People Spotlight Issue 2, Belfast: NIHE.

Northern Ireland Social Care Council (2012) *Background to the review of social work in Northern Ireland*, www.niscc.info/SocialWorkStrategy2012-22-115.aspx

Offer, J. (1999) *Social workers, the community and social interaction*, London: Jessica Kingsley Publishers.

Office for Public Management (2011) *Complaints about privately funded and arranged social care*, London: OPM.

Oliver, M. and Barnes, C. (1998) *Disabled people and social policy: From exclusion to inclusion*, Harlow: Longman.

Oliver, M. and Sapey, B. (1999) *Social work with disabled people*, Basingstoke: Macmillan.

O'Neill, C., McGregor, P. and Merkur, S. (2012) 'United Kingdom (Northern Ireland) Health Systems Review', *Health Systems in Transition*, vol 14, no10, pp 1-91.

ONS (Office for National Statistics) (2010) *National Population Projections, 2010-based Statistical Bulletin*, London: ONS.

Parker, G. and Lawton, D. (1994) *Different types of care, different types of carer: Evidence from the General Household Survey*, London: Her Majesty's Stationery Office.

Parker, G., Arksey, H. and Harden, M. (2010) *Meta-review of international evidence on interventions to support carers*, York: Social Policy Research Unit, University of York, www.php.york.ac.uk/inst/spru/profiles/gp.php

Parker, G., Corden, A. and Heaton, J. (2011) 'Experiences of and influences on continuity of care for service users and carers: synthesis of evidence from a research programme', *Health and Social Care in the Community*, vol 19, no 6, pp 576-601.

Parr, S. and Nixon, J. (2009) 'Family intervention projects: sites of subversion and resilience', in M. Barnes and D. Prior (eds) *Subversive citizens: Power, agency and resistance in public services*, Bristol: The Policy Press, pp 101-17.

Patient Client Council (2012) *Care at home: Older people's experiences of domiciliary care*, Belfast: Patient Client Council.

Payne, J. (2012) *Social Care (Self-directed Support) (Scotland) Bill*, SPICe briefing, Edinburgh: Scottish Parliament.

Penhale, B. and Parker, J. (2008) *Working with vulnerable adults*, Abingdon: Routledge.

Petch, A. (2008) 'Social work with adult service users', in M. Davies (ed) *The Blackwell companion to social work*, Oxford: Blackwell Publishing.

Petch, A. (2012) 'Tectonic plates: aligning evidence, policy and practice in health and social care integration', *Journal of Integrated Care*, vol 20, no 2, pp 77-8.

Phillips, K. (2009) 'Learning in complex environments', in J. McKimm and K. Phillips (eds) *Leadership and management in integrated services*, Exeter: Learning Matters.

Pickard, L. (2004) *The effectiveness and cost effectiveness of support and services to informal carers of older people: A review of literature prepared for the Audit Commission*, London: Audit Commission.

Pickard, L. (2008) *Informal care for older people provided by their adult children: Projections of supply and demand to 2041 in England*, report to the Strategic Unit and the Department of Health, London: Department of Health.

Platt, D. (2007) *The status of social care: A review 2007*, London: Department of Health, www.dh.gov.uk/en/publicationsandstatistics

Poll, C. (2007) 'Co-production in supported housing: keyring living support networks and neighbourhood networks', *Research Highlights in Social Work: Co-production and Personalisation in Social Care*, vol 49, pp 49-66.

Pollard, K., Thomas, J. and Miers, M. (eds) (2009) *Understanding interprofessional working in health and social care*, Basingstoke: Macmillan.

Powell, J. and Steel, R. (2011) 'Policy, governance and governmentality: conceptual and research reflections on ageing in England', *Journal of Social Research and Policy*, vol 2, no 2, pp 111-20.

Princess Royal Trust for Carers and Crossroads Care (2011) 'Written evidence from the Princess Royal Trust for Carers and Crossroads Care (SC 60)', www.publications.parliament.uk/pa/cm201012/cmselect/cmhealth/1583/1583we14.htm

Reilly, S., Challis, D., Donnelly, M., Stewart, K. and Hughes, J., (2007) 'Care management in mental health services in England and Northern Ireland: Do integrated organisations promote integrated practice?', *Journal of Health Services Research and Policy*, vol 12, no 4, pp 236-41.

Review of Public Administration (RPA) (2005) *The Review of Public Administration in Northern Ireland: A further consultation*, Belfast: Review of Public Administration in Northern Ireland.

Riedel, M. and Kraus, M. (2011) *Informal care provision in Europe*, Brussels: Centre for European Policy Studies.

Robinson, K. and Webber, M. (2012) 'Models and effectiveness of service user and carer involvement in social work education: a literature review', *British Journal of Social Work,* doi: 10.1093/bjsw/bcs025

Robson, P., Sampson, A., Dime, N., Hernandez, L. and Litherland, R. (2008) *Seldom heard: Developing inclusive participation in social care*, SCIE Position Paper 10, London: Social Care Institute for Excellence.

Rosen, R. and Ham, C. (2008) *Integrated care: Lessons from evidence experience*, London: Nuffield Trust.

Roulstone, A. and Morgan, H. (2009) 'Neo-liberal individualism or self-directed support: are we all speaking the same language on modernising adult social care?', *Social Policy and Society*, vol 8, pp 333–45.

Roulstone, A. and Prideaux, S. (2012) *Understanding disability policy*, Bristol: The Policy Press.

Royal College of Psychiatrists (2009) 'Reduction in psychiatric beds', www.rcpsych.ac.uk

RQIA (2012) Corporate Strategy 2012–2015, Belfast: RQIA.

RSM Robson Rhodes (2004) *Review of the Supporting People Programme: Independent report*, London: Office of the Deputy Prime Minister.

Rubery, J, and Urwin, P. (2011) 'Bringing the employer back in: why social care needs a standard employment relationship', *Human Resource Management Journal*, vol 21, no 2, pp 122–37.

Rummery, K. (2007) 'Modernising services, empowering users? Adult social care in 2006', in K. Clarke, K. Maltby and P. Kennett (eds) *Social policy review 19*, Bristol: The Policy Press.

Rummery, K. (2011) 'Personalisation: risk v benefit?', www.publicservice.co.uk/feature_story.ASP?ID=15839

Rummery, K., Bell, D., Bowes, A., Dawson, A. and Roberts, E. (2012) *Counting the cost of choice and control: Evidence for the costs of self-directed support in Scotland*, Social Research Findings, no 110/2012, Edinburgh: Government Social Research.

Sadd, J. (2011) *'We are more than our story': Service user and carer participation in social work education*, SCIE Report 42, London: Social Care Institute for Excellence.

SCIE (Social Care Institute for Excellence) (2007a) *Participation: Finding out what difference it makes*, London: SCIE.

SCIE (2007b) *Developing social care: Service users driving culture change*, London: SCIE.

SCIE (2009a) *Personalisation: A rough guide*, London: SCIE.

SCIE (2009b) *Building user and carer involvement in social work education*, London: SCIE.

SCIE (2010a) *Personalisation: A rough guide*, London: SCIE.

SCIE (2010b) *Commissioning to develop and sustain user-led organisations (ULOs)*, At a Glance 25, London: SCIE, www.scie.org.uk/publications/ataglance

SCIE (2011) *Learning from the experiences of older people and their carers,* Personal Budgets Briefing, London: SCIE.

SCIE (2012a) *People not processes: The future of personalisation and independent living*, London: SCIE.

SCIE (2012b) *Reablement: A guide for families and carers*, London: SCIE.

SCIE (2012c) *Reablement: Emerging practice messages*, London: SCIE.

Scottish Executive (2003) *Partnership for Care: Scotland's Health White Paper*, Edinburgh: The Stationery Office.

Scottish Executive (2006) *Changing lives: Report of the 21st century social work review*, Edinburgh: Scottish Executive.

Scottish Executive (2004) *Community Health Partnerships Statutory Guidance*, Edinburgh: The Stationery Office.

Scottish Government (2007) *Report of the independent review of regulation, audit, inspection and complaints handling of public services in Scotland* (The Crerar Review), Edinburgh: Scottish Government.

Scottish Government (2009) *Better health, better care*, Edinburgh: Scottish Government.

Scottish Government (2010a) *Reshaping care for older people*, Edinburgh: Scottish Government, www.scotland.gov.uk/news/releases/2010/03/24111551

Scottish Government (2010b) *Caring together: The carers strategy for Scotland 2010–2015*, Edinburgh: Scottish Government.

Scottish Government (2010c) *Getting it right for young carers: The young carers strategy in Scotland 2010–2015*, Edinburgh: Scottish Government.

Scottish Government (2010d) *Self-directed support: A national strategy for Scotland*, Edinburgh: Scottish Government

Scottish Government (2010e) *Community Health Partnerships delivering better outcomes and use of joint resources*. Available at: www.scotland.gov.uk/publications

Scottish Government (2011) *Reshaping care for older people: A programme for change 2011–2012*, Edinburgh: Scottish Government.

Scottish Government (2012a) *Integration of adult health and social care in Scotland*, Edinburgh: Scottish Government, www.scotland.gov.uk/publications/2012

Scottish Government (2012b) *Public services reform (social services inspections) (Scotland) amendment regulations*, Edinburgh: Scottish Parliament.

Scottish Office (1966) *Social work and the community: Proposals for reorganising local authority services in Scotland*, Cmnd 3065, Edinburgh: Her Majesty's Stationery Office.

Scottish Parliament (2011a) *Report on inquiry into the regulation of care for older people*, Health and Sport Committee, 3rd report, Edinburgh: Scottish Parliament.

Scottish Parliament (2011b) *Official report*, 15 September, cols 1818-1821.

Scourfield, J., Holland, S. and Young, C. (2008) 'Social work in Wales since democratic devolution', *Australian Social Work*, vol 61, no 1, pp 42-56.

Scourfield, P. (2010) 'A critical reflection on the involvement of "experts by experience" in inspections', *British Journal of Social Work*, vol 40, no 6, pp 1890-907.

Scragg, T. (2006) 'An evaluation of integrated team management', *Journal of Integrated Care*, vol 14, no 3, pp 39-48.

Sharkey, P. (2000) *Essentials of community care*, Basingstoke: Palgrave Macmillan.

Shutes, I. (2012) 'The employment of migrants in long term care', *Journal of Social Policy*, vol 41, no 1, pp 43-61.

Simmons, R. (2011) 'Leadership and listening: the reception of user voice in today's public services', *Social Policy & Administration,* vol 45, no 5, pp 539-68.

Simmons, R. and Birchall, J. (2005) 'A joined up approach to user participation in public services', *Social Policy & Administration*, vol 30, no 3, pp 260-83.

Simmons, R., Birchall, J. and Prout, A. (2011) 'User involvement in public services: "choice about voice"', *Public Policy & Administration*, vol 27, no 1, pp 3-29.

Skills for Care (2007) *National Survey of Care Workers*, London: Skills for Care.

Skills for Care (2010) *The workforce implications and employment aspects of people employing their own care and support*, London: Skills for Care.

Skills for Care (2011a) *The size and structure of the adult social care sector and workforce in England 2011*, London: Skills for Care.

Skills for Care (2011b) *Capable, confident, skilled: A workforce development strategy for people working supporting and caring in adult social care*, London: Skills for Care.

Social Services Improvement Agency (2005) *Social work in Wales: A profession to value*, Cardiff: Social Services Improvement Agency.

Social Work Education Participation (2011) *Definitions: Service user and user controlled*, www.socialworkeducation.org.uk/content.asp?contentid=200

Stein, W., Asenova, D., McCann, C. and Marshall, A. (2010) 'Modern concepts of quality and risk: challenges for older people in Scotland', *Public Policy & Administration*, vol 25, no 3, pp 305-26.

Stevens, S. and Tanner, D. (2006) 'Involving service users in the teaching and learning of social work students: reflections on experience', *Social Work Education*, vol 25, no 4, pp 360-71.

Sturgeon, N. (2011) 'Integration of health and social care', news release, 12 December, www.scotland.gov.uk/News/Releases/2011/12/12111418

Sullivan, H., Knops, A., Barnes, M and Newman, J. (2004) 'Central–local relations in an era of multi-level governance: the case of public participation policy in England 1997–2001', *Local Government Studies*, vol 30, no 2, pp 245-65.

Syson, G. and Bond, J. (2010) 'Integrating health and social care teams in Salford', *Journal of Integrated Care*, vol 18, no 2, pp 17-24.

Taylor, I. and Le Riche, P. (2006) 'What do we know about partnership with service users and carers in social work education and how robust is the evidence base?', *Health and Social Care in the Community*, vol 14, no 5, pp 418-25.

The King's Fund (2010) *The King's Fund response to the NHS White Paper*, London: The King's Fund.

The King's Fund (2011) *Social care funding and the NHS: An impending crisis?*, London: The King's Fund, www.kingsfund.org.uk/publications/social_care_funding.html

Thistlethwaite, P. (2011) *Integrating health and social care in Torbay*, London: The King's Fund.

Think Local, Act Personal (2012) *Progress Report Summer 2012*. Available at www.thinklocalactpersonal.org.uk

Thomas, C. and Rose, J. (2009) 'The relationship between reciprocity and the emotional and behaviour responses of staff', *Journal of Applied Research in Intellectual Disabilities*, vol 23, no 2, pp 167-78.

Titterton, M. (1994) 'Managing innovation and change in community care', in M. Titterton (ed) *Caring for people in the community*, London: Jessica Kingsley Publishers.

Tizard, J. (2010) 'Afterword', in C. Needham, *Commissioning for personalisation: From the fringes to the mainstream*, London: Public Management and Policy Association.

Townsend, P. (1962) *The last refuge: A survey of residential institutions and homes for the aged in England and Wales*, London: Routledge & Kegan Paul.

Tucker, H. (2010) 'Integrating care in Norfolk: progress of a national pilot', *Journal of Integrated Care*, vol 18, no 2, pp 32-7.

Tucker, S., Baldwin, R., Hughes, J., Benbow, S.M., Burns, A. and Challis, D. (2009) 'Integrating mental health services for older people in England: from rhetoric to reality', *Journal of Interprofessional Care*, vol 23, no 4, pp 341-54.

Turner, M. (2012) 'Co-production: contributing on equal terms', in *Scieline*, March, London: Social Care Institute for Excellence, www.scie.org.uk/publications/corporate/scieline/scielineMar12.pdf

Twigg, J. and Atkin, K. (1994) *Carers perceived: Policy and practice in informal care*, Buckingham: Open University Press.

Tyler, G. (2006) 'Addressing barriers to participation: service user involvement in social work training', *Social Work Education*, vol 25, no 4, pp 385-92.

UK Sector Skills Assessment (2010) *UK wide sector skills assessment*, Exeter: Asset Skills.

UKHCA (United Kingdom Home Care Association) (2012) *UKHCA Commissioning Survey 2012: Care is not a commodity*, London: UKHCA, www.ukhca.co.uk/pdfs/UKHCACommissioningSurvey2012.pdf

UNISON (2011) *Caring for our future consultation: Submission to the Department of Health December 2011*, London: UNISON, www.unison.org.uk/acrobat/A13845.pdf

UNISON and the College of Social Workers (2012) *Community care 2012: Personalisation Survey results*, www.communitycare.co.uk/the-state-of-personalisation-2012

Vickers, T., Craig, G. and Atkin, K. (2012) 'Addressing ethnicity in social care research', *Social Policy & Administration*, doi: 10.1111/j.1467-9515.2012.00851.x

Vickerstaff, S., Loretto, W., Milne, A., Alden., Billings, P. and Whiteraus, M. (2009) *Employment support for carers*, DWP Research Report no 597, London: Department for Work and Pensions.

Victor, E, (2009) *A systematic review of interventions for carers in the UK: Outcomes and explanatory evidence*, London: Princess Royal Trust for Carers, http://static.carers.org/files/systematic-review-15-jan-3840.pdf

Wallcraft, J. and Sweeney, A. (2011) *User involvement in adult safeguarding*, Adults' Services Report 47, London: Social Care Institute for Excellence.

Wallcraft, J., Fleishmann, P. and Schofield, P. (2012) *The involvement of users and carers in social work education: A practice benchmarking study*, SCIE Report 54, London: Social Care Institute for Excellence.

Ward, N. (2008) 'Multi-agency working and partnership', in A. Morris (ed) *Social work and multi-agency working*, Bristol: The Policy Press.

Warren, J. (2009) *Service user and carer participation in social work*, Exeter: Learning Matters.

Watters, C. (1996) 'Representation and realities: black people, community care and mental illness', in W. Ahmad and K. Atkin (eds) *'Race' and community care*, Buckingham: The Open University.

Weatherly, H., Mason, A., Goddard, M. and Wright, K. (2010) *Financial integration across health and social care: Evidence review*, Edinburgh: Scottish Government Social Research.

Webb, S. (2008) 'Modelling service user participation in social care', *Journal of Social Work*, vol 8, no 3, pp 269-90.

Weeks, S. (2006) *Report on the integration of health and social care services in England*, London: UNISON.

Welsh Assembly Government (2000) *Carers strategy in Wales*, Cardiff: Welsh Assembly Government.

Welsh Assembly Government (2007) *Fulfilled lives, supportive communities: A strategy for social services in Wales over the next decade*, Cardiff: Welsh Assembly Government.

Welsh Assembly Government (2010) *Carers Strategies (Wales) Measure (2010)*, Cardiff: Welsh Assembly Government.

Welsh Assembly Government (2011) *Sustainable social services for Wales: A framework for action*, Cardiff: Welsh Assembly Government.

Welsh Assembly Government (2012) *Refreshing the Carers Strategy for Wales*, Cardiff: Welsh Assembly Government, http://wales.gov.uk/docs/dhss/consultation/121113documenten.pdf

Welsh Government (2012a) *Social Services (Wales) Bill: Consultation document*, Cardiff: Welsh Assembly Government, www.wales.gov.uk/consultations/healthsocialcare//bill/

Welsh Government (2012b) *Giving citizens a voice in social services*, Cardiff: Welsh Assembly Government, www.wales.gov.uk/newsroom/healthandsocialcare/2012

Wenger, G.C., Scott, A. and Seddon, D. (2002) 'The experience of caring for older people with dementia in a rural area: using services', *Aging & Mental Health*, vol 6, no 1, pp 30-8.

Wilding, H. (2010) 'Integrated care: from horizontal to vertical integration', *Journal of Integrated Care*, vol 18, no 3, pp 15-20.

Williams, F. (1996) 'Race, welfare and community care: an historical perspective', in W. Ahmad and K. Atkin (eds) *'Race' and community care*, Buckingham: The Open University.

Williams, C. (2012) 'Care: new major challenges', *Local Government Chronicle*, 13 September, www.lgcplus.com/topics/social-care/care-new-model-challenges/5048705.article

Williams, I., Dickenson, H. and Robinson, S. (2010) 'Joined up rationing? An anlaysis of priority setting in health and social care commissioning', *Journal of Integrated Care*, vol 14, no 1, pp 3-11.

Williams. P. (2012) 'The role of leadership in learning and knowledge for integration: managing community care', *Journal of Integrated Care*, vol 20, no 3, pp 164-74.

Williams, P. and Sullivan, H. (2010) 'Despite all we know about collaborative working, why do we still get it wrong?', *Journal of Integrated Care*, vol 18, no 4, pp 4-15.

Wilson, D. and Game, C. (2006) *Local government in the United Kingdom*, Basingstoke: Palgrave Macmillan.

Wiseman, D. (2011) *A 'four nations' perspective on rights, responsibilities, risk and regulation in adult social care*, York: Joseph Rowntree Foundation.

Wistow, G. (1994) 'Community care futures: inter-agency relationships', in M. Titterton (ed) *Caring for people in the community*, London: Jessica Kingsley Publishers.

Wistow, G. (2011) *Involving older people in service commissioning: More power to their elbow?*, York: Joseph Rowntree Foundation.

Wood, C. and Salter, J. (2012) *The home cure*, London: Demos, http://dementianews.wordpress.com/2012/07/02/the-home-cure-demos/

Worth, A. (2001) 'Assessment of the needs of older people by district nurse and social workers: a changing culture?', *Journal of Interprofessional Care*, vol 15, no 3, pp 257-66.

Wright, K.G., Cairns, J.A. and Snell, M.C. (1981) *Costing care*, Social Services Monographs: Research in Practice, Sheffield: Joint Unit for Social Services Research, University of Sheffield.

Wright, F., Tinker, A., Mayagoitia, R., Hanson, J., Wojgani, H. and Holmans, A., (2010) 'What is the "Extra" in Extra Care Housing?', *British Journal of Social Work*, vol 40, no 7, pp 2239-54.

Yeandle, S. and Buckner, L. (2007) *Carers, employment and services: Time for a new social contract?*, CES report no 6, London: Carers UK.

Young, P. (2000) *Mastering social welfare*, Basingstoke: Palgrave Macmillan.

Index

Note: The following abbreviations have been used – f = figure; *t* = table